TRANSATLANTIC
TOPOGRAPHIES

Cultural Studies of the Americas

EDITED BY GEORGE YÚDICE, JEAN FRANCO,
AND JUAN FLORES

TRANSATLANTIC TOPOGRAPHIES

Islands, Highlands, Jungles

ILEANA RODRÍGUEZ

Cultural Studies of the Americas, Volume 17

UNIVERSITY OF MINNESOTA PRESS

MINNEAPOLIS • LONDON

Published by the University of Minnesota Press
111 Third Avenue South, Suite 290
Minneapolis, MN 55401-2520
http://www.upress.umn.edu

Library of Congress Cataloging-in-Publication Data

Rodríguez, Ileana.
Transatlantic topographies : islands, highlands, jungles / Ileana Rodríguez.
    p. cm.—(Cultural studies of the Americas ; v. 17)
Includes bibliographical references and index.
ISBN 0-8166-4223-0 (hc : alk. paper)—ISBN 0-8166-4224-9 (pb : alk. paper)
    1. Caribbean Area—Description and travel. 2. Central America—Description and travel.
    3. Amazon River Region—Description and travel. 4. Geographical perception—
Latin America. 5. Place (Philosophy) 6. Latin America—Historiography. I. Title. II. Series.
F2171.3.R63 2004
917.2′904—dc22
2004006902

Printed in the United States of America on acid-free paper

12 11 10 09 08 07 06 05 04   10 9 8 7 6 5 4 3 2 1

*To Alejandro Cesar
and Gabriel Aurelio*

CONTENTS

ACKNOWLEDGMENTS

Many granting agencies and institutions supported the research to write this book. In particular I thank Fulbright, the American Council of Learned Societies, the Social Sciences Research Council, and my institution, the Ohio State University. I also express my gratitude to the chairman of my department, Professor Dieter Wanner.

In this book I am indebted to the following persons. First, to Professor Derek Petrey, who walked with me the entire length of the project and read every sentence of this manuscript several times without losing his kindness or patience. Professor Linda Grabner-Coronil professionally and meticulously edited the first version of this manuscript. The editors of the series Cultural Studies of the Americas (Jean Franco, Juan Flores, and George Yúdice) offered detailed and invaluable advice in final revisions and encouraged me to edit the manuscript one more time. My friends and colleagues from the Columbus Translatina Women Writing Collective (Catriona Rueda-Esquibel, Ildeasela Buso, Tori Saneda, and Lillia Ramírez) read chapters of this text and offered expert advice. Professor Luz Calvo helped me considerably in the revision of the first chapter. I am also grateful for the help of Professor Muge Galin. My editor at the University of Minnesota Press, Richard W. Morrison, guided me through the long process of rewriting and editing, providing his sound, qualified advice. My dear *compañero* Roberto Guibernau and my endearing friends Monica Szurmuk and Robert Carr have always understood that strong people also need emotional support. Their companionship is a perennial source of bliss.

LAND AND PEOPLE

SPACE AS CULTURAL AND
NATURAL GEOGRAPHIES

Concepts of space as cultural and natural geographies have been in circulation for some time. The bibliographies on the subject are vast and transdisciplinary. Interest in space has gone hand in hand with large-scale projects of social engineering such as colonial expansion and colonization, and the social imaginaries of development. Interest in space as culture has been the province of colonial and postcolonial scholars; the former are interested in documenting the continuity of Europe in America, the latter in underscoring the ruptures.

In the sixteenth-century European imaginary, American space was conceived as "new" and empty; after the eighteenth century, it was reorganized following a post-Enlightenment logic of counting and accounting, leading to the formation of disciplines. In either case, American space was a seedbed for the exercise of European invention, be it in the form of religious projections, the fabulous and wondrous, scientific discourse, or the criticism of all of the above. This tradition reaches down to our day. America is still the consummate blank space of twentieth-century narratives of research and development that Latin American writers, as well as foreign-born travelers, naturalists, and geographers, defined as borders, orillas, and emptiness—the U.S. concept of the frontier—and that postcolonial scholarship combats as oppression and the extermination of peoples.

The story of the representation of American space begins with a series of lethal misunderstandings. These misunderstandings are the indelible legacies of colonialism to the identities of this continent. At the moment of the initial Euro–Amerindian confrontation, the specialized lexemes each party has of organizing territories is absolutely illegible on both sides. Hence, for those who write the bulk of the corpus, it is not so much culture and natural geographies that are at stake, but the perplexity and enthusiasm, the fear and giddiness of the colonial and imperial I for whom the "new" appears as undecipherable and obscure, as inspiringly and pleasurably rich.[1]

If we examine the first sign that marks the transcontinental debate, the sign *tierra*, this is conceived as a social space. When Rodrigo de Triana sights *tierra* from his caravel, no one on board imagines it as empty space, *terra nullius*, a natural geography, but that cultural landmark a fatigued seaman is confident to find at the end of his journey—not just empty space, *tierra*, land, but a port; not geography, nature, but cities, culture, civilization—the fabulous and fantastic lands of the Great Khan, Cipango. In the first reading of the sign *tierra* as a disappointment, the signs find themselves at odds with the European universe, and all analogies in this transcontinental confrontation are placed in jeopardy and subjected to adjustments. *Tierra* is the sign where all the familiar landmarks of Western thought must be renegotiated, and where renditions of familiar hypotheses, religious hermeneutics, and profitable investments find a threshold. We can read the sign *tierra* in the style of Michel Foucault as the sign where "all the ordered surfaces and all the planes with which we are accustomed to tame the wild profusion of existing things" break up.[2] If exploration and "discovery" inaugurate early modernity, early modernity starts as a head-on collision between various imaginaries. The arduous attempt to disengage *tierra* (which subsequently will become nature, the sites of conflict, jurisdictions, agrarian reforms, research and development, and nonrenewable resources) from culture (the sites of epistemological and hermeneutical interpretations and interpellations of people, their consciousness, performances, and differences) originates with trying to resolve matters concerning the distinction between seeing, hearing and interpreting, data gathering and disciplining. Representation, as we all know, is not solely a reflection of the social relations of production, but also a social relation itself.

It is not possible to think about the "new" *tierras* (people and languages) using the existing technologies of knowledge prevalent in the sixteenth century. In observing American space, the crack between signs and words widens and the relationship between new and old becomes very problematic. Foucault is right in observing that without the use of semantic chains it is not possible to think about what is seen, heard, and observed. In America, the four forms of analogy Foucault outlines—*convenientia, aemulatio*, analogy, and sympathy—go awry and belie a lack of fit in explaining the hermeneutical predicament the imperial subject encountered in colonization. Therefore, the enormous confusion created by colonial writing can serve as the basis to ground the invention of the new taxonomies that, in Foucault, correspond to the invention of the sciences of life.

It seems self-evident that logical space is tied to physical space, the history of science and representation to that of colonialism. It is colonialism that places the fracture at the heart of representation. Explorers did not see with scientific disciplinary eyes because there was no such knowledge then. They proceeded by accumulating, examining, and storing information in all the archival systems made available to them—encyclopedias, museums, catalogs, filing systems, libraries, indexes, inventories. Documents are thus "unencumbered spaces in which things are juxtaposed [and] in which creatures present themselves one beside another grouped according to their common features."[3] This is, then, a primitive accumulation of knowledge, a hoarding that will make sciences possible later on. The understanding of the New World is then predicated on the invention of classificatory systems, which will later be segmented into the different sciences. But at the time of colonization, colonizers operated within their own conceptual frames. Things not belonging in that order became objects of wonder. This is precisely the blueprint necessary to express the realities and fictions of what Stephen Greenblatt calls the (awesome) "rhetorical machinery" of the West.[4] In either case, Europeans were not interested in understanding the new systems, but in appropriating them.

From the display and interpretation of signs, Europeans move to the exchange of gifts and the bartering of goods, and from there to the learning, teaching, and kidnapping of languages and possession of *tierras*. The three modes of communication are then mute signs, material exchange, and the learning, teaching, and kidnapping of language.[5] In the face of the unknown, Europeans had no remedy but to use conventional, intellectual, and organizational structures that greatly impeded a clear grasp of the radical otherness of the American lands and peoples.

ISLAND, HIGHLAND, JUNGLE

For students of colonialism, the geographies represented in the colonial documents are not just natural environments or landscapes, but vast corpuses of cultural and economic practices that play a pivotal role in the formation of social identities. This book takes this proposition seriously and studies the cultural representation of these three topographical sites. I begin by looking at continental social realities as if they were merely physical geographic entities. Subsequently, I highlight the confusion created by the interaction between geographies, peoples, languages, and cultures, and lay down the chaotic elements structuring the initial identities of a continental reality in which very little, if anything, was understood. After having established this original chaotic structure, I move to the more orderly universe of representations of space in the eighteenth through the twentieth centuries.

My main quest is to understand the logical development of the construction of these identities, focusing on space and the representation of space as it mutates from landscape into sugar fields, milpas into haciendas, forests into plantations, rivers and lakes into transoceanic canals. The logic of the construction of continental America passes from *terra nullius* and awesome wilderness to aesthetic pastoral, from pastoral into exciting narratives of travel and exploration, and from there into discourses on mining, industry, commerce, and research and development. The natural process, once narrated as disorder, ignorance, and entropy, follows a curve that, briefly passing through a moment of positivistic scientific order, seems to lead again toward narratives of entropy and chaos.[6]

Part I studies the representation of the Caribbean islands using the trope of paradise. The founding image is provided by Christopher Columbus, but it is subsequently used, first, by colonial, and second, by postcolonial scholars to discuss a vast array of topics ranging from the foundation of scientific knowledge to the invention of the new marketing techniques and colonial entrepreneurial subjectivities and projects. The trope of paradise serves as a pivot to move from scientific invention to the exploitation of people and from aesthetics to the hard-and-fast prose of research and development.

To make this possible, chapter 1 discusses how colonial scholars (such as Antonello Gerbi, Tzvetan Todorov, and Edmundo O'Gorman) and postcolonial scholars (such as Margarita Zamora, Beatriz Pastor, José Rabasa, Mary Louise Pratt, Stephen Greenblatt, and David Spurr) engage this issue. Simply put, the difference between these two types of scholarship resides in their focus of interest. For colonial scholars, America is a "discovery." For postcolonial scholars, America is an "invention." Colonial scholars are invested in arguing the continuities and projection of Europe in America, and the type of discursive tradition it gave rise to. They argue that the "discovery" of America was a scientific enterprise that gave birth not only to the scientific disciplines themselves but also to a theory of knowledge based on the direct observation of empirical reality. In contrast, postcolonial scholars are invested in arguing the discontinuities and differences between Europe and America, and the type of epistemic confrontation they originated. They argue that the "invention" of America is a colonial enterprise, a business, that gave rise to the erasure of the past and present contributions of indigenous cultures. Both corpuses depart from the analysis of the observations of nature, but whereas colonial critics are vested in underscoring the contemplation of nature as aesthetics, postcolonial critics see aesthetics as a decoy to obscure the realities of colonialism. The founding image, paradise, based on Columbus's perception of nature and the temperate climate of the tropics, is taken by colonial scholars as a pretext to speak about stylistics and argue rhetorical influences tying the writing style of the new to the European classics. In contrast, postcolonial scholarship overrides any question relative to aesthetics, beauty, or sensibility, leaving the performance of colonial lies, exploitation, and ethnocide in its bare bones.

Chapter 2 discusses how, at the end of the nineteenth century, the representation of the Caribbean islands undergoes a drastic about-face and the perception moves from paradise to inferno. This radical shift is obtained by moving away from the marvelous Orientalist cosmographies and geographies of encounters, travels, and discoveries into the realities of agricultural production. Inferno is the appraisal of land and people at the end of slavery. A detailed description of soil erosion is coupled with the description of the customs and habits of the population. In stark contrast with the narratives of early cosmography and the fantastic voyages of Columbus and his policies on population, these narratives claim to be more objective and are based on symmetry, enumeration, and subtle ridicule. If the gardens of Hesperides are dry and worn away, the customs of the people constitute a rich field of behavioral psychoethnography that, together with the narratives of naturalists, lay the groundwork of a burgeoning *costumbrismo*.[7]

Comparing the conduct of the islanders to the laissez-faire convention of the conduct of Europeans renders Afro-Caribbean Americans' way of life simply ridiculous. Encouraged by a budding social Darwinism, the social types that are to be enfranchised and that constitute the seedbeds of the new civil society are derided. Their socialization of space, time, and life in their language, dress, festivities, and work habits takes the appearance of an embarrassing parody of Europe, a simulacrum that, mediated by high culture, will constitute the telling sign of a European mind reluctant to consider these people as equals. At this moment, a multiethnic and heterogeneous society of Creoles, whites, mulattoes, and blacks begins a polemic on the possession of land and land-tenure systems. Surveillance and surveyors vie to eliminate from the concept of British all those not fitting the standards of whiteness, an ethnic identity synonymous with culture and civilization.

I have chosen the works of one absentee planter, the novelist Matthew Gregory Lewis, and one English abolitionist commissioner, R. R. Madden, to introduce the ideas of a tradition that will come to slide into the narratives of research and development. As we can prove, the second narrative moment expands the notion of *tierra* as cultivated or productive land, and gives birth to all the narratives on agriculture and agricultural projects. *Tierra* feeds the narratives of positivism, and its representation is predicated on the idea of utility, progress, and productivity. *Tierra* is at the root of Francisco de Arango y Parreño's essay on agriculture, Andrés Bello's "Zona Tórrida," Ramiro Guerra's *Azúcar y Población*, and Edward Long and Bryan Edwards's *History of Jamaica*.

Part II examines how the notion of the socius changes. In the American mainland, Spaniards found well-organized societies and a land-tenure system, milpas, they did not know. In addition, unlike the islands, the highlands were densely populated and the types of languages spoken so varied that they could not differentiate one from the other. My take on this confusion is to begin by discussing how phonetic misunderstandings trace a labyrinthine topography in which a very small place is blown up into an immense number of fragments, many of which simply repeat the same referent. I construct my argument around the city of Utatlán, also known as Utatán, Uclatán, Gumarcaaj, and Kumarcaaj, depending on whether it is being spoken by the Quiché-Maya, Tlascaltecan, Mexican, or Spaniard. Utatlán, the most powerful center of Quiché-Maya power, is immediately reterritorialized (1524) as a new Spanish pueblo, Santa Cruz del Quiché. A different form of organizing the socius, through attempting to gather the dispersed populations of milpas, becomes the new symbol of the struggle for hegemony. The *Títulos* constitute the first claims of land made by the old lords. They form part of the testimonial corpus of the Conquest.

Speaking of languages and language instruction and differentiation, chapter 4 examines the argument of anthropologists (such as Linda Schele, Joy Parker, and David Freidel, David Tedlock, and Quetzil Castañeda) who maintain that the absence of common conventions and understanding creates as many grammars as there are researchers. From the very beginning, the Amerindian documents and testimonials, strongly marked by the presence of the indigenous voice, are translated from Quiché-Maya into Spanish, and then into English and French, and then back into Spanish. Thus, a mutilated bibliographical body is paired with a mutilated topography, which yields old jurisdictions and ends up, at the end of the fifteenth century, with the establishment of the city of Santiago de Guatemala or Antigua, to the south of Utatlán/Santa Cruz del Quiché, as the center of the new Spanish administration.

Based on this fragmented layout, chapter 5 discusses how nineteenth-century geographers and naturalists, such as E. G. Squier and Arthur Morelet, using selections from earlier colonial texts written by Spanish conquerors or English pirates and captains, set the records straight. The same principles followed by planters and commissioners remain operative with geographers and naturalists. If in the islands the principal problems were soil erosion and the illiterate and ungovernable character of civil society, in the Guatemalan highlands the problem is that of measurement and the self-subsistence economies of Amerindians. If in the islands the problem is sugar production and slavery, in the Guatemalan highlands it is the construction of transoceanic routes and railroads to link the U.S. East and West, and the nature of *mestizaje*. The metaphor "Banana Republics," used to name the Central American nations, comes to reflect this moment with accuracy.

In Part III, my geographical site is the Amazon. Nature is represented as a cross between ornate garden, landscape, and wilderness. In jungle, the mixture of poetic categories underscores the lack of differentiation between gardens as cultivated nature and nature as empty lands or wilderness. I begin by unraveling the terms *forest, wood, wilderness,* and *jungle,* and comparing them to their Spanish counterparts *manigua, selva,* and *jungla* to point out their semantic dependency on the modern ideas and concepts of development. If there is no concept that can really encompass the idea of the jungle, jungle becomes a chaotic organization of nature, impenetrable and ungovernable by definition.

Chapter 6 begins the analysis of jungles by reading Fray Gaspar de Carvajal, the first European to travel the Amazon with Francisco de Orellana, and compares the different tropes he used to describe his journey with the pilgrimage, retracing the same journey undertaken by the German and U.S. film industries today. I show the latter to be cultural heirs of the former. My point of contrast is the different narratives of confrontation, such as Sir Walter Raleigh's, Alexander von Humboldt's, and modern fiction writers' accounts of Guyana, Colombia, Peru, and Brazil. I also read the writings of the Portuguese Jesuit António Vieira and governor Antonio de Mendonça to underscore the writing of chaos, not only as the impossibility of finding a way through nature, but also as the hopelessness of understanding people and languages. The barbarian as cannibal and as unintelligible creature, and the cultures of anthropophagi, emerge from these pages where frustrated entrepreneurs face the ungraspable jungle. In chapter 7, I analyze the novels of Wilson Harris, Mario Vargas Llosa, and Alejo Carpentier.

It is over the (virgin or cultivated) land (*tierra*/nature) that the first epistemic exercise is organized. I argue that in the marketing of the intellectual projects, the poetic and religious notion of *locus amoenus,* utopia, the marvelous, Arcadia, paradise or El Dorado, *hortos conclusus,* namely, aesthetics and high culture, comes to mediate and serve as a rhetorical conduit for the mapping of the natural and cultural geographies of earlier modernity. I concentrate in this book on the impurity of discourse production and localize the place where one narrative type crosses and intersects the others. These narrative moments, which begin by adopting the notion of nature as *terra nullius,* later move into their opposite: settlement, fencing, claiming, delimiting, bordering, dividing, ruling, invoking the notion of privacy. Private property, first royal and imperial, then *encomendada*, privatized, staticized, corporativized, in turn implies that the old forms of holding *tierras*, the *ayllu*, the small garden/plot, the *ejido*, the milpa will become hacienda, latifundio, transnational corporations' strongholds.[8] Narratives of early colonialism, as well as of postcolonial globalization, fit this classification and profit from it. My claim is that the topographies of jungle tie all these morasses together.

In sum, my thesis is that the confrontation between indigenous peoples and the European colonial powers has persisted throughout the centuries; that this confrontation permeates all aspects of cultural production in Europe and in America, and that it lies at the bottom of the creation of the disciplines; that the principles of construction of these topographies are the solid referents conditioning the perception of continental America prevalent in the popular and elite minds and permeating the whole corpus of continental American studies, ranging from academic institutions, founding agencies, and governmental offices. Two parallel notions run through this book: one is resistance and the other is appropriation. In what follows, we will examine how resistance and appropriation vie against each other for the production of meaning at all levels.

PART I

THE CARIBBEAN ISLANDS

chapter 1

PARADISE

During his return trip to Hispaniola he confided to his Diary an extraordinary alternative: either the land which he had found was a "great terra-firma," or else it was "where the Terrestrial Paradise is to be found," which according to the general opinion "is at the end of the East," the region of the earth where he believed himself to have been.

—EDMUNDO O'GORMAN, *The Invention of America*

The earthly Paradise is at the end of the Orient, because it is a most temperate place, and so those lands which he had now discovered are, says he, at the end of the Orient.

—TZVETAN TODOROV, *The Conquest of America*

THE CARIBBEAN ISLANDS AS PARADISE

The representation of the Caribbean islands as paradise, promoted by tourist guides and brochures, is a trope that enjoys a long scholarly genealogy. Scores of enticing pictures of pristine greenish-blue waters, gracefully swaying palm trees, and gardens of radiant exotic flowers in full bloom subtend the idea. But the trope of the paradise itself is brimming with a history that grinds its way through several important debates in the field of colonial and postcolonial studies. This chapter examines the nature of these debates at two different historical junctures: one in the twentieth century, and the other at the beginning of the nineteenth.

Chapter 1 examines the works of colonial and postcolonial scholars.[1] The entry point for both scholarly traditions is the trope of paradise, but then research forks into two different directions, one concerned with

3

scientific knowledge production and aesthetics, the other with entrepreneurship and politics. The difference between the two types of scholarship is that whereas colonial scholars are invested in documenting the projection and continuity of Europe in America, underscoring all the cultural benefits the clash of worlds accrued to knowledge and aesthetics, postcolonial scholars want to pinpoint the ruptures and deconstruct all types of cultural performances as a way of exposing the entrepreneurial nature of the European project that accrued wealth, destroyed cultures, invented lies, and massacred people. For colonial scholars, America is a scientific "discovery," data; for postcolonial scholars, America is a rhetorical invention and intervention.

Chapter 2 examines travel and plantation diaries and maps and grapples with the turning of the trope of islands as paradise into its exact opposite, namely, the trope of islands as inferno. Travel narratives and plantation diaries directly address soil production and labor. In this regard, they are closer to postcolonial studies in that they openly accept the entrepreneurial character and purpose of the colonial enterprise, move away from science and aesthetics, and come straight back to ethnicity by openly discussing the racial profiles of people in reference to soil production and labor.

My intervention in this debate is not to provide yet another analysis of Christopher Columbus's navigational diaries, but rather to underscore the extraordinary generative power of the representation of nature as paradise that scuttles back with glee to its original source and demonstrates how a localized motif hit on by Columbus after a long and uncertain journey over uncharted waters becomes a foundational image of American nature. In the long history of colonialism, this image of nature as paradise mutates from gardens into soils, lands, land grants and land-tenure systems, productivity, property, propriety, and labor, jurisdictions, natural and nonrenewable resources. These mutations give rise to a vast array of agrarian narratives defining the identities of the continent and the people inhabiting it. Actually, all of America's foundational tropes subtend the same idea of America as paradise, a utopian Arcadia grounded in nature as a human resource. The purpose of this study is to follow up the arch of these mutations for which significant samples have been selected. But before the real discussion on nature as natural resources, we must pass through the crucible of multiple intellectual discussions whose intent is to unravel the imbroglio created by the clash of worlds that the voyages of Columbus and his prose of the world instigated. Therefore, before analyzing the works that address the ideas of nature as productive sites, spaces of labor and profit, and sources of identities and hermeneutical wars, there is a need to review the intellectual polemics that move from aesthetics, high culture, elite historiographies, and knowledge production to ethnocide, politics, and subaltern historiographies.

I argue that rhetorical tropes are the points of entry for understanding the continuities and mutations of this idea of nature as paradise, whose flip side underscores the chaos produced by the clash of worlds and the radically different views of reality of the contending parties involved. Disciplinary knowledge was the only way to come to terms with the nature of nature understood as "new" lands, a "discovery." Actually, the protracted discussion on knowledge and knowledge production originates in the attempt to bring some order and discipline to the chaos created by the confrontation between two worlds rendered evident in travel narratives of exploration.

What are the terms of this historical debate and how is the discussion thematized? Three large themes run through twentieth-century works: natural and geographic determinism, scientific empiricism, and entrepreneurship. The first theme works with the idea of "discovery" and focuses on the aesthetic contemplation of the "new" lands. The second theme also works with the idea of "discovery" but focuses on the theory of knowledge and method. The third theme works with the idea of "invention" and focuses on profits. The first two themes are closely intertwined, one leading to the other, or one serving as the pretext for the other. These themes reveal that the idea of the representation of the Caribbean islands as paradise is the effect of a more complex set of circumstances that involves the confusion of a theologically oriented mind facing an unedited world. The third theme is radically different and takes us to Columbus himself, a cunning, shrewd entrepreneur who invented the trope of paradise for its purchase. With the wisdom of hindsight, nineteenth-century works more clearly outline a discussion grounded on a change in the organization of labor and the extraction of surplus value. The important points of the debate here are (1) the nature of soil and soil erosion as it impinges upon production, (2) the nature of slave culture and the distinction between truth and deceit, and (3) the incipient discussion on governance and the emerging subjectivities of ex-slaves as citizens.

In this manner, the discussion of the trope of islands as paradise becomes extraordinarily productive. If the point of departure is paradise, as a form of the aesthetics, the end point is inferno, as the politics of colonialism. The connecting thread is a methodology that demonstrates how culturally fabricated ideas cross over the liminal spaces of disciplines, from geography to economy and politics, via the aesthetic, and how their discussion serves to lay the groundwork for an intriguing reflection on knowledge and politics.

I have deliberately discussed the last century first to demonstrate the historical endurance and resiliency of foundational images that are more than five hundred years old. I placed the study of nineteenth-century texts second to underscore how the ending of slavery also brought to sharp closure the trope of the Caribbean islands as paradise, and how, from then on, the image of inferno also belies everything we know and discuss about them.

NATURAL AND GEOGRAPHIC DETERMINISM

Knowledge of the "new" lands begins with the extrapolation of the geographies of the Caribbean islands onto an imaginary religious plane, that of paradise. On February 21, 1493, Columbus writes: "The sacred theologians and wise philosophers were right to say that the earthly Paradise is in the farthest orient, for it is a most temperate place, and the lands which I have discovered are indeed the farthest orient."[2] The interpretation of nature in religious terms is thus a foundational colonial gesture. Paradise is that rhetorical device that informs scholars that the Europeans are adjusting their perceptions of the newly found geographies and natural resources to their own familiar epistemes. From now on, the idea of nature as paradise cannot be separated from the culture encoding it. The trope of the islands as paradise is thus inescapably and indelibly attached to history, and more specifically to the colonial history of Christianity that subtends it. This is a momentous enterprise and an extraordinary invention because implicit in the trope of paradise, a garden of bliss, is the idea of a harmony between nature and people. The effects are twofold: a grounding of all subsequent American narrative developments and identities in nature and geography, and a longing for covering up the devastating results of the history of colonialism. What matters now is to underscore how a small nucleus of signification, a religious trope, is set loose and becomes the extended metaphor for obscuring the politics of colonialism.

The story really begins with a kind of weather report entered by Columbus on October 21, 1492:

> Here and all over the island the trees and plants are as green as in Andalusia in April, and the song of the birds makes a man want never to leave. There are flocks of parrots so big that they darken the sun, and birds of amazing variety, very different from our own. The trees, too, are of a thousand kinds, each with its own fruit and pleasant fragrance; it grieves my heart not to recognize them, for I am sure they must all be useful. I am taking samples of them all, and of the plants.[3]

Here Columbus writes the pleasures of arrival by conflating beauty with a temperate climate. These two tropes will be repeated ad nauseam throughout all of his voyages and will serve as the basis for the foundational image of America as paradise.

Based on this geographic observation, only a huge hermeneutical leap allows colonial scholars to harness the production of beauty to the production of scientific knowledge. Of all the tendencies implicit in Columbus's observation of nature—the purely geographic, the hermeneutical, and the aesthetic—they privileged the latter, because it served them as a vehicle to move from the hermeneutics of faith to those of scientific certainty. As a postcolonial scholar, my trouble with this interpretation is that beauty coupled with temperate weather is used as a pretext to erase the indigenous contribution to the discussion on colonialism. A vast disciplinary corpus overlay European ideas in order to cover up other epistemological organizations of the meaning of the world. To take stock of the issues at hand, we must attend to each implication separately but be a bit wary of the disciplinary intersections that cannot simply be done away with and that, in fact, turn out to be the most productive regarding the discussion of knowledge. Strategies of containment, deterrence, and prevention are all implicit in the polemic over Columbus's prose style, and, by extension, in that of all the early colonial chroniclers.

DISPLACEMENTS: FROM RELIGION TO AESTHETICS
TO NATURAL AND HUMAN SCIENCES

The displacement from religion to aesthetics, and from aesthetics to natural and human sciences, sets in motion the logic underscoring disciplinary intersections, the stuff colonial interpretations of earlier texts are made of. This is because the mission of colonial scholarship is to rend asunder and separate science, protoscience, nonscience, and fable and lies.[4] What matters to colonial scholars is to trace the borders between forms of knowledge and retroactively prove that early colonial writings partake of modernity. But in all cases, it is the constitution of scientific knowledge as the sole arbiter of colonialism that interests them. Would finding the scientific in the explorer justify the colonial enterprise?

One of the most enduring explanations of the shift from religion to science is Antonello Gerbi's. In his two groundbreaking books—*The Dispute of the New World: The History of a Polemic, 1750–1900* and *Nature in the New World: From Christopher Columbus to Gonzalo Fernández de Oviedo*, first published in 1955 and 1975 respectively—he argues that the chroniclers were avid information seekers, truly Renaissance minds who broke away from the old European *imago mundi* and established empirical evidence as the sole criterion of truth. To prove his point, Gerbi uses the mediation of aesthetics. He begins by explaining the prose style of the early chroniclers in terms of stylistics. His claim is that in order to accurately describe the "new" geographies of the world, the only figurative apparatus available to Columbus, and, after him, to all the early colonial chroniclers, is that of literature. The Latin classics and the bestiaries and fiction of the medieval world (Pliny, Dante, Petrarch, Boccaccio, Amadís of Gaul) are the blueprint to speak the "new."[5]

America is first encoded within the language of literature, because it is the only rhetoric available to describe what was fabulous and wondrous, and odd, and because it was the language of prestige. And although this classical apparatus was to crack before the realities of the "New" World, as Foucault demonstrated in his studies on the crisis of the analogue, it fully served its purpose in conveying the subjective understanding of the "new," alongside the joy and pleasure of the seeing eye contemplating the immensely rich geographies of the new global empire.[6] Thus, the imitation of the classics is intimately related not only to the absence of a conceptual grid in relation to the wonder of the "new," but also to aesthetics and pleasure, mostly the pleasures of the contemplating eye.

Explaining early colonial prose in terms of stylistics is a masterful strategic move: first, because it attenuates the confrontation between the "old" and the "new"; second, because it enables scholars to read the early colonial writings simply as the empirical evidence of an unknown world; and third, because it produces a more muted and safe discourse that treats confrontations as encounters. Furthermore, the style of the classics not only enables but also explains multiple juxtapositions—gardens with natural geographies, and natural geographies with paradise and utopian lands. The most profitable aspect to this move is the precipitation of the "new" into the idea of the "natural" that secures and seals up all inquiries and identities about the American continent within the realm of geography.

It goes without saying that nature itself, geography, is the site of utopia because it enjoins a paradisiacal climate with astonishing fecundity, the mutual harmony of all living creatures with the blessedness of nature. In this context, the ideoscape of paradise becomes an empty signifier holding together and containing the unbound images of a limitless nature. To round things to perfection, an anti-utilitarian caveat is added to the formula. On the other side of this world, European entrepreneurs who drool at the sight of this wealth envision a mode of production opposed to the artificial nature of the world of value, of money, of institutional structures, of repression, of colonization. Hovering in the shadows is the idea that the nascent capitalist imperial world is going to be perversely imagined as a world "without weights or measures . . . without the fatal curse of money, living in the golden age."[7]

Keeping this idea in mind, we can understand why the Caribbean islands, and, by extension, continental America, are the image of paradise. This image is predicated on the lack of structures and boundaries, the abundance of goods, and the absence of property, a world where "the land is the property of all, like the sun and the sea, and Thine and Mine, seeds of all evil, are unknown amongst them."[8] The key idiom is the absence of property. America is *terra nullius*. People and people's cultures are immediately and mercilessly factored out of this formula, and when they are included in the equation, they are made into tropes to support the scaffold of paradise. "They live in gardens open to all. Without laws, without books, without judges, but by their own nature they cultivate the right. They judge that man to be bad and wicked who delights in doing injury to others."[9]

This way of thinking Amerindians constitutes the seedbed of a tropical and sentimental indigenism (or nativism and even naturalism) that comes to supplement the construction of America through the geographic and natural narratives of exploration. The whole Americanist field will be permeated by this idea that expands in all disciplinary directions throughout the centuries with the force of a blast, an idea that is grounded on the emptying of the land coupled with the rhetorical idealization of the naked man set against the splendor of a natural paradise.[10] *Los naturales* (the naturals) are praised for a wisdom that is forever wedded to nature and geography. Their own sense of property and propriety and, at times, even their political and military savvy are all crisscrossed together and subsumed in the straightjacket of geographic determinism.

Nevertheless, nature, written in the style of the classics, subtends Renaissance utopias, which, in turn, underscore that America is a worthwhile enterprise, big business. Actually, geographic and natural determinism and entrepreneurship, deceitfully formulated as opposite poles, as an "either/or," reinforce one another as an "either/and." In a heavily entrepreneurial age, large inventories of natural resources and detailed descriptions of nature, disingenuously defined as the opposite of utilitarian, are the vehicle to carry the heavy cargoes of unprecedented wealth from America back to Europe on the back of literature, as in the following Columbus quote:

> It is only sensible to go where there is good potential for trade. . . . there is no point in lingering when one can set off and explore a large area until one finds a country which offers profit, although I do believe that the place where we are now may provide an abundance of spices. It is a source of great regret to me that I know so little about spices, for I see an enormous variety of fruit-bearing trees, all as green as the trees in Spain in May and June, and many kinds of plants and flowers, and the only one we have recognized so far is this aloe, of which I have a large quantity brought on board today to bring to Your Majesties.[11]

The imitation of the classics in such early colonial geographic writing does not detract in any way from the commercial purposes of Columbus's enterprise—so much so that we can safely conclude that Columbus's style inaugurated modern marketing techniques. Rhetorical figures come to assist his purpose. Analogic expressions become hyperbolic expressions—"like" becomes "bigger, higher, and larger than." Hyperbole makes possible the maximization of the metaphor of paradise. Continental America, like the islands, becomes a superior measurement, a superior production, not only the contemplation of the marvelous but also the inexhaustible production and then knowledge and possession of the marvelous. The recurrent turning back to nature, the reiteration of the organic relation between people and the environment, and the absolute dependence of humans on nature, which resonate in the narratives of environmentalism and research and development today, echo these founding narratives.

In an ironic twist, utopia becomes cornucopia and is tied to the admiration and governance of the naked man. Wisdom in the ordering of nature is later enjoined to all the ensuing productive narratives that counterpose paradise to inferno, the exaltation to the oppression of the naked and natural man. The entwining of all these diverse points of view requires the assistance of disciplinary knowledge, but, at this point, all we have is a subjective positioning and repositioning, written in a classic rhetoric and a hyperbolic mood that skews the conquering subjects as it foregrounds the natural man. It goes without saying that the mapping of these contours sharply silences any other voices that do not fall within the European purview and that aesthetic contemplation alongside the anti-utilitarian qualification of the colonial enterprise takes the edge off oppression. Ignoring people buttresses the European enterprise, anathematizes difference, and stems the swelling tide of the epistemological discrepancies to which the colonial relationship between the worlds gives rise.

SCIENTIFIC EMPIRICISM

Another way of understanding the relationship between the natural geographies of the "new" lands and the "old" epistemological descriptions and images apprehending them is to move the discussion away from the realm of aesthetics and into the natural and human sciences. In this regard, colonial scholars tread very carefully to pinpoint the crossover of narratives. In an attempt to knit up the loose ends, they carefully classify these crossovers following the modern division of disciplines. They know that, in the early documents, ethnography, natural sciences, astrology, astronomy, political geography, and history are deeply and structurally embedded into each other, and that they vie with theology and Christian tenets to obtain the precision the knowledge of the "new" lands demands. They admit that in the first chroniclers the ethnographer assumes the stance of the historian or naturalist; the political geographer becomes an ethnographer or an anthropologist; forensic, military, moral, and political history are all intertwined, tangled, and confused with ethnography. However, the genealogy of disciplines and of disciplinary knowledge is not paired to the history of colonialism. Their intent is to claim that natural sciences are in command of the new prose of the world.

Natural sciences are important because what is "new" is perceived in terms of nature. "New" means that the whole world is one global datum, the object of interpretation. The problem lies in how to separate the natural world from hermeneutics, how to disengage natural from human sciences. Colonial scholars do not bother with this question. Nevertheless, the glitch of how to come to terms with the relationship between empirical observation and faith as opposing methods to know the world remains. And if the chroniclers are held to be the admirers and panegyrists of the "new" in terms of nature, all evidence shows that their minds press on not so much to bridge the chasm separating one epistemology from the other, one discipline from another, or, for that matter, one world from the other, but to appropriate one world by another. Therefore, any discussion on knowledge and knowledge production, any debate on the formation of disciplines, must explain the relationship between those Europeans who emphasized conquest and markets and treated America as the biggest fair, and those who were stimulated by the "new" and worked on the hermeneutics of difference. My whole point is that it is impossible to sever business from science, or science from aesthetics, and that what early-twentieth-century colonial scholars do is to moralize, attenuate, or simply gloss over the devastating effects of colonialism. Their aim is to prove that the "discovery" of America was a big benefit to humanity because it laid the foundation of scientific and disciplinary knowledge.

METHOD

In the discussion just outlined, the question of method becomes relevant. Empiricism is the method used to override the religious interpretation of the world. What is argued is that knowledge production entails the intervention of the senses, and that it is impossible to inaugurate sciences without their concurrence. Direct observation accrues value and sense perception—seeing, hearing, touching, tasting—and installs a new way of apprehending the world. Empiricism is the method for bridging the chasm between the "new" reality and the European subjective understanding of it. It is the new technology to know the world. It is sense perception that launches the division of disciplines.

Knowledge is experiencing, seeing with the naked eye, being an in situ witness of what one describes. The physical experience of a place, of a specific location, claims the epistemological privilege that counting, measuring, and accountability will have for the nineteenth-century positivistic sciences. Seeing and experiencing are not only the necessary condition for obtaining knowledge, but also a lesson learned in the body politic: "a knowledge of the things of these parts can only be acquired with much thirst . . . hunger . . . weariness, in war with the enemy and in war and peace with the elements . . . wounded without surgeon, sick without doctor or medicine . . . tired without being able to take a rest." [12] Epic and knowledge are grounded on the flesh and blood of the explorers, the new entrepreneurs.

The caveat introduced by direct empirical observation of the local and the regional, by the real presence within the "new" geographies as a prerequisite of knowledge, was the cause of many a great and grave problem to cosmography, oceanography, and religion. The heated and resentful polemic between those who came to America, the *Indianos*, and those who stayed in Europe has direct observation as a central point. Presence splits local from global knowledge, arguments, and sensibilities. The "new" lands were dividing the scholastics and empiricists, the national vernacular languages—such as Spanish—from Latin. Presence also demarcates a polemic between institution-bound *sapientia* and freelance intellectuals, between experience and tradition, between the *letrado*, the court humanist, and the explorer or mine inspector—the new intelligentsia. In personal experience, the modern takes precedence over the traditional and seeing possesses intrinsic value. It is in this manner that geography and traveling are set over and against theology and sacred history as the source of authority. Here we come back once more to entrepreneurship. Scientific knowledge is inextricably bound up with it. Each of these observations elicits a myriad of polemics. For instance, when seeing, a single witness is no witness at all; two people seeing the same thing in two different locations makes the data believable; two similar hypotheses over the same data observed at dissimilar times are likewise believable.

Local knowledge becomes a commodity to buy and sell, to exchange and to profit from. By 1513, long before Sir Walter Raleigh was to explicitly state the concurrency of the eyes as a method of knowledge, the *Suma de Geografía* (1525) by Martín Fernández de Enciso stands poised on the empirical ledge. The interpretation of this work is important because it denotes that, by the time of its publication, something very important had come into being and that is the intervention of the indigenous cultures in the dispute. The Spaniards no longer believe in what they hear, or they have acquired the rudiments of language to hear what the aborigines are saying. "They say . . . but the truth of the matter is not known."[13] Enciso already admires fabrics, garments, colors, and even people who write books, people "like us." The culture of the *naturales* makes its way into the hermeneutic world and *terra nullius* becomes densely populated land.[14] Natural geography becomes political history. Narratives of the marvelous give way to narratives of arms. Bestiaries yield to politics entwined with rudimentary biology to explain the move away from the "noble savage" and into the naked man. He is written as animal and hence deprived of the rights to his lands and entitlements. But from the very beginning there is a vested interest in keeping natural and political histories apart. Natural history is constructed as an independent subject, not as the context of the events. Political history is at best relegated to the space of fable. This clash of knowledge accounts for the superimposition of narratives, and in turn it is accounted for by the impartiality required of the observer, an impartiality that refers to the world of nature but not to the society of men. Only eyewitnesses write sciences, but only eyewitness write political history too.

COLUMBUS'S PROSE OF THE WORLD

A glance at Columbus's prose allows the reader to immediately grasp the non sequiturs of a narrative of the world where the contemplating subject is profoundly confused when not altogether lost. In the following quote it is easy to discern the tension between what Columbus sees and the way he is interpreting it:

> I have always read that the world of land and sea is spherical. All authorities and the recorded experiments of Ptolemy and the rest, based on the eclipses of the moon and other observations made from east to west, and on the height of the Pole Star made from north to south, have constantly drawn and confirmed this picture, which they held to be true. Now, as I said, I have found such great irregularities that I have come to the following conclusions concerning the world: that it is not round as they describe it, but the shape of a pear, which is round everywhere except at the stalk, where it juts out a long way; or that it is like a round ball, on part of which is something like a woman's nipple. This point on which the protuberance stands is the highest and nearest to the sky. It lies below the Equator, and in this ocean, at the farthest point of the east, I mean by the farthest point of the east the place where land and islands end.[15]

It is clear from this quote that two impulses, one triggered by the senses and the other by dogma, spill over into several areas that today we organize into different regimes of knowledge—religious, geographic, cartographic, astronomic, navigational—but that in Columbus's day and in his prose are all entwined. It is evident that all his sensations must be passed through the crucible of religious imagination, which constitutes the main frame hovering over and overlooking all of his practices. The trope of the Caribbean islands as paradise is a clear sign of this religious hegemony, but as a rhetorical figure it is useful because it allows a condensation of functions—imaginaries, imagination, invention, history and fable, geography and astrology.

In Columbus's disorientation, *fabula* and imagination prevail and lend their mediating services to the new prose of the world. Yet, although it is clear that fable works in tandem with the subjective ambitions of an entrepreneur, colonial scholars prefer to read Columbus's early colonial perception of nature as protoscience, a truly modern and revolutionary prose that expands the understanding of the natural kingdoms and promotes new sciences and fresh research. This is the way the Eurocentrism of colonial scholars is foregrounded. Located on the threshold between colonial and postcolonial scholarship, the works of Tsvetan Todorov (mainly *The Conquest of America: The Question of the Other* [1984]), and Edmundo O'Gorman (mainly *The Invention of America: An Inquiry into the Historical Nature of the New World and the Meaning of Its History* [1961]) will rehearse the aesthetic and the scientific argument once more. What is of relevance in Todorov's argument is the reiteration of the anti-utilitarian covenant. What is important in O'Gorman's is his disengagement with the scientific position and his decisive move toward invention. I will examine these two moments separately.

Todorov's anti-utilitarian argument rests its case in the pleasure of the gaze. Contemplating the "new," Columbus surrenders to beauty and "loves a tree because it is lovely . . . not because one might make use of it as a mast for one's ship or because its presence promises wealth."[16] Bartolomé de Las Casas, on whose authority Todorov bases his argument, had already stated that, in the contemplation of nature, Columbus preferred beauty to utility: "He said that even if there were no profits to be gained here, if it were only the beauty of these lands . . . they would be no less estimable" (23).

In Todorov's work, the aesthetic argument reinforces the idea that Columbus's concern is nature and nature alone. This explains why Columbus attentively observes every sign that might concern natural phenomena. His abilities as a navigator rely on this most keen of interests. He can make the distinction between winds, discerning their direction and speed, which is how he becomes informed enough to compare the weather to Andalusia in April. He can accurately read those signs in the sky that come to bear upon navigation, and that is how he finds his way through the waters. There is nothing wrong with this view except that Columbus's intransitive admiration for the land becomes intensively profitable. Furthermore, in Todorov as in Gerbi, beauty is grounded on empiricism, empiricism lies at the foundation of sciences, and sciences are the shortest road to profit. In a roundabout way, aesthetics always becomes a partner of the colonial enterprise.

But there is another problem here and that is that Todorov's interpretation sidesteps the fact that Columbus's main interest was commercial; that he was looking for new commercial routes; that that was the project he sold to the Spanish monarchs. The caveat is that Columbus's commercial enterprise was predicated on finding a shorter route to the Indies and it is paradoxically in his not finding the route, on his error, that colonial scholars ground their hypothesis on the discovery of America as the foundational moment of sciences. There is no problem in granting that Columbus's project was mediated by a scientific hypothesis, that his scientific hypothesis was geographic. There is a problem in correlating scientific inquiry with gross error. Thus, if there is a point to be made here, it refers to the intersection and crisscrossing of entrepreneurship, religious dogma, science, and aesthetics.

Moreover, Columbus's style, his penchant for exaggeration and hyperbole, is directly related to his enterprise—more concretely to the selling of his enterprise—but it is also related to his own inability to distinguish between his own navigational hypothesis, the "new" geographies he is navigating, and the religious dogma that informs his own ways of the world. All these different forms of approaching a subject are tangled in his head. He is totally confused and totally disturbed. His prose cannot be read but as a huge mixture of the fabulous and wondrous that is key to his conundrum. The easy way out of this dilemma is to focus on aesthetics—and there are so many passages supporting this reading that it is easy to fall prey to them; but aesthetics and sciences do not go together, for while one enjoys the privileges of exaggeration—Columbus's hyperbole is a case in point—the other demands precision and accuracy. Thus, when Columbus claims that the land is "the fairest," that "no other land under the sun can appear finer, nor more magnificent," that "a thousand tongues would not suffice to express it, nor his hand to write it, for it appeared that it was enchanted" (Todorov, *The Conquest of America*, 24), he is obviously appealing to beauty to market his project, but also giving his errancy and error an exalted aesthetic flare. In doing so, he is simultaneously disclosing his own lack of parameters, and hence his own disorientation. This is not to say there is no beauty in Caribbean nature, or no possibility of reading an incipient development of sciences in Columbus's prose, but rather that cultural critics must be aware of the implications of the readings we choose to make.

Todorov's reading of aesthetics into Columbus's prose sidesteps Columbus's own disorientation and covers up the politics of colonialism. Actually, his is a way of justifying colonialism. Thus, even if Columbus did not find the new commercial routes to Asia, he did all of us the favor of "discovering" a new world. But if we were to admit this statement as true, it would be tantamount to acknowledging that Columbus's discovery of America was indeed a scientific error. There is nothing wrong with accepting that, except that it reveals the flaws inherent in colonial scholarship.

In sum, we are led to conclude that Columbus's enterprise is neither aesthetic nor scientific; that science and aesthetics are by-products of European hermeneutics; and, as proven by the endurance of the trope of America as paradise, that both are also wealth, riches to be accumulated and profited from. Furthermore, Todorov's own underscoring of Columbus's insistence on being called Colón, which is part of the word *colono* (colonist), equally enjoins the aesthetic and the symbolic in the profitable scientific. The same holds for the names he chooses for the landscapes, such as Monte de Plata, Río de Oro. The possessive *de* qualifies nature and marks its wealth. The hypostasis of mountain and silver, river and gold, markets the new possessions. And, finally, the fact that Columbus is only interested in proper names addressed to nature and that nature becomes his sole referent proves that people are of no importance to him. In fact, people are referred to as animals: "I shall take from this place six of them" (ibid., 30), or "I had nothing with me which I might show them to make them come near" (32). Postcolonial critics will make him pay for this.

On the opposite side of this discussion, Edmundo O'Gorman totally dismisses the scientific interpretations of Columbus's enterprise. He does not for a moment believe that Columbus discovered America because he "was sensitive to the beauty of tropical nature, which enabled him to announce the existence of a truly new world" (ibid.). O'Gorman's obsession is the nature of the "new," of which the "old" existing world of European culture had no awareness. For him, Columbus is a feudal man and his prose of the world, far from being scientific, is still deeply grounded in the religious. In his pathbreaking study on the invention of America, O'Gorman sets out to prove that for knowledge to be scientific, it first has to pass through the filter of consciousness. Culture, consciousness, and writing are here the preconditions of being and of arguing the old/new dichotomy.

O'Gorman's thesis is that Columbus never knew the "new," because he was never conscious he had arrived at any continent other than Asia; he never admitted, based on his empirical evidence, that he was in error. No amount of significant data revealed by experience will ever make him doubt his findings. His lack of awareness of the difference between empirical reality and his subjective understanding of it tells us he did not break with a functional Christian paradigm created by faith and punishable by fire. He could not imagine a different way of relating to his Creator, and, for that reason, he is, in O'Gorman's view, a premodern man.

O'Gorman argues that Columbus's method is based on "invention," and that his son's thesis in defense of his father is flawed: "Ferdinand Columbus not only takes advantage of the current concealment of his father's true opinions, but also deliberately fosters it with the hope of hiding them permanently. . . . [He] accompanied Columbus on his fourth voyage, when the Admiral . . . convinced himself, finally and absolutely, that all the shores he had explored belonged to Asia."[17] Thus, Columbus's proclaimed aesthetics is nothing but scientific error and religious stubbornness. O'Gorman believes that although Columbus was forced to accept the magnitude of his enterprise, he still took refuge in speculations. The observations he wrote down in his diary concerning the variation of the compass, the astonishing mildness of the climate, and the fine proportions and light skins of the natives indicate that the admiral was mulling over some other explanation. During his return trip to Hispaniola he confided to his diary an extraordinary alternative: either the land he had found was a "great terra-firma," or else it was "where the Terrestrial Paradise is to be found," which, according to the general opinion "is at the end of the East," the region of the earth where he believed himself to have been.[18]

In sum, the discrepancies examined by modern scholars of colonialism regarding early colonial writings are based on the incongruity between America's nature (as empirical data) and European culture (as an interpretive device). The problem is how to encode the relationship between the physical and the cultural in landscapes. Modernity requires that the new explorers move away from the ideas of landscapes as the physical geographies of the divine. They must provide evidence, learn to see, gauge, evaluate, account for, and experiment with the "unknown" with new eyes and fresh sensibilities. It is in this sense that narratives of exploration and discovery are enterprises, what Michel de Certeau calls "industries"—the art of writing possession into a writ, and of underwriting it.[19] The point is that neither aesthetics nor natural sciences relate to the politics of colonialism. On the contrary, both serve as a decoy to obscure issues relative to the clash of the worlds. Therefore, the discussion on aesthetics and knowledge is a way of covering up the real issues concerning peoples and their cultures under colonialism. And that to the degree that colonial studies buttresses the arguments of aesthetics and the foundation of knowledge, it is complicit with the politics of colonialism, part and parcel of the same enterprise.

THE AESTHETICS OF OPPRESSION AS
A HERMENEUTICS OF SPACE

The aesthetic function within the colonial writings of space is precisely what postcolonial criticism most takes to task. In total agreement with Enrique Dussel (*El encubrimiento del Otro: hacia el origen del "mito de la modernidad"* [1492]), David Spurr reminds us that "colonial discourse takes over as it takes cover," and that the aestheticization of foreign realities is made possible by accentuating distances, both cultural and geographic.[20] "[T]he aesthetic stance itself is taken from within a position of power and privilege," which makes possible "the digestion [of unpalatable realities] into art" (47). In tune with Spurr, José Rabasa states that the phrase "Andalusia in April," Columbus's emphasis on the sweetness of the weather, the invocation of the orchards of Valencia in April, are an enabling referent that fabricates the "new" as a *locus amoenus*. In his reading of the diary, idyllic landscapes are linked to the purchase of the "experience of exotic lands," to the oppression of "noble savages," and the promotion of "the so-called literature of going native."[21] This type of criticism focuses on the ideological debate on cultures, in terms of knowing them through Eurocentric historiographies, and on the hermeneutics of space. In Columbus's diary, landscape is encoded in the lexemes of Orientalism, "immersed in a symbolic field where deserts, the plains of Eurasia, or volcanoes lack particularity, and function as scenarios for the inscription of the monstrous and the otherworldly. . . . Paradisiacal landscape is a legendary phantasm, but not an actual locus given for description."[22] The actual locus of description is ideology, defined as the problematic relationship between the subjective and colonial understanding of the problematic relationship between a "new" world and "exotic lands."

Along with aesthetics, the pleasure argument is also thrown overboard. Readings of space are no longer concerned with pleasure or the contemplation of nature. Macro-tropes like the *gusto* of arrival and the peacefulness of the sight are all submerged into the hermeneutics of space viewed as the project of colonialism. Actually, what postcolonial scholars propose is a reading of continental data against the grain and through the eyes of the *naturales*.[23] The relationship between the literary or cultural model and empirical continental data is of much less relevance than the intersections between the beautiful and the profitable, pragmatics and intellect, the pleasure of the subjective moment of arrival and politics. The new interest lies in the production of knowledge as the culture of colonialism. These are readings that privilege the learned, or the ideological, over the seen object.

Speaking about exploration literature, Mary Louise Pratt (*Imperial Eyes*) and David Spurr begin their studies by accentuating visual observation and by isolating the privileging role of the gaze as cultural activity, and of the eye as an instrument of appraisal. A gaze fixes upon an object. The eye's task is to describe it. Description refers to the pragmatics of a choice that discriminates, appropriates, renames, and disengages. The mechanics of description are then predicated on privilege and power, rights and availability. The eye is authorized to inspect, to examine, and to look; a legality is somehow implicated. Descriptions are then mediated de facto by language and power, culture and legality, and presume not only the distance between observed and observer, but the notion of passivity and activity. What we encounter here is a disempowerment of that which is being observed, and an espousal of the dynamics of the economies of uneven exchange as plotted in narratives. Obedience and passivity are the predominant aspects of the contemplated. The effect of the gaze, coupled with the action of writing and remodeling, is paralyzing.

By phrasing cultural encounters in this manner, these studies claim that early colonial travel narratives engineer the ideas of colonialism. In accordance with W. J. T. Mitchell's theory, the master strategy of colonial students is to naturalize, that is, to remove agency from whatever is contemplated, to transform culture into nature.[24] In contrast, for postcolonial critics, supported by Foucault's studies on disempowerment, the analytical, symbolic, iconographic, and semantic arrangement of that which is seen immediately guarantees control. Taking control, grasping power, debilitating, and disempowering are among the cultural stylistics that suppress human and civil rights as politics of discovery. According to postcolonial criticism, the metaphor of the panopticon as private or public eye best fits such a conflation of the concepts of surveyors, surveying, and surveillance as applied to the reading of places, cultures, and peoples undertaken by early colonial writing.

Making the analysis contingent on the eye renders a visual-arts perspective—a mathematical, geometrical, or pictorial representation—of that which is being observed and enjoins aesthetics to the hermeneutics of space, and both areas to the geographies of oppression. This creation of perspectives marks the birth of human, social, and natural sciences, as they can be said to start in travel narratives of encounter. From the horizon to the ground, from the horizon to the instrument, and from subject to object, the eye aims at capturing general outlines, a point of focus, some measure of spatial order. The first scanning combines quantified impressions of distance, spatial arrangement, order, and symmetry. Part of this counting is accounting and accountability, the investment vested in both the value of the object and the reliability of the seen subject. But how do pragmatics and pleasure merge in the gauging gaze of the colonialist?

In Spurr's reading of Pratt, "the landscape is first aestheticized, then it is invested with a density of meaning intended to convey its material and symbolic richness, and finally described so as to subordinate it to the power of the speaker" (18). Aesthetics enters as a way of enticing investment by enhancing the value of lands, first by conferring strategic value upon them, and second by underwriting the authority of the eye. The sensorial and the subjective probably contribute to the perceptual appetite of that which is being narrated—*contado, raconté*. Literary erudition is another factor adding to the density of meaning and, consequently, of value. The privileges of the gaze only serve to reproduce the privileges of a larger political hermeneutical sphere. When it comes to interiors, and to the bodies of the peoples themselves, to human rights, survey becomes surveillance. Cultural encodings and hermeneutics work as surveillance, and turn the politics of Christianity, democracy, and the rights of man into submission to science, discipline, and narrative genres.

Coming from this perspective, we can concede the myriad of convergences found in Columbus's "sight unseen." However, the sight that is given the greatest currency in past and present narratives is that which plots islands as the site of paradise, an always sublime or picturesque geography. We are obliged to explore the intersections between the pragmatic act of seeing a pristine ecological sight, and the heavy downloading of a European rhetoric upon the object to make it fit into the colonial project.

We must ask, what was Columbus actually seeing? Reading Columbus's tropes and methods through the ideologies of representation alone does not avoid the pitfalls that are to be found in reducing the Caribbean islands to the position of floating signifiers, to be accommodated within major European texts. It does not preempt the reading of the Caribbean islands solely as European tropes.[25] The object of knowledge as empirical data, as an object described by the natural sciences (geology, ecology, biology) cannot possibly be dislodged from the object of knowledge filtered through the structures of meaning of subjective understanding—at least not in the sixteenth century. A reading of the object is always culturally overdetermined, and at best crossed by doubt and placed halfway between the vision of the gauging eye and writing. We can argue here that what mediates between nature and culture is political hegemony, and that political hegemony comes across in the form of aestheticized scientific and mercantile concerns. The problem is how "the real," as empirical data, is positioned in writing and what writing does for the construction of localities, accumulation of capital, and power.

THE "OLD" AND THE "NEW"

Cultural critics have excised the simile of island paradise to unravel not only the "new" and old continents and their epistemes, but also the hermeneutics of space that reads aesthetics as the politics of colonialism. The problem is how to speak of the relationship between two continental segments of the world and their data, how to decide what is "new" and what is "old." Substituting this dichotomy for "written" and "oral" has not freed postcolonial scholars from becoming embroiled in the same kind of hermeneutical riddles besetting colonial scholars. Transferring the adjective *new* from *world* to navigational routes or to mappings and cartographies has not made the situation any better. Walter Mignolo's idea of coevalness underlines the simultaneity of productivity, ingenuity, and dexterity in and of cultures, but does not sidestep the new/old dichotomy of the narratives of encounter and exploration. He simply renames them using the adjectives *advanced* and *behind*. Margarita Zamora takes up this very same question of old and new and traces its genealogy to the relationship between Columbus and Amerigo Vespucci, arguing that for Columbus, the (New) World was already there; that is, the (New) World is just an "other" world, the *urbis alterius* "well known to the ancients," pagans, whereas for Vespucci, "none of these countries were known to our ancestors, and to all who hear about them they will be entirely new."[26] Discovery, then, Zamora states, "was the product of a rhetorical tour de force, not of an empirical observation" (130). Neither Columbus nor Vespucci "made a definitive contribution to our knowledge of the true configuration of post-Discovery geography. Yet each made a profound contribution to the ways in which we think about the world" (132). The unknown "new" is that which is not particularly attached to any given place and that could be even part of an imaginary site. The "known" is that which has already been articulated and therefore can be used as an objective point of reference.

Rabasa's reformulation of O'Gorman's term *inventing* into *reinventing*, to signify the appearance of the "new" in knowledge, lays out the process whereby a given piece of data comes into being. His point is to read against the reproduction of definitions and categories that mar the possibility of the knowledge of "new" cultures and their contexts. He does not so much oppose the metaphors used for describing and encoding the "new" as he points out the preconditions of its fabrication. All knowledge has the status of a sign within a structure (e.g., Columbus in the New World, or the Caribbean in Columbus). Knowledge is, then, a product of the intersection of signs within narrative clusters, and of narrative clusters among themselves. Contextualizing is the placing—or re-placing—of signs, the transposing or sliding of a referent from one hermeneutical space into another. Contextualizing is changing vocabularies.

The method and power of placing, displacing, and replacing old and new data is what makes postcolonial critics the warriors of words. Words, signs, and their chains of meaning are the only permanent witnesses of cultural hegemonies, and they make possible over and again the uncontestable realization that in colonial narratives every thing is mixed and it cannot be even momentarily disengaged. The positions just outlined have one mission and one mission alone: to prove that there is no knowledge without the mediation of cultures, that cultures are known through discourse, be it that of drawing, singing, or weaving. Knowledge is writing, and writing is a technology—the technology for building empires—an awesome mimetic machinery. The intersection of narratives, the hybrid, is what becomes the site of "the real" fabric of cultures, and a most profitable place for the discussion of knowledge as the hermeneutics of encounters. Speaking about the world, the "old"/"new" dichotomy loses all hermeneutical value because looking at them from the cultural standpoint, both are old worlds.

THE MODERN IN THE POSTCOLONIAL

Directly connected to the debate on the old and the new is the question of what is or what makes something modern. As we have already seen, the works of Gerbi, Todorov, and O'Gorman negotiate this question. In judging what is or makes modern, the critical difference between colonial and postcolonial scholars is not the scientific but the utilitarian aspect of the colonial enterprise. Columbus is a modern entrepreneur, an inventor who proposes a new subjectivity, a new space, and a new discourse. The great image of the geographer-cum-cosmographer becomes projected in tandem with the realities of the ambitious businessman. To divorce the man of science from the businessman is of no use. It only serves to condone the appropriation of lands and to value individual entrepreneurship as a desirable subjectivity. Thus, ideologies of science as civilization (later to be taken over by the ideologies of progress, modernism, and modernization) are already coupled to a pre-post-Enlightenment historiography that privileges individualism, dexterity, and invention as the basis for colonialism. Enterprise, knowledge, and colonialism coalesce in modern science; Columbus is therefore a modern man, and modernity implies the use of counting and accounting as method, but also the extraction of wealth and the exploitation of peoples.

Insofar as the modern is concerned, the hypothesis of manufacturing is worth considering too. In dialogue with Michel de Certeau, Rabasa argues that Columbus's industry is the fabrication of images as investment. His product is a new discourse that entails changing the notions of subject, space, and narrative. His expertise is similar to that of a code breaker. He must produce "new signs" (narratives). Columbus's narrative intersections are viewed as his errancy through a semiotic universe in search of the signs that will permit him the reconciliation of the old and the new symbolic fields of reference: America and the Latin classics, the Bible, Pierre d'Ailly, Marco Polo, all raw material from which to fabricate resemblances. Proper names not only are meaningful in their analogies

with silver and gold but they also underscore the phonetic interference
and entwining of the codes, as in Caniba, Civao, Cipango. The semantic
transformation of the territories back and forth from the known into the
unknown and from Spanish into the indigenous languages also highlights
the boundaries of the European codes and foregrounds how the unknown
constantly eludes paradigmatic assimilation.

An examination of the modern also brings up the pressing question
of the wild eye. Thus, what of the knowledge of Amerindians? Columbus's
gaze stands poised on the brink of what the cultures inform one another.
This is a point that carries over into what Sylvia Wynter studies as the
abduction of signs from their contextual environments and inherited
stocks of knowledge. It is transferring meaning from one data bank into
another, making signs circulate among different information loops.[27] The
savage gaze leans in the direction of the exotic as satanic or monstrous.
Do wild and naked *naturales* and their perception have the same epistemic
status as animals? Can they also be read as a lack of correspondence
between sights and seen, data and legend, a description of unedited phenomena as a semantic asset?

Beatriz Pastor (*The Armature of Conquest*) argues that the Amerindian
knowledges never reached the pages of the European texts. Her hypothesis on Columbus's writings is also one of construction and fabrication. In
her opinion, Columbus engineers the realities of the "New" World by
following the blueprint of three basic manuscripts: those of Marco Polo,
Pierre d'Ailly, and Aeneus Sylvio. The "New" World was, then, not presented as unknown, but as a summary of all available knowledge at the
time. The process by which Columbus reproduces a summary of the
model of the "New" World against the backdrop of radically distinct landscapes is adjustment. Adjustment turns the idea of discovery into verifica-
tion, and whatever is not verified is dismissed or dumped. Dumping and
dismissal are methodologies providing knowledge of the non-European
"new," Janus-faces of a method of distortion and destruction, part of the
coverup that ultimately leads to the destruction of the "new"—or to its
(re)invention—in the form of depopulation and deculturization. There is,
then, a relationship between inventing, deforming, and covering up as the
technologies for building the localities of "the new." Previous narrative
encodings of exotic lands lend their exuberance and hyperbole. The same
methods are used on indigenous people and their cultures. This is the

method of sustaining the objectives of Columbus's project, but what is his project?

For some critics, Columbus's project is the patenting of his findings, for others, the duplication of a model that, in contact with cultural diversity, proves as rigid as an ideological parameter. The goal is to prove that Columbus already knows what the lands are destined for, or that they lead toward the Oriental riches, because knowledge for Columbus is an a priori condition that precedes all empirical evidence. Where critics disagree is in whether or not invention is a summary of previous readings, attributing to the "new" that which is the most prestigious in the old, or whether invention is a conscious injunction of signs. One piece of evidence is Columbus's duplication of databases that were available only to himself, in which the "duplicitous distortion of time"[28] signals the alteration of the space–time relationship in order to conceal the parameters of the true route, a political praxis that certainly agrees with the protocols of modern industrialists protecting their trade secrets and patents, and with the classified nature of research and development reports and grant applications today.

CONCLUSIONS

Along the lines of the discussion on method examined earlier, we can argue that there is a threefold rupture in the reading of early colonial texts: first, between geographic and religious imaginaries—that information that was encoded in the Latin classics; second, between the modern scientific and the premodern feudal—marked by the insistence on empirical data and method; and third, between aesthetics and science and entrepreneurship—based on the profitable nature of the colonial production of knowledge and marked by the turn from aesthetics into ethnocide. The first rupture between the geographic and religious imaginaries works in tandem with the second rupture between the modern scientific and the premodern feudal, but not so with the third between aesthetics, science, and entrepreneurship.

In contrast with colonial scholars, for postcolonial scholars the primordial concern is not the divide between geography, aesthetics, and religion, or between natural sciences and dogma, but one between cultural confrontations and knowledge put at the service of colonialism. Their thrust

is to move the discussion away from aesthetics and scientific invention
into entrepreneurship and ethnocide. They take for granted that in each
and every colonial manuscript, the "new" continent constitutes itself into
an epistemological limit or riddle, which confronts the Europeans with
their own picture of the world. The "new" in fact splits asunder the scientific and religious imaginaries. After the first contact with the Caribbean islands, the European *imago mundi* must go. But this is just the
beginning of a massive mental revolution. America triggers the necessity
for a radical rethinking of European interpretive parameters and demands
a momentous epistemological change, a severance between Europeans' own
cultural parameters and the geographies and cultures of the "new" world.
This shift places people and their cultures at the center of the debate. To
make European critical faculties operative, Europeans must commit their
discourse to the difficult task of speaking outside their own ideological
perceptions.

The new scholarship reads the colonial manuscripts along the lines of
entrepreneurship. In Columbus's prose of the world, they pay attention to
the pragmatics of the trip, to gold, conquest, colonization, dis- and repos-
sessions of land. Reading Columbus's approach to aesthetics gives rise to
a whole different set of intersections. It becomes the cross between the cultures of monoculture economies, ethnographic studies, and research-and-
development projects, and the pleasures of arrival and the beauty of the
place are rendered into business, to which tourist narratives, tourist industries, and postcolonial criticism all bear witness.

Colonial scholarship is thus given the deserved and long-awaited
ethnic twist. Stephen Greenblatt acknowledges that Columbus is more intense a reader than an observer of signs, that his aim is to compile significant markers rather than to represent difference. His point is that the idea
of discovery as entailing an act of sustained and highly particularized narrative representation of differences is quite alien to him. Instead, he hoards
signs. Signs are read favorably, hopefully, with a reckless epistemological
and strategic optimism. Words are written as vacant spaces. Columbus
assumes the transparency of gestures and sounds and rushes from wonder
to possession. He reads the signs to confirm his theory and to fulfill his
desires. Writing is contingent on a structure of expectation and perception
in which the ear is at least as fully implicated as the eye and analogies are
possible. Columbus's method is to register material sighting first and then

aim at its significance. But between seeing and naming, there is a caesura, which is the place of discovery. Bluntly put: "Should we not say then that the words do not matter, that the discursive tactics are interchangeable, that the language is a mere screen for the brutal reality of power?"[29]

The unknown is a vacant slot to be filled by mimesis, the troubled analogue. But some of the pressing questions are, "How does one read the signs of the other? How does one make signs to the other? How does one reconcile the desire for transparent signs with the opacity of an unknown culture? How does one move from mute wonder to communication?"[30] Is it possible for one system of representation to establish contact with a different system? The answer lies in a series of propositions that connect geography, commerce, and science to the ethnic policies of racism.

Methodologically, there is an interest in crossing borders and in paying attention to the intersection of disciplines in narratives of exploration and colonization.[31] The radical difference is that geographies are not viewed solely as geographic but as cultural spaces, and *culture* is the word that permits scholars to veer in the direction of reading all kinds of ethnic confrontations in texts. There is a rejection of all the old Columbian geographical commonplaces—notions of the Caribbean islands as paradise, *terra nullius*, "unclaimed lands," and "uncultivated wilderness"—and a proclivity to examine the intersection of culture and nature within the dynamics of colonialism. Nature is always a cultural construct, and in order to unravel nature from cultures, critical readers must pull apart the rhetorical models to find answers within narrative intersections.

In narratives of discovery and exploration, as in travel narratives, critics contend, the fundamental dissonance, the flaw inherent at the moment of encounter, is that the grammar that encodes geographies does not fully correspond to the object being described. Knowledge begins with a troubled disjunction between thinking, seeing, and writing. What is being written (discourse) is just an approximation that does not quite properly fit the object (the Caribbean islands/America). And once again, this disparity between object and discourse that discusses the divide between nature (landscape as the physical geographies of the Caribbean islands as paradise) and culture (the Caribbean islands as inhabited lands and the new object of knowledge for European cultures) is centered on method. Stylistic resources play an important role in this discussion. The implications of rhetorical devices and their interplays are many: they underlie the ideological constructions of continental identities and strap them to nature and geography. In this, rhetoric is not only instrumental to the discussion of knowledge and knowledge production, it is also inextricably linked to the business of colonialism, the possession and exploitation of land, the dispossession of peoples, as much as to the creation of disciplinary fields and common sense.

chapter 2

INFERNO

THE ANTITHETICAL DISCOURSES OF AESTHETICS
AND PRODUCTIVITY

At the end of the eighteenth and the beginning of the nineteenth centuries (1770–1830), as the English legislature became engaged in debates on the abolition of the slave trade, colonial narratives shifted radically to soil cultivation and deterioration. Mood and tone were no longer the same. Although a set of literary tropes and motifs borrowed from English garden aesthetics and the Spanish colonial tradition of the literature of the Golden Age was preserved and even embraced by the traveler diaries of absentee planters and visitors, the portrayal of the islands was no longer that of Columbus's gardens of Hesperides. Sugarcane fields rendered that trope unwieldy and forced a drastic reversal in representation, transforming paradise into inferno. Islands became sugarcane-producing plains, sites of high-intensity agriculture and labor. Thus, the productive or economic discourse became positioned antithetically to the discourse on aesthetics, aesthetics itself being shifted from the sublime to the picturesque and the grotesque; the narratives of utopian investment were superseded by the hard-and-fast prose of research and development, undoing all kinds of identities—national, ethnic, and cultural.

Written at the end of slavery and situated in the liminal zone of a structural change, plantation diaries, travelogues, and consulting reports on agricultural and economic investments also showed their concerns with the emancipated and the new relations of production. They seemed to theorize the chasm of these in-betweens and to invent new parameters of action. My claim is that although the prose interweaving these changes still avails itself of aesthetics, mainly literary tropes and styles, it is in the description and study of soil erosion, balances, losses, and yields that it makes its point. However, when it comes to narrating culture directly, irony is the rhetorical instrument to map the new social relations of production.

To discuss this transition, I have selected the works of English commissioner R. R. Madden (1798–1886) (*A Twelve Month's Residence in the West Indies, during the Transition from Slavery to Apprenticeship; with Incidental Notices of the State of Society, Prospects, and Natural Resources of Jamaica and Other Islands* [1835]) and novelist and absentee plantation owner Matthew Gregory Lewis (1775–1818) (*Journal of a West Indian Proprietor* [1834]). These two books address two different, albeit related, questions.[1]

Madden's text is invested in a detailed description of the agricultural production of the islands. He examines in detail the nature of the soil and its production, pays close attention to production statistics, examines the nature and infrastructure of ports, and undertakes a comparative analysis of the islands. Madden's book is also attentive to historical detail. He includes important data about slave rebellions, explains the connections between them and the ill-treatment of slaves, and introduces a comparative analysis between the dispossession of the Amerindians and that of the African slaves. His pages are filled with ethnographic data and detailed descriptions of uses and customs. This narrative trait is proper to the age and situation of the writer and, in a certain sense, mandatory to a man who has traveled extensively throughout the Orient, America, and Australia. His keen sense of observation and excellent gift as a raconteur were a result of his extensive traveling and experience. His narrative skills had earned him some important positions, such as that of foreign correspondent for the *Morning Herald*. He was special magistrate in Jamaica, colonial secretary in western Australia, superintendent of liberated Africans in London, special commissioner of inquiry into the administration of British settlements in the west coast of Africa, and judge arbitrator of the mixed court of commission in Havana. His zeal for the cause of slaves is very well documented. Here I will examine how he looks at the relationship between material production and the culture of free blacks (the so called "brown" people), poor whites, and Creoles.

In contrast, Lewis's narrative is more literary and offers the reader a complete description of the culture of the island and the character of its people. Lewis's cultural landscapes betray an inclination toward taste and the cult of sensibility proper to a man of his position. As a novelist, he was part of the literary European circles. He knew Goethe, befriended Sir Walter Scott, and was a friend of Shelley, Byron, and William Wilberforce. In his diary, he carefully observes the subjectivity of people and his characters come alive as real flesh-and-blood human beings. However, Lewis's main purpose is to make careful arrangements for the welfare of his slaves, to legislate. He is a legalist. He firmly believes in codes and rules as a means to better the slaves' miserable lot. In fact, throughout his writing he is drawing a codicil to provide any future holder of plantation property with guidelines. His hope is that through law, slaves will be properly treated and tended. He was accused of injudicious indulgence toward slaves. This study will focus on Lewis's representation of slaves, civic rights, and the distribution of justice.

In Madden's assessment of the islands' landscape, all notions of beauty are suspended, and more realistic and rigorous studies of landscapes as productive spaces are laid out. In Lewis, the new and distressed English structures of sensibility are now enframed in a self-contained and manageable picturesque. But despite the differences, the favorite mood of both writers is irony, which is used as a weapon against the local cultures in all and every one of its flanks. Irony sidesteps the classic and creates the comic alongside the picturesque and grotesque, low mimetic modes that mediate between the rhapsodic narratives of agricultural prosperity and the melodramatic narratives of soil decay depicted by the historians of the planter class, William Beckford, Edward Long, and Bryan Edwards.[2] Irony also marks the distancing between two colonial projects (one English, one Spanish) and two English economic plans (mercantile protectionism and laissez-faire liberalism). The picturesque holds on to aesthetics but downsizes it, framing it in a self-contained and well-managed minimalist tableau. Minimalism is a way of managing environments and a technique to idealize the social relations of labor. The notion of space as supple, abundant, easily organizable, together with the pictures of effortlessly laboring people, although at the slow pace later suggested by Lewis, is a vision of Arcadia already inflected by the overwhelming problems of production. The grotesque is reserved for the representation of local people—Creoles, "brown" people, and slaves. Thus aesthetics continues serving as a medium for seeing and interpreting the geographic layout of the land and its people in the West Indies.[3]

THE TRANSATLANTIC JOURNEY

The entry point to the Caribbean is still the transatlantic journey. Lewis treats it in more detail than does Madden. In Lewis's *Journal*, the journey is both a cultural and a natural experience. He seems to be a high-spirited fellow, a gentleman whose gaiety provides a counterbalance to all the "scary" tropes of the Middle Passage. His readings and quotes ease away all displeasures and make the trip into an aristocratic Caribbean cruise, what Alejo Carpentier would call a "promenade en bateaux" (a walk by boat).[4] All Lewis wants, he gets: "a very clean cabin, a place for [his] books" (4).

During the Atlantic Middle Passage, irony serves this writer to brace the master tropes of the literature of the Spanish Golden Age, but whereas Columbus's master tropes of islands as paradise are maintained, all of his theoretical anxieties are ridiculed. New and better instruments of measurement, modern scientific hypotheses, and expertise have rendered them obsolete. Fretting about uncharted waters and uncertain places has become totally passé. Crossing the ocean now only means registering the few bodily discomforts of seafarers, sprinkled and tenderized with abundant literary quotes that render them ludicrous.

Although English literature scoffs at Columbus's tales of monsters, it retains his tropes: the Caribbean landscapes are still the enchanted April Andalusian gardens. For Lewis, Santa Cruz is "the Garden of the West Indies" (46), and Jamaica, "the Land of Springs" (48). English politics always rides piggyback on the narratives of the Spanish canon. The novelty here is that by rendering Columbus's difficulties of his voyages null, the English traveler elides another kind of traveling that he now combats, that of the Middle Passage. The slave ship focuses the attention of the English public not on high culture or aesthetics, but on plantation economies and the debate over the abolition of slavery, which is to create rifts between home and abroad. Home is no longer the "new lands," but the "new era."

The new era opens with the emancipation of the slaves, after which the nineteenth century in the Caribbean is a long, staggering period of reflection and accommodation, of adjustment. Because both wealth and production are attached to land, to the possession and management of land, the discussion of the nature of the soils and labor is paramount. By 1838, with the abolition of slavery, the cultural landscape of neglected plantation and peasant farms is set as the central worry. A rural population, such as that in Claude McKay's *My Green Hills of Jamaica* (1979), became the main landscape of the West Indies before the twentieth century would again switch the topographies of identity from mountains and plains to beach, from feeding to entertainment, from production to service industry— relaxation, sex, and drugs.[5]

THE NATURE OF SOIL AND SOIL EROSION AS IT IMPINGES ON PRODUCTION

In the first half of the nineteenth century, R. R. Madden observed that an island that was no more than thirty-five square miles, "seven leagues in length . . . five in breadth, attained, in less than forty years, to a population of 100,000 souls, and to trade that employed 150,000 tons of shipping. Never . . . had the earth beheld such a number of planters collected in so small a compass, or so many productions raised in so small a time" (33). This statement describes the Golden Age of plantation economies, a story whose conclusion was unraveling before Madden's very eyes. It took well over a century, from 1655 (when the English captured Jamaica) to 1805, to set the island on a course toward a pattern of settlement, stability, and production. It took only thirty years, a single generation (from 1805, when the sugar economy reached its peak, to 1838, when it crashed), to bring plantation economies and the landscaping of plains to a close. In thirty years, the internal layout of large agricultural units (plantations and pens), the land-tenure and regional settlement patterns, and the internal structures were all laid waste.

By the end of the eighteenth century, the land is reported as being totally impoverished, with yields approaching zero. By the beginning of the nineteenth century, narratives of land surveyors and land appraisers have reduced culture to numbers. The written literature of the epoch betrays two split interests: one fixed on soils, proper to the economic and financial narratives of research and development, the other, on culture, proper to the narratives of rural sociology and ethnology. It is the task of

nineteenth-century consultants and local intelligentsia to work out the
relationship between these two disparate interests.

Two prominent methods for unraveling this relationship are (1) measurement, which is sometimes made analogous to symmetry and often
used as an aesthetic category, and (2) comparison, an analogical device
serving to contrast the characters of nations in relation to the idiosyncrasies of colonies. Both measurement and comparison work through
reduction, a rhetorical device consisting of narrowing down the focus of
interest and restricting the discussion to numbers.[6] In the colonial documents that concern plantation economies, the data is organized in sets of
repetitions that are subsequently drilled throughout the reports. The only
variables are related to numbers in the form of production figures. Established typologies and taxonomies, such as pounds of sugar produced and
acres of land cultivated, make up the listings that ground the story of organized property and its products.

Insofar as soils are concerned, writers face a matter-of-fact condition:
the "erosion of the uplifted limestone plateaux has created a typical karst
landscape, the drainage network commonly disappearing underground
except in regions where underlying formations have been exposed."[7] Madden's opinion is that many of the soils are beyond repair, notwithstanding
the richness of the island's verdure. Climate is considered a contributing
factor. Heavy rains "tear up the soil, and wash away all that is rich and
valuable in it" (35–36); scant rains dry up streams and springs; hurricanes
devastate houses, plantations, shipping, crops. Because of soil deterioration, most of the plantations are mortgaged or in ruins. One of Madden's
exhibits is his old uncle's dwelling house. He says: "about two hundred
feet above the works, the remains of a little garden . . . was still visible. . . .
the soil was now covered with weeds. . . . The Negro huts, at some distance from the house, were all uninhabited; the roofs of some of them had
tumbled in. . . . I took the liberty of walking into the house of my old
uncle. The room I entered was in keeping with the condition of the exte-
rior; every plank in the naked room was crumbling into decay" (167).

To reverse the situation, consultants recommend drastic changes. The
discussion on soil production and culture would then affect the whole
development of the region, whose prosperity was now contingent on the
substitution of "wages for supplies, and agricultural machinery, to a large
extent, for manual labour" (36). The use of new technologies was to

definitively alter the relationship between capital and labor, natives and citizens, nations and geographies. One way to bring about a solution was to stem the sources from which English citizens purchased or retailed slaves. Agricultural production and yields thus account for both strong pro-slavery and abolitionist sentiments. Thus, a contextualized reading of the abolitionist movement reveals not only the humanitarian interest in the civic rights of the slaves, but also a concern for agricultural prosperity and the economic reconstruction of the islands' economies in tandem with the interest of English laissez-faire.

Part of the discussion on soil erosion and deterioration is labor productivity and labor management. The English Caribbean is not alone in this debate. Reproducing English laissez-faire ideas, Cuban planter Francisco Arango y Parreño spoke forcefully in favor of importing machinery and reforming the system of labor.[8] José Antonio Saco vehemently argued against slave labor; Domingo del Monte organized a literary club to discuss the damaging aspects of slavery and to promote the works of Plácido, the mulatto poet, and of Juan Francisco Manzano, the emancipated slave.[9] Manzano's work was translated by R. R. Madden and taken to England as testimony against planters and in favor of the abolition of slaves. Cirilo Villaverde addressed similar issues in his novels. In all these narratives, the nature of slave labor is completely revamped and, as a category, labor will intersect all narratives and turn a discussion on the nature of the soils, agronomy, agriculture, and geology into politics, sociology, and cultural anthropology.

LABOR MANAGEMENT AND ETHNIC PROFILING

Debates on labor begin haltingly with an attack on the slave trade, and end with advocating the radical abolition of slavery. Once considered a source of prosperity, slave labor has now become its impediment. What is significant about the discussion of slave labor, however, is that it is not related to soil deterioration alone but that it constitutes an attack on ethnicity and culture. Nonproductive labor is either attributed to the nature of "the negro character" or blamed on the bad management of the planter class. Management is reproved because it relies on severe punishment, which in turn breeds "indolence and inactivity." Slave "industry ha[s] no stimulus, [slave] exertion no reward" (Madden, *A Twelve Month's Residence*, 94).

Labor is, then, a pivotal category used for discussing all kinds of divides and oppositions.

Looking at it from the viewpoint of managing people, the English abolitionist discussion in the Caribbean begins at the time the captured Africans have been broken. At that moment, they are classified on the basis of their color and place of origin. Origin provides a good measurement for the productivity of labor. Geographic determinism is a tool to explain character, personality, and the cultural traits of people. The classification of Africans works as follows: first, ethnic "tribal" groups and places of origin are coupled, and subsequently, catalogs of virtues and vices are outlined. In this sense, Mandingos are from Senegal and their distinct feature is that they can read and write Arabic, some are well versed in the Koran, and thus they are distinguished from the others by their literacy, their learned and scholarly activities. The Coromanties are from Fanlyn country and are distinguished by their "ferociousness of disposition," that is, their "courage," "stubbornness," an "elevation of soul which prompts them to enterprises of difficulty and danger, and enables them to meet death in its most horrible shape with fortitude or indifference" (ibid., 102). Eboes come from the borders of the Benin River and they are "the least valuable of the negro race—as timid, feeble, despondent creatures, who not infrequently used to commit suicide in their dejection" (104). The Congos are from Angola and they are "less robust than the other negros, but more handy as mechanics, and more trustworthy . . . the most useful slaves merely as machines of toil" (ibid.). From the point of view of management, the most meaningful traits of "negro character" that are recorded, and ones that will lay the foundation of racist stereotypes because they disturb labor, are that "they are addicted to stealing, prone to dissimulation, and inclined to dishonesty" (ibid.). However, in Madden, a caveat immediately follows to distinguish between the vices of "his nature" and those of "his condition." Moral idiosyncrasies negative to development, such as cunning, falsehood, dissimulation, are, as described by Lewis,

> the result of power and injustice. . . . But where the negro labours on his own ground, for his own advantage . . . where the wages he receives for his services are at his own disposal—where his own time is duly paid for, not in shads and herrings, but in money . . . the negro is not the indolent, slothful

being he is everywhere considered, both at home and in the colonies. I am well persuaded in respect to industry, physical strength, and activity— the Egyptian fellah, the Maltese labourer, and the Italian peasant, are far inferior. (105–6)

Here, the abolitionist bent of the writer underscores a liberal program of labor management. Whether or not this is a more democratic project will be debated later on by the philosophers of Pan-Africanism and the critics of modernity.

But nineteenth-century discussions on labor management and production must also take notice of slave agency, and, like all narratives of research and development, they also focus on the intersection between political and economic stability. Lists of rebellions and conflagrations are incorporated into the text with the purpose of underscoring the relationship between bad management, decay, and slave labor. "In 1771, Georgetown was consumed by a dreadful fire; in 1775 it was again destroyed by fire"; "in 1792 another conflagration in the same town destroyed property to the amount of about 100,000 pounds" (Madden, *A Twelve Month's Residence*, 59). Before England took control in 1763, "[t]he Grenada governor was executed by his subjects in 1656; the governor of Barbadoes was executed by his successor in 1631; the governor of Antigua was executed by the people in 1710" (62). Discussions on deterrence appear to be concerned with the civic rights of slaves and related to citizenship when they are, in fact, related to production and linked to management: rebellions bring production to a halt, destroy property, and are hence converted into economic data. Talks on deterrence are important in measuring the impact of slave labor on the narratives of research and development. The humanist discourse of the abolitionists, which is part of the Enlightenment discussion on the universal rights of man, is in this case constructed inevitably as part and parcel of productivity, good management, progress, and modernization.

The discussion on the productivity of labor also broaches the subject of white people. Poor whites are considered feeble people, unable to endure the climate. They were once employed in clearing land "that was once a forest, and of the hardest timber" (39), but they live on the island, in a "state of complete idleness, and are usually ignorant and debauched to the last degree," they are "the most degraded and the lowest. They subsist too often, to their shame be it spoken, on the kindness and the charity of slaves. I have never seen a more sallow, dirty, ill-looking and unhappy race; the men lazy, the women disgusting, the children neglected" (ibid.).

In fact, Madden's position on settlers, buckras whose cultural status verges on the native—merchants, attorneys, overseers, and bookkeepers, whose interest, emoluments, dearly earned stipends, and allowances from the estate are enough alone to account for the decay—suffices to give an idea of the workings of the colonial mind with respect to labor and its management, which turns into an indictment of all West Indian inhabitants, including white people, for whom he has the harshest criticism. In fact, his research has demonstrated that West Indian whites are neither industrious nor prudent. They are not hardworking or moderate. They do not practice self-restraint or savings. Their cultivation of the soil is traditional and routine, using ancient implements—the hoe—rather than the horse-drawn plow. As Moreno Fraginals will describe the Cuban planter class a century later, Madden reports on the English Creoles here: they have no capacity for invention, no desire to experiment with crops, no wish to change. In Jamaica, white settlers object to the introduction of steam engines for the sugar mills because, they argue, the scarcity of firewood is too great. And yet, "if the first geologist of Europe were to visit Jamaica, and state that the indication of coal was evident in the formations of the neighbouring mountains . . . no effort would be made to obtain it . . . in fact, no adequate effort has yet been made to develop the one twentieth part of the available resources of this naturally rich and fertile country" (87). Planters are neither industrious nor ambitious. If "they want to build a house: they send to England for the bricks rather than cut stone from the quarries which everywhere abound" (ibid.). For Madden, the only worthwhile whites are the leading members of the House of Assembly, English government representatives, because they can practice restraint, and they are moderate in their views.

PROPERTY MAPS—A SAMPLE

The discussion on management and labor, as on soil erosion and deterioration, provides an accurate example of how seriously land and labor were thought of and how lopsided the representation of property in writing is, compared to drawings. For example, in his book on eighteenth- and nineteenth-century plantation maps, B. W. Higman illustrates the perfection of plantation economies through drawing, and permits us to see why the planter class was so upset about the abolition of slavery. His illustrations are realistic and very abstract representations of plantation land use. Some of them include the works, the mill, trash, boiling and curing houses, and the great house of the master and slave huts. I have chosen some of the maps to illustrate the different perspectives of representation.

Figure 1 (Figure 3.44 in Higman) represents types of soil relief in Jamaica. Although most plantations were located in relatively leveled plains, or flat and gently sloping land, relief was also a concern. In this picture, soil relief is the theme. Engineers and regional cartographers rather than land surveyors carried out this job. This picture is perfect not only because of the accuracy of its representation but also because for Higman it describes a range between the realistic and the symbolic moods. The difference between one mood and the other parallels the ascending and descending curve of plantation economies and roughly coincides with the period of the discussion of the abolition of the slave trade in England, which takes place approximately between 1770 and 1840. The picture on the upper-right-hand corner moves in the direction of the picturesque. Small hills and trees with some scattered palm trees constitute the essentials of a minimalist tableau. The two pictures on the left-hand side top and bottom (which Higman labels realistic and hill shading, respectively) appear more symbolic to me. This is owing to their size and abstract character. The rest of the pictures are more within the realistic mode and follow the conventional protocols of ordinary topographical representation with all the specified hachures the caption indicates.

Figure 2 (Figure 4.18 in Higman) is the 1851 plan of Drax Hall Estate in St. Ann, the property of historian William Beckford, the leading landholder in Jamaica. This illustration contains abstract diagrams that outline ideal and specific characteristics and land uses for each portion of the property. At the bottom of the illustration we can read "Woodland and provision grounds," and on the upper portion "Guinea grass" and "Common pastures." Some of these illustrations even listed the functions of each of the parts of the properties with their corresponding arrangements and numbers. In this one, the little squares in the upper portion indicate number of acres and functions. We can read signs such as "Windmill," "Garden," "Long corner," "Gully." Some of these illustrations even contained

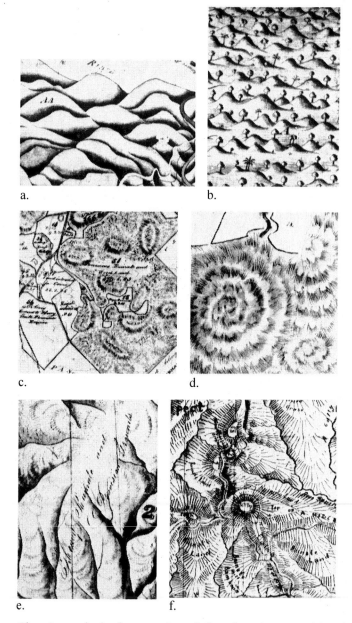

Figure 1. Changing methods of representing relief on plantation maps: (*a*) realistic perspective drawing (1770); (*b*) symbolic perspective (1800); (*c*) simple hachures (1808); (*d*) layered hachures (1850); (*e*) hill shading (1851); and (*f*) graduated hachures (1860). From B. W. Higman, *Jamaica Surveyed: Plantation Maps and Plans of the Eighteenth and Nineteenth Centuries* (Kingston: Institute of Jamaica, 1988). Courtesy of the National Library of Jamaica.

tables labeled "Explanation" or "Reference," that summed up the protocols of representation. Diagrams delimited each area with absolute symmetry and accuracy, two of Madden's requirements. The names of the other estates (Windsor, Bay) border the property.

Figure 3 (4.6 in Higman), a picture of Edward Long's Lucky Valley Estate, provides architectural detail that permits a fuller identification of the buildings and the organization of the works. There are two levels in this plan: one distinguishes the works and great house, the other, the slaves' huts. The works are located in the foreground. To the left is located the trash house and the mill; to the right, the boiling house with its cupola and chimney. Behind it, there is the curing house and far back, the hog sties. The great house, or the overseer house, is on the right-hand side of the picture in front of a palm tree. Behind the palm tree, in the background, are the small duplex-like buildings that housed the slaves. Puffs of smoke coming out of the boiling house at the center of the picture indicate that the production of sugar is in full swing. On the top part of the map we see a drawing of the plantation specifying the soil relief with its hills and hachures. A river runs through the property, supplying the much-needed water for the works. Sketches of the living quarters in the style of the picturesque are reproduced today in a style called "Primitive" or "Naive." Pictures of landscapes in the same style are found for sale in markets in Haiti and Jamaica, and more refined versions can also be purchased at art galleries everywhere.

Figure 4 (Figure 4.50 in Higman) offers a partial view of Meylersfield Estate in 1790. Here we can appreciate the layout of buildings within the works yard. Mills usually stood at the center. The two chimneys in the picture reveal intense work activity and production. The representation of people is always downsized. Although in this particular instance the difference in size between buildings and people may be attributed to perspective, the fact is that they are very small in comparison to the buildings. They are carrying something on their heads that could be canes, water, or vegetables from their provision grounds. The woman in the foreground is carrying an infant on her back. Observe that the only male of the picture has his hands free. The conic structure of thatched roofs is one of the cultural traits in house construction of the epoch in the region. The fact that the image is situated right at the center of the picture is proof of symmetry and order.

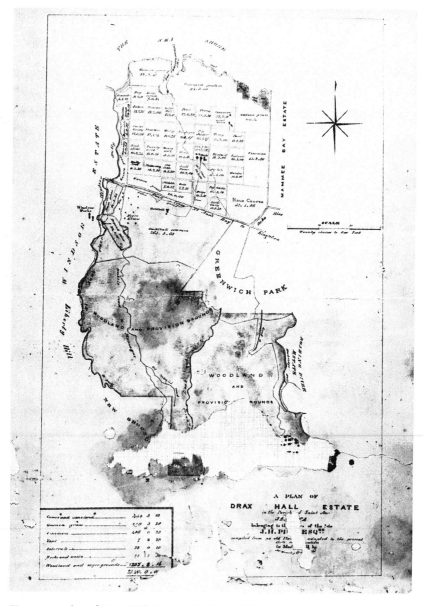

Figure 2. A plan of Drax Hall Estate, 1851. From Higman, *Jamaica Surveyed.* Courtesy of the National Library of Jamaica.

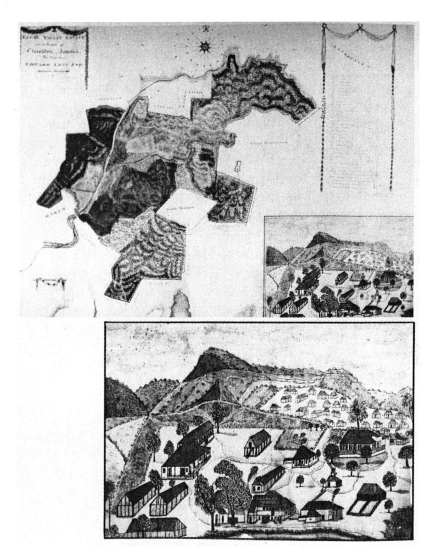

Figure 3. Plan of Lucky Valley Estate, Clarendon, 1861, by Benjamin Haynes. From Higman, *Jamaica Surveyed.* Courtesy of the National Library of Jamaica.

My favorite picture is the 1817 view of Petersfield State in St. Thomas (Figure 5; Figure 3.51 in Highman) because it brings up a more modern and stylized portrayal of soils that anticipates Vincent van Gogh's style. This view emphasizes the cultivated fields of sugarcane planted in well-defined and measured rows. Abundance is portrayed in the multiplication of the cultivated fields that extend to the horizon and are interrupted only by the mountains. The works are subdued. Located on the left-hand side, they are barely discernible in the picture. The crops take the center. On the right there are some people. Women are always holding baskets on their heads and in the company of children. Men are empty-handed or tending herds. Palm trees frame the pictures and are the trademark of islands. Inside one of the cultivated fields, right at the center of the picture, there are some cattle; and on the field behind it, to the right, there seem to be some working people. Overall it is significant that lands are empty, and that when people are added to the picture, they are usually represented as minuscule, barely discernible. In some illustrations they look like ink spots.

Figure 4. A view of Meylersfield Estate, Westmoreland, c. 1790. From Higman, *Jamaica Surveyed.* Courtesy of the National Library of Jamaica.

In sum, the highly detailed close-ups, together with the extremely well-defined portions of terrain marked in accordance with their useful-ness and ease of access and the exact depiction of the numbers of acres assigned to each function, are indications of well-tended works. This neatly delineated representation contrasts with the smallness and sparse-ness of the laboring people. Their microscopic dimension makes them look like laboring ants carrying sugarcane sticks on their heads. The ubiq-uitous puffs of smoke invariably highlight the presence of ongoing pro-ductive activities even in the absence of human presence. Contemporary aerial views today underscore the outcome of a tradition that began with very refined ground surveillance lenses and equipment and is now per-fected in the sophisticated electronic ware that can cover distances and details from the air with accuracy.

THE NATURE OF SLAVE CULTURE—GROTESQUE AND PICTURESQUE

As with all research-and-development reports, Madden's success lies in his formal advice on agriculture and commerce. His empirical data and esti-mates on yields and shipping and his analyses of soils are all unobjection-able. However, the same does not hold true for his observations on culture. In dealing with culture, he has to grapple with the fact that his subjective

Figure 5. View of Petersfield Estate, St. Thomas, 1817, drawn by G. C. J. Kennion. From Higman, *Jamaica Surveyed*. Courtesy of the National Library of Jamaica.

understanding must also be factored into the analysis.[10] And here is where
the discussion on productivity dovetails with the discussion on culture. In
Madden, culture is argued as productivity, growth, and progress and not
as the civic rights of people. His cultural analysis is rooted in the mode of
production. Abolitionism is nothing more than a step in the direction of
modernization. Thus, if soil narratives stress erosion, cultural narratives
speak with irony of prosperity to underscore the exact opposite, decadence
and decay.

The difference between prosperity and decadence is numbers. Whatever accrues value is by definition prosperous; what does not is decadent.
Gross earnings, good city planning, and solid infrastructural works are an
indubitable measure of prosperity. Concrete figures are offered: Barbados
exported 541,707 pounds sterling in 1831 and only 150,000 forty years later.
Prosperity is contingent on the resources of a country, the intensity of production, the ratios yielded per square mile and tons shipped, but also on
the industriousness of the people. And here is where problems begin. Culture is placed under the rubric of prosperity and becomes manageable
through numbers. It is an English habit, a modern method, and Madden's
narrative strategy is to measure and count everything—from acres, input/
output, taxes, shipping tons, inhabitants, and gross earnings to the fre-
quency of festivities, time spent in serving at an inn, the weight of people,
hours sitting in front of a house. Culture is time and timing, and time
is products, growth, money. The behavior of people, their habits, their
bodies, their pace are the surfaces on which the traveler will write the distance between prosperity and decay, and where he will ground his definition of the "negro character" as "prone to dissimulation, and inclined to
dishonesty" (104).

IRONY AND RIDICULE: THE CONSTRUCTION
OF THE GROTESQUE

The colonial imaginary in the Caribbean chooses numbers to undergird
the serious aspects of production, and utilizes culture in the form of services, festivities, and the "character of negro people" to construct the
nature of colonial culture as grotesque. When applied to public life, the
grotesque is tantamount to the denial of a civil society in the colonies. The
grotesque is also a scaffold to enhance the norm, which is English character

and nationality. This is defined as progress, enterprise, courage, humanity, and amiability. The creole, white, brown, and black character is no
character at all. It is the antipodes of English, jealous, fanatic, and, more
important, opposed to progress. Women's services—cooking, washing,
nurturing—become the paradigmatic samples of colonial culture as grotesque. I will present two samples of Madden's portrayal of women. One
is the two innkeepers, Miss Betsy Austin and Miss Hanna Lewis; the other
is Mary Logan, the washerwoman of Annotto Bay.

The presentation of services through the good or bad conduct of
women is set against the backdrop of laissez-faire parameters. Misconduct
is defined as a disregard or, better yet, ignorance of the rules of market
competition. Miss Austin and Miss Lewis get very upset when Englishmen-
men choose the services of one over the services of the other. The point is
that they do not understand, much less like, the fact that when it comes
to services there is freedom of choice. Both innkeepers interpret personal
choice (who goes to one or the other inn, who uses Austin's or Lewis's
services) as an insult, thus investing commercial transactions with personal drama and reading the customer's freedom as personal compliment
or rejection. Freedom of choice takes Madden straight into defamation of
character. Here is one passage illustrating what he sees and hears:

> [T]he ferocious yet vacant gaze of baffled desperation of Miss Austin, the
> unmeaning yells of her slaves, and the uproarious merriment of the negroes
> outside, all combined, made a scene which Cruikshank might do justice to,
> but which I cannot. . . . The ill-mannered slaves all the time kept tittering
> and giggling, with an occasional "hi! hi! you no hearie dat!" and "MiGar
> Amighty, whara say misis! nebber in no passion!" (30)

It is out of the question for a distinguished English gentleman to
empathize with these habits, lest he lose all proper restraint and "go
native." His goal is to combat these norms and propose alternatives. Distancing and the proper eschewing of anger and aggravation will become
normative techniques to write the productive contrast between an Englishman as a consumer of services and a brown creole woman as a service
provider. Irony is the only appropriate way to write the observations of
customs, and the hysterical behavior of local innkeepers. Here we are
completely in the business of colonial cultural production. English wit

is honed by brown creole women's dullness, and put to the service of his project. Women's linguistic idiosyncrasies, their oral exchanges, are reproduced verbatim to be interpreted in the most quaint and charming comedic style. Glossaries of ungrammatical terms document cultural oddities, while overtly reprimanding the uncouth enunciator of these deviancies. Who would ever entertain the idea that these cultures can dialogue with each other?

First, Madden notices the lack of sophistication in the repetition of vocabulary, "the same unvaried greeting, the same drawling courtesy, the same apathetic reply . . . the same moaning excuses. . . . she only drawled out a few sentences strung together for similar occasions" (24). Second, phoneme alteration pinpoints inferiorities and superiorities; for instance, the difference between sir/sa, god/gar, almighty/amighty, what do you/ whara, never/nebber, first/fuss, thief/teef, master/massa, that is, "the vile French patois . . . is still spoken a great deal by the negroes" (46). In spite of the fact that Coleridge speaks highly of West Indian hospitality, and, Madden observes, "has done much to immortalize the brown ladies of the West Indies" (23–24), he probably did not meet specimens like Miss Lewis and Miss Austin. What nerve, may I ask, have these women touched to deserve such a cultural offensive in which art and literature join to deal them such a blow? What is it in those two women that Madden wants to control, attenuate, discipline, or erase? Who does he think he is to position himself so separate and apart from the women mocked, scoffed, and derided? My answer is that what makes "the two fat ladies" repulsive is the incapacity—or, better yet, unwillingness—of England to make dissimilar alike. What makes him angry is the total disdain and disregard of people for the sacred, universal values of English liberalism. But there is more to it. Madden does not stop at language and pronunciation. Body traits and cultural habits make him hysterical, and age, the fact that Miss Lewis is "verging on her grand climacteric; she was evidently conscious of her natural advantages—a sedate, sensible woman of some two hundred weight" (24), provokes his laughter. Here is another instance of his representation:

There sat the pink of Barbadian dignity, the pride of the Creole aristocracy. . . . [h]er head and the upper part of her body thrown back nearly in an angle of forty-five degrees with her lower extremities . . . elevated on a

foot-stool. A black damsel stood behind her chair, taking advantage of her
situation to grin at the passengers instead of plying her large fan carefully
and sedulously for the result of her grinning was flapping the said fan
against the side of her mistress's head-gear, and receiving a volley of virago-
ism . . . that would have startled an adder, and a box on the ear that would
have produced a vermilion suffusion on the skin of a white waiting-maid.
(27–28)

Madden does not like women to sit, to laugh, to talk, to get older. In the
quoted passage, what is at issue is more serious. Relaxation and enjoyment
are simply repulsive and turned into laziness. And laziness is a capital
sin, because it contradicts the philosophies of labor. So Madden defines
laziness: it is to work oneself into stupor and stupidity, and stupidity
underwrites the idea of "brown" women as the "specimens of the species."
But what does that mean? It means that the body becomes the intense
focus of attention: movement, repose, weight, age, and posture are carefully surveyed. A perennial state of siege and surveillance is evident in a
sharp tongue at the ready. English perversity in poking fun at what hurts
the most amply documents the sadism of colonialism, which a century
later Frantz Fanon would deconstruct and combat.

But by means of what inner mechanisms does the English mind move
from women's anger to men's pride and prejudice? Let us go carefully
through Madden's logic. First, he observes the excessive demonstrations of
feelings—which are construed as lack of urbanity and decency, a kind of
excitability that is explained in terms of climate and "climacterics." Second, there is speech pattern, ungrammatical sentences, and loud noises.
Third, there is relaxation and repose. These three idiosyncrasies drive
Madden crazy and add fuel to the discomforts of the place and to the deterioration of the economy. As a result of this irritation, other small and
apparently insignificant cultural items are also brought under scrutiny. For
instance, sitting in front of an open doorway is labeled indolence. That
the two innkeepers are seated with "indolent tranquility" (23) and "imper-
turbable repose" (24) becomes a trait of "the luxury of native indolence"
(ibid.), and something that rubs him the wrong way. But what is un-
forgivable is that the lady "specimens" display these gestures as correct
postures and attitudes appropriate to a landlady—however much these

landladies' natural urbanity and gentleness of disposition can be ruffled by the squabbles with their guests.

An alternate reading of this passage will construe a different chain of meaning, one that exposes the limits of liberalism in abolitionism. In this example, there is no civic space, no performance of choice, no possibility for West Indian Creoles to feel at ease in their habits or to negotiate their cultures. The verdict offered is always negative, not pride but prejudice, not dignity but indolence, not urbanity or gentleness but squabbles of another sort. All these indignities are added to numbers such as body weight and age, which become the significant markers of nativeness, one woman being "a female member of the Creole aristocracy [tracing ancestry] back to the dusky antiquity of a century and a half ago" (23). This passage turns human beings into exhibits, and the two misses into creole Aunt Jemimas. The moral of the story is that ignorance or neglect of the rules of competition turns citizens into specimens.

The story of Mary Logan, "an old brown woman in Annotto Bay" (92) offers a somewhat different set of possibilities. This is an example of a brief encounter between a washerwoman and an Englishman. It is mainly the story of an Englishman who, disgusted with the patriots of South America, arrived on the Jamaican shores almost destitute and was assisted by Mary, a Jamaican woman. That she is given a name and a place of residence in the text is already a sign of deference, a recognition that Mary cannot be written as were the innkeepers. Not only is Mary Logan the antipode of those other two women, she is also wise. She knows how to administer herbs, that is, she is positioned as a "doctor-feuille," as Simone Schwarz-Bart would call her character Ma Cia, or Jean Rhys would think of Christophine, two of the best personifications of African American West Indian women in contemporary Caribbean writings by women.[11]

Madden gives Mary a ring as a token of his gratitude, and, in return, she gratefully reassures him she is a servant by calling him "her good master" (93). Exchange of objects for services prompts Madden to speculate on payments, exchanges, and services, and catapults him back to his laissez-faire frame of reference, expecting the washerwoman Mary to begin asking for more when she discovers the man she helped is back in Jamaica and no longer impoverished. Would she, he speculates, return the ring and ask for some pecuniary reward? Would she show her true character?

To his pleasure, he finds the woman truly pious: "the old brown woman had her own exceeding great reward in the satisfaction of knowing that she had done her duty to a fellow-creature [her equal?] in sickness and distress, and to one who was not unworthy of her kindness, or forgetful of it" (ibid.).

Symmetry between masters and emancipated slaves, or between English commissioners and washerwomen, is possible only through the mediation of Christianity. Christianity tends a bridge between masters and servants by recognizing feelings between people, however much in Madden the example serves some utilitarian purposes. The image of a good black woman helps his proselytizing in favor of abolitionism. As a reward for being pious, for making him feel good without risking anything, for providing an alternative to the otherwise degraded uses and customs of the place, Madden rewards her again by paying her a visit in her house, and by sitting with her "for . . . a good hour" (94), until the neighbors begin to look at him as a "walk and nyam" (ibid.), that is, an indigent white man without a horse. Mary Logan thus stands in contrast to the innkeepers Miss Hanna Lewis and Miss Betsy Austin, whose portrayal serves to illustrate the undesirable in creole colonial women. But what is the real divide between them? To all appearances, it is a matter of services, good versus bad. To be recognized as a person by the colonial self, then, means to serve well, that is, to be a slave or a maid.

Although Madden will ascribe women and the mores of "colored" people to the low mimetic and make them the object of derision, in the following quote, he makes amends. He asks: "what weapons beside falsehood, cunning, and duplicity, has the slave to oppose to oppression?" (104–5). And before that, Madden had already struck a chord in defense of the creole character by writing:

> The defects of the Creole character are more than counterbalanced by its virtues. If they are easily moved to anger, they are still more easily incited to kindness and generosity; if they are "devils being offended," they are frank and honest to their enemies, and faithful beyond any people I know, to their friends. I wish they were less proud, because their noble qualities would be more appreciable, and I would be glad to find them less captious, because their personal courage has no need of such demonstration on slight occasions. (81)

IRONY AND RIDICULE: THE CONSTRUCTION
OF THE PICTURESQUE

Good government and productive labor are the two horns of the dilemma and the last bequests of the slaveholder to inform the debate over slave societies and their limits. In reading their narratives, one wonders if labor has come to a complete halt, or if the narratives overdramatize the lack of discipline. The truth is that there is an obsession about slave behavior that focuses on their bodies and culture. Narratives of soil production keep the body and its movements and expressions under strict and constant surveillance. Moods are also carefully supervised. Happiness comes under suspicion, and is then argued within the sphere of labor and productivity. Being merry is also related to labor, in that it is interpreted as being thoughtlessness and improvidence. Age is the object of commentary. We are told that slaves do not foresee the future because they know they will have something somehow, and that old slaves, seventy or older, are still able, healthy, strong, and cheerful, but do not work. Dancing is under the vigilant eye of the master. But Obeah practices are the most untrustworthy aspects of black culture. Obeah stories shed light on the infractions and negotiations between slaves within the restraints of slavery. In the view of masters, slaves always seem to be able to negotiate everything—holidays, time, justice, punishments.

This deeply ingrained anxiety about slaves, the new citizenry, takes us directly to a discussion of culture that looks at slaves no longer as ciphers but as real flesh-and-blood people. Their ways about the world are puzzling and seem to have the power of interrupting English certainty. Are there other interpretive devices to properly assess the mores of slaves? What is the true nature of the slaves' character? To answer these questions, direct cultural contact is necessary. Real knowledge begins at the moment of physical contact, but physical contact is no guarantee of certainty. In point of fact, physical contact triggers all the sensors. What is interesting in Lewis is that he confesses not to know who the slaves really are or what they really mean. Many discrepancies are noticed between what they think, say, and feel. Particular interest is shown for those cultural idiosyncrasies that refer to labor—for instance, laziness, cheating, cunning, and rebelling. In understanding what we might call civil disobedience lies the (re)-construction of the subjectivity of the slaves. Perhaps there is intelligence in them; perhaps slowing down work denotes the will to resist. Planters notice a gap between words and deeds, and hence must pay close attention. Doubt on the side of the master and lying on the side of the slave does not make for fluid communication.

The dominant perception governing the relationship between masters and slaves is that of an invisible thread dividing being and pretending. Dissimulation and mimicry are at the heart of the master–slave exchange. From the point of view of governance, or management, to find the divide is key, because it provides the criterion separating what works from what does not. For instance, regarding labor it will tell the difference between illness and health, working and idling. It does not go unnoticed that this invisible divide is a space of negotiation: freedom for the slave and uncertainty for the master. For a laissez-faire mentality, which relies on counting, gauging, and measuring, the divide renders all epistemological practices fussy. How to know if slaves are taking advantage of a kind master or just taking a break? How to know if they are tired or despondent? Thus, interpretation and negotiation are essential tools of management and governance. Three instances illustrate how colonial English literature comes to terms with this doubt. One is a scene welcoming the master; another is a scene of John-Canoe, a popular festivity; and the third refers to the rebel Plato.

WELCOMING THE MASTER

Upon Lewis's arrival in Savannah la Mar, a reception committee is waiting at the gate. His trustee has rallied some people to welcome him. He is startled to see that all, even "hogs, dogs, geese and fowl and turkeys," "came hurrying along by instinct, to see what could possibly be the matter" (60). "The works are instantly abandoned" (ibid.); and "[u]proar and confusion" (ibid.) is the law of the land. All of it defies description. The first impressions of his property cannot be grasped with words. The rituals of welcoming, "[t]he shouts, the gaiety, the wild laughter, the strange and sudden bursts of singing and dancing" of his slaves can only be found in literature. He believes these cultural practices are "an exact counterpart of the festivity of the witches in Macbeth" (61). To his great bewilderment, women slaves offer their babies to him—"him nice lilly neger for Massa" (ibid.).

In his view, the merriment of the welcome party serves two purposes: to interrupt work and to please him. The mixture of work and affect,

coupled with exaggerated body gestures, splits the otherwise secure hermeneutics of the imperial self, and divides genuine from feigned behavior,
authenticity from performance. And although these are all ordinary practices for the West Indies, Lewis does not know how to interpret them. He
knows that whether his slaves like him or not, they will serve him all the
same. Slavery is a compulsory system, but what he wants to know is if the
expressions of feelings are compulsory too. The question is, are the slaves
sincere? Do they really love him? Or are they simply using the opportunity to stop working? Why is he so interested in affect? He is interested
because understanding affect is key to understanding culture and understanding culture is key to management. Therefore, the planter observes
attentively, always keeping in mind the English proverb that Negroes "are
excellent cajolers, and lay it on with a trowel" (Lewis, *Journal*, 120). However, at this transitional moment, the real question is how slaves themselves feel about slavery and what kind of relationship they are willing to
establish with their master. In the welcoming party, this population has
to all appearances learned to negotiate the master's emotions and to collaborate with the attorney's wishes to appear to be welcoming to the owner
of the plantation.[12]

   The master carefully compares gestures and words to see if they coincide and then writes them down as ethnic profiles—kindhearted,
flamboyant, boastful, drinking, noisy, insincere, cunning, promiscuous,
thoughtless, unrestrainable, heedless, inattentive—terms that conform to
the internalized portrait of the colonized, which the literature of Pan-
Africanism is to deconstruct.[13] The master carefully transcribes the phonetics and syntax of creole English, believing that in the interstices of
language, in the in-between of dialect, he will find answers.[14] But creole
language is unwieldy, and sounds disturbing and irritating. What Lewis
wishes for is moderation, well-regulated and proper behavior. What he
really wants is good and proper management. His real problem is that he
is touched by the performance of affect because these people are his property. But whereas ownership gives him pleasure, happiness provokes
doubt. Overall, the interaction makes him feel embarrassed. The word
slave makes him feel "a pang at the heart" (62). So he says, "say that you
are my negro, but do not call yourself my slave" (ibid.). The shift from
slave to Negro denotes the transition between slavery and free labor. Considered from a social perspective, welcoming parties offer the mistaken

impression that slaves are well tended. From the perspective of the slaves, welcoming the master is truly a party, a way out of the daily drudgery of work.

JOHN-CANOE, A POPULAR FESTIVITY

As stated earlier, doubt inflects all of Lewis's assessments of the relationship between metropolitan epistemologies and his own observations of West Indian societies. His description of social festivities is no exception. They are riddled with the difficulties of interpretation. The John-Canoe festival is one of his examples. In this carnival-type parade, the locals stage a parody of an English national celebration. Two parties, the Reds and the Blues, compete to build the most beautiful floats and thus vie for the favors of the "brown girls"—such is the fairer sex called in Jamaica. The rivalry is evident through investments in "taste" and "magnificence." However, in the staging of the John-Canoe festivities, the "national" is called into question, and a bizarre patriotism is staged. The names of Waterloo and Nelson, the titles of king, queen, princes, the throne, and the flag— all invoke the presence of England. The faux elegance of the colors and materials used for dresses, the heavy sun, the interpretation of history, and the impersonation of royalty all become oxymoronic. The rendering of wealth using the material conditions of poverty and the social and political imaginary of subalterns brings the colonizers face-to-face with their own signs turned upside down. Reds and Blues stand for English and Scottish and Guelphs and Ghibellines—they reenact the War of the Roses.

At the beginning of this narrative, the color line is blurred and it is not clear who are the protagonists of this festivity. Yet a pervasive sense of ridicule or irony leaves no doubt that Lewis is narrating "color." Here, the incontinence of people's culture, their flamboyance, is being underscored. However, what Lewis ridicules is the uncivil behavior evidenced by the letting out of emotions for public display. This sense of the ridiculous turns against the narrator himself because his own laughter, formerly a sign of his joy, turns out, in this case, to be nothing more than embarrassment about something that has not been done properly. Laughter here betrays a feeling of being ill at ease, the emotions of someone who could not help but see his own nation parodied. To get rid of this feeling, he directly criticizes Miss Edwards and Britannia, the two women representing England in the floats, and then, the whole colored community that pretends to appropriate the genuine—namely, the history of their rulers through performance. The scene culminates with blazing torches that light up the town, giving it a beautiful effect that combines with "the excessive rapture of the black multitude" (58). "Excessive" always connotes colored or black, and in this context it most likely refers to the emancipated population.

A contemporary reading of the John-Canoe festivities would render the differences between the earlier English view of the spectacle and the social functions it performs today, if not as a parade for tourists, then as popular entertainment. But for our purposes, that is irrelevant. What matters is the illustration of a local West Indian social event in which much of the relevant data is subtracted in order to privilege the sense of shame that overcomes the imperial self. The gaze is clouded by the parody of his own history enacted in earnest, by the presence of the grotesque embodied in "poor Britannia, who hung down her [head] in the most ungoddess-like manner imaginable" (57).

As readers, we are left with questions, all concerning the constitution of civil society and the public space in the colonies at this moment in time. Who came to watch these events? Where were the slaves, and how did they relate to the public spheres at the moment of this festivity? These questions are left for anthropologists and historians to answer. But whatever answer we may provide and whatever reconstruction we may undertake, the fact is that this is an example of transgression. It supersedes mimesis and only creates the shadow image of what it pretends to interpret. Hence, facts become elements of parody. But, on the flip side of the mock-historical parade, there is the industry of people. They are ingenious engineers, making and repairing machines. Describing how John-Canoe himself speaks about his float, Lewis says, "To be sure . . . it was not so large nor so showy as the other but then it was much better proportioned and altogether much prettier" (75).

In narrating the John-Canoe festivities, Lewis recognizes cleanliness, intelligence, good temperament, and industriousness: "[a]nd indeed [the carousel] was as fine as paint, paste-board, gilt paper, and looking-glass could make it!" (ibid.). It is as good as can be made with whatever material is available in the country. He also recognizes good performance, for Mr. John-Canoe "performed the part of an impromptu . . . with so much fun and grotesqueness, that he fairly beat the original performers out of the pit, and carried off all the applause of the spectators, and a couple of my dollars" (ibid.). It is here that we know who finances the operation, the rich Negroes, who later on distribute the money they make in the performance. A carnival is a local industry, a way of attracting and redistributing money.

THE REBEL PLATO

Now, if for a moment we turn our sight to Plato, the rebel from the Moreland Mountains, we can argue that his representation introduces the reader to a narrative of disobedience, which is a narrative of cunning, intelligence, and resistance. In Plato, Lewis exposes his feelings about a transgressor. As a runaway slave of some success, established in the Moreland Mountains, Plato's character is caught up within webs of ambiguous propositions. One tells us that he "robbed," "murdered," and "raped"; another that he was "young," "strong," "tall," "athletic," and "swift"; a third portrays him as a drunkard, womanizer, and Obeah man. Thus Plato is compressed within sets of opposites that distinguish a high mimetic hero from a nonheroic lowlife. So, who is Plato? Is he a maroon and bandit chieftain? Does his disobedience make him stand apart from the norm of obeisance and enslavement?

The three points of view framing Plato contradict each other. He is simultaneously a positive and a negative character. This indicates that a doubt intersects the point of view of the narrator and cracks the line of his story, revealing the ambiguities of colonialism. Two moments are important in this logic. One is related to Lewis's inability to weave the moment of treason into the narrative of resistance. The other is tied to the form of the story that must be embedded in the fable in which two black protagonists (Plato and Taffy, his betrayer) play out the narrative of resistance and betrayal. It is only through fable that the betrayal of one by another is related, but it is the law of the fable that the most cunning must win, and in this instance both protagonist and antagonist are winners. A parity of skills reestablishes the equilibrium between two black people and two types of disobedience. That which in the past must have been a narrative of law and order now becomes a eulogy of insurgency.[15]

The image left of Plato for future noncolonial imaginaries is that he is daring, brave, and skillful at avoiding capture. That other Negroes feared him, emoting a feeling that borders on respect and is a sign of deference, for he defends himself with Obeah and with guns. His supportive network is made available to a readership, because we are told that he has informants, friends, a cohesive and wide network of people and confidants to help him. In other words, Plato fits the description of a human being, and, like Mary Logan, the character in Madden, he transcends his labor and ethnic condition and is hermeneutically emancipated.

After all is said and done, figuring out who the slaves really are is daunting. The planters seem to have no clue. The grin of a slave is like that of the Sphinx. Being lost in the codes mars the interpretation of African-American cultures and leaves them at the mercy of stereotypes that are the result of doubt and misguided interpretation of cultural behavior. In spite of it all, Lewis, the planter, enjoys his lands. Pleasure tends a bridge between doubt and understanding, and pleasure in him is constituted into knowledge. Pleasure has the virtue of providing an immediate grasp of the object. Writing joy and enjoyment, pleasure and beauty into his journal underscores Lewis's own sensibility and fabulous aesthetics in relationship to the people; likes and dislikes account for taking a side. In many ways, his narrative acts as a bridge between two sensibilities and two economic and political perspectives, those of the quasi-native buckra Creoles, and those of his English compatriots at home.

In pleasure, the colonial/imperial self relaxes, and the imperious image of England that regulates perception gives in. When this happens, the English subject dares to imagine the new geographies as possible new homes. Lewis writes: "I am as yet so much enchanted with the country, that it would require no very strong additional inducements to make me establish myself here altogether" (68). In the West Indies, both the nature of geographies and the nature of humans are so quaint that they firmly stand for the picturesque: "light-coloured houses with their lattices and piazzas completely embowered in trees" (51); places that "exceed in beauty all that [Lewis has] ever seen" (65).[16] Picturesque also is the human figure of Mary Wiggins, a much-too-pretty mulatto girl whose "form and features were the most statue-like. . . . her complexion had no yellow in it. . . . it was more of an ash-dove colour. . . . her teeth were admirable. . . . her eyes equally mild and bright; and her face merely broad enough to give it all possible softness and grandness of contour: . . . Mary Wiggins and an old Botton-tree are the most picturesque objects that I have seen for these twenty years" (69–70).

Picturesque is framing landscape and peoples into a picture, a technique that illuminates the view and the composition alongside human
relationships. Picturesque is to recast her figure against the sentimental
Yarico, the "good black woman" sensualized.[17] The contemplation of
Mary Wiggins can be read as a cross between literary moods, expressing a
shifting political sensibility via the sentimental picturesque. But it can also
be read as a trope, the permissive white master's gaze contemplating his
mulatto women slaves. What his fixed look selects—white teeth and eye-
balls, his careful rendering of body parts—intersects the economic narratives of slavery that record the purchasing habits of masters within the
semantics of sentimental and picturesque romanticism. In this, as in many
other subsequent scenes, the picturesque provides the clue that this gaze
leaves no doubt that a (white) man is looking at a (mulatto) woman, very
much as Cirilo Villaverde saw his characters looking at Cecilia Valdés, the
icon of Cuban liberal nationalism. There is an attraction in Lewis's gaze.
What is speaking here, if not lust, when he tells us that Psyche, a creole
girl, smells of orange blossoms emanating from an orange bough she
brought to fan away disturbing insects?

GOVERNANCE AND THE SUBJECTIVITY OF EX-SLAVES AS CITIZENS

Lewis's *Journal* can be read as a treatise on governance, although not necessarily on citizenship. He touches on all matters concerning the flow
between civil rights and labor as public and private spheres. Fairness and
justice, for instance, are broached through a comparison between free versus slave forms of labor. In this comparison, there is a profitable theoretical chasm separating English citizens from colonial subjects. The contrast
is unfavorable to the citizen, and his narrative produces the evidence to
prove his point. It is clear from his journal that Lewis knows that citizenship rights governing West Indian former slaves are about to be reformu-
lated in England. The reform is a corollary of the debates on commerce
within laissez-faire parameters. He is interested in comparative cultures,
and specifically in the contrast between human labor relations at home,
which are already in the hands of the state, having been codified into law,
and human labor relations in the islands. At home, concepts of civil society and public space are already in place. They constitute part and parcel

of Lewis's ideoscapes and political imaginaries of the state that mediate all relations between people and prohibit any and all personal exercise and execution of justice. In England, justice is not a private affair but a public business. Perhaps this constitutes the gist of citizenship. In the islands, justice is still a personal matter. Planters are justices. Justice is predicated on the good management of the plantation estates, which at best function like small republics, small places, the borders of which mark the edges of the hyphenated estate-state. Inside the plantation, there is no distinction between the execution of justice and the management of labor. Planters' authority can often cross the boundaries, and in the case of absentee owners, slaves can appeal to other slave owners for justice.

In his journal, Lewis speaks from the position of a plenipotentiary statesman: "I gave [the slaves] a holiday for Saturday next" (63); "This was the day given to my negroes as a festival on my arrival" (73). When slaves show ingratitude and bad manners, "they are treated like English soldiers and sailors" (119). He feels proud to have "positively forbidden the use of [the cart whip] on Cornwall; and if the estate must go to rack and ruin without its use, to rack and ruin the estate must go" (ibid.). He relates inhumanity and abuse to class and education, and thereby projects it onto the proverbial behavior of less illustrious whites, bookkeepers and attorneys who act in flagrant disobedience of the orders of their more liberal (absentee) masters, like his father, "one of the most humane and generous persons that ever existed. . . . his letters were filled with the most absolute injunctions for [the] good treatment [of slaves]" (115). If justice depends on the planters' residence in their plantation, injustice is explained by their absence. In their absence, plantation managers exert their brutal power over the slaves.

In this regard, Lewis argues that freedom under slavery means destitution, that a slave without a master is like a boat cast adrift; that the death of a master can signify eternal slavery for an offspring about to be freed during his lifetime. For a slave, the greatest fear "is not having a master whom they know" (68). Not having a master has legal and economic consequences, for in an economy that only hires blacks as slaves, in which the conditions of ethnicity and labor are identical, where is the slave to labor? The problem of manumission is related to the spaces of insertion: Where in the slave economy can they belong? Given that slave society is predicated on providing basic needs, what kind of occupation can a free person lacking a master obtain? The sick one, the lame, dropsical, and aging, all share the same problem of allocation. "I rather be an under-work-man on Cornwall, than a head carpenter any where else," "me wish make it good neger for massa" (77–78), Lewis has them say.

Here the argument becomes one related to the nascent civil society that underscores some of Lewis's economic concerns. In other nineteenth-century Caribbean novels, such as Cirilo Villaverde's *Cecilia Valdés*, there is a civil society constituted by "colored" free laborers—tailors, carpenters, masons.[18] In Lewis, the festivities of John-Canoe also speak of the labors of a free population. In Madden, innkeeping is a self-employment area for "brown ladies." In addition, there is already in existence the tradition of self-subsistence economies, the small plots of land, or gardens, that will constitute the main West Indian landscape during the nineteenth century—forms that have always run parallel to plantation and hacienda economies. They constitute the internal market, the site of industry, the description of which is a source of pleasure for Lewis as it is for so many other West Indian writers.[19] Claude McKay states: "in our village we were poor . . . but very proud peasants. We had plenty to eat. We had enough to wear, a roof against the rain, and beautiful spreading trees to shade us from the sun."[20] In Jean Rhys's novel, Christophine cultivates her own plot of land and this capacity to feed herself makes her free from law-enforcement agents, and proud.

By this time, the nature of Lewis's intervention is philosophical, a hypothetical abstract that, with the advantages of hindsight, ponders the difference it would have made to have practiced a more liberal administration of slavery. It is obvious that the personalized and privatized application of justice signals the absence of a well-structured state and the presence of a strong estate. What are both absent and at stake in him are the strict mandates of organized capital. This establishes the sharp contrast between the lax personal governance conditioning the administration of justice in the West Indies at the end of slavery, and the stern rules of governance of English laborers. The distribution of justice is not any better. It is simply different. A gentle lord is paternalistic, a harsh state, tyrannical. In comparison, he finds the former more humane.

My reading of Lewis's records is located at the intersection of the personal and the political. Inasmuch as production determines venality and penalty, it writes into law the distinction between slave and citizen (a free laborer). Some of the redeeming aspects of his discussion on justice and injustice are the possibilities he offers for the (re)construction of subjectivities in relationship to the pressing secular issue of citizenship rights and entitlements. He argues that diligence and indolence are categories related to labor and hence to exploitation; that diligence only works within the context of freedom, understood as the freedom to sell one's own labor power; that slavery begets timid, feeble, and despondent human beings; and that flamboyance and moderation are simply two types of human behavior whose full meaning is only displayed within the narratives of modes of production. In his text, probity and humanity, the conditions for the exercise of justice, define the English character. In defining justice, a by-product is the construction of the English self as the new modern liberal male democrat. The emancipated new citizen is yet an unknown quantity.

CONCLUSIONS

The debate on free and slave labor profoundly and decisively affected the English representation of Caribbean cultures during the nineteenth century and created a deep rift between the English metropolitan and the local intelligentsia.[21] The two works considered in this chapter are the products of the metropolitan elite, and they discuss this issue differently. Lewis addresses the distinction as the nature of citizenship and governance in relation to state and state formation; Madden sets up the parameters of citizenship as the nature of English character.

In Madden's narrative, self "implicate[s] the character of a nation" (110) and therefore constitutes the essence of citizenship. In fact, one of the paradigmatic axes of his report is character, the constitution of the English imperial self. But what in essence is English nationality or character? The attributes of Englishness are self-control, self-restraint, and discipline, or, what is the same, to be prudent, discreet, and moderate. Measurement, symmetry, and restraint are the golden rules the English self displays for purchase in the big market of the world. When these predications are brought together, they make up the profile of the new laissez-faire liberal democratic personality. This is the character of the free trader, a man who adventures into distant lands guided by his spirit of enterprise, a fact that gives him joy, and enhances his courage, which is his humanity.

Thus, English narratives of national character formation, as plantation owners are to lean on their narratives of economic formations, are indeed technologies to assert what Gayatri Spivak calls "the [intellectual] international division of labor."[22] And within these narratives, the rights of the enunciating subject—here, the English character, nation, subject, and citizen—are emphasized over and against the other obscured characters such as the African or the white West Indian bukra. The real sticker is that while these narratives foreground the English self as a sovereign subject, they make believe they are supporting the rights of others. Embryonic multicultural civil societies, where other forms of self could perform their choices, stand no chance. The definition of Englishness and the English self weaves its way through culture and law and always stands as "the norm." The topographies of regularity (moderation and symmetry) betray the modalities of home as the structuring structure. The opposite of moderation is excess—in the case of the West Indian Negroes, flamboyance, the grotesque.

Yet, for an English gentleman living in the West Indian islands at the end of slavery, this definition of citizenship becomes problematic. As properties and nations become disengaged, citizenship rights will become dislodged. Citizenship is a right of birth that stems from the place of birth, and, in the case of imperial nations, is always extended to the place of residence. However, at this point in time, the change over from mercantilism to laissez-faire liberal policies has rendered this right null. The predicament for planters is either to build an alliance with the natives and start the process of nation construction, or to go back to England. Many chose to return.

The quandary of the local intelligentsia is very well expressed in the works of the three most renowned Jamaican historians, William Beckford, Edward Long, and Bryan Edwards, who, in their books, narrate their disenchantment with their native country, England. They begrudge English policies and determination, and hold England responsible for their bankruptcy. In their view, England is tampering with their rights and withdrawing its protection over their wealth and property. What is most interesting about this local intelligentsia is that their dystopic narratives of decay are not grounded in a sense of nationality but in one of territoriality, property rights—a seedling "native land" nativism. However, this type of nativism is moot, for, as Philip Curtin, Richard Pares, and Gordon Lewis, among others, have demonstrated, the radical difference between the English colonies in the North and in the West Indies in the Caribbean is none other than nation building.[23] Whereas the former choose to construct their citizenship different and apart from England, the latter choose against it. And in no other texts is this choice more evident than in the works of the three Jamaican historians just mentioned. In their work, they limit themselves to defending their property rights based in their rights as citizens of England, and lamenting the break of the cultural paradigm. My contention is that the planter intelligentsia embodies the type of mentality of governing colonial elites, Creoles whose styles and modes of domination and traditions will be reproduced by the planter's white and mulatto heirs. But what I want to remark in this historical performance of choice is the loss of the possibility of a reconfiguration and modernization of ethnicity, together with the early formation of an incipient native creole intelligentsia and sensibility.

The trope of a betrayed or doubtful nationalism is typical of the planter class across the Caribbean and is grounded on the distinction between free and slave labor. Manuel Moreno Fraginals has documented these feelings of ambiguity between nation and property in the Cuban planter class.[24] He sets their apocalyptic views side by side with the paradisiacal names of their *ingenios* (plantations). Some of the plantations' names in Jamaica— "Lucky Valley" (Edward Long's); "Drax Hall" (William Beckford's); "Friendship" (Lord and Lady Holland's); "Worthy Park" (John Price's)— parallel the Cuban and the French. They all portray sugarcane fields as gardens, linking their aesthetic tradition to the sublime of the commercial narratives of the Spanish Golden Age. Their immaculate cartographic representation speaks of a very orderly productive universe that clearly demarcates their structures of feeling, while the names of their slaves— Plato, Priam, Pam, Hercules, Minerva, Psyche, Venus—invoke the Orient via Greece.

That from here a sense of nationhood and nationality might be developed explains the shift from plantation (estate) to *factoría* (state)—as the new form of government is called in the Spanish Caribbean—making the sugarmill stand as the metonymy of nation and governance. This is the same predicament of sugar planters elsewhere. In Cuba, planters like Francisco Arango y Parreño, Domingo del Monte, and José Antonio Saco harbor ideas of a troubled independence. The paradigmatic fiction addressing this moment in Cuba is Cirilo Villaverde's *Cecilia Valdés*. Madden, Lewis, Beckford, Long, and Edwards represent the English national and the white creole English native intelligentsia at odds with each other in the Caribbean. They engage in the civic debate by focusing their representation of nature on plains, plantations, and native lands—not as recreational grounds, Columbus's gardens of Hesperides, but as industrial sites producing sugarcane.

Sugar fields, planting sites, and plantation geographies are narrated in a legalistic tone, through the close scrutiny of labor as culture. Culture is understood as habits and habitat, people's character and manners, the host of idiosyncratic types of creole societies placed in the position of subaltern nonsubjects within their own natural geographies. The quaint and colorful rhetorical palette of "Negroes," "blackies," "sambos," "niggers," "mulattoes," "octoroons," "quatroons," "mestee," "mustefee," poor whites—that is, the vast array of social types—provides the tropes, moods, and styles that stand poised on the ledge of Pan-Caribbean and Pan-African movements. They in turn constitute the stuff on which new disciplines and approaches to citizenship and civil rights are spawned.

chapter 3

BEACHES

THE POSTCOLONIAL CARIBBEAN

On the other side of the postcolonial debate, contemporary narratives about the Caribbean have selected beaches to represent the region. The Houghton Mifflin Company, a producer of educational and tourist books, the San Francisco Sierra Club Books, concerned with environmental issues, and government publications from all kinds of political regimes center on beaches as they become the metonymy for development, the panacea to bring in dollars. Beaches have become natural, economic, and poetic frontiers. The best minds of the Caribbean are invested in making this project succeed. The Houghton Mifflin tourist guide on Jamaica, for instance, counts among its collaborators the novelist V. S. Reid; the one on Puerto Rico, the historian Gordon Lewis. One must also mention the political work of the Cuban Communist Party cadres working with Spanish capital in Cuba to make the tourist project succeed.

Tourist guides to the Caribbean make use of the enchanted-island paradigm found in the traveling diaries of Christopher Columbus. Most of these texts capitalize on the disoriented prose of the admiral, selecting the passages where he speaks about the weather and the beauty of the islands, or remarking upon his erroneous location, much to the chagrin of postcolonial scholars. What the Caribbean is, is contingent on where the Caribbean is. The Caribbean is a site between two oceans/seas, a ridge of islands separating two large bodies of water, a tropical archipelago some fifteen hundred miles in length uniting the southern and the northern parts of the continent, from Cuba in the north to Trinidad in the south, a place that must resemble another place—Asia, the Hesperides, paradise. What Beatriz Pastor reads as the site of adjustment is for tourism a geography that extends from the southern United States all the way into the Amazon basin, making Manaus/El Dorado into a remote romantic Caribbean inland port in the middle of the Amazon jungle. The names refer to tangled geographies, a tradition initiated by the admiral and perpetuated by all travel narratives of colonialism.

Tourist guides, then, emphasize what Margarita Zamora calls the pragmatic and commercial aspects of travel narratives; they rewrite Columbus to support their business and promote industrial cultures while marketing for profits; they enhance and support the vision of the admiral that tourism wants to promote, for instance, stressing confusions to extract profit from narratives of intersection, very much in the tradition of the *Diaries*. The crisscross of the knowledge of geology, geography, and history turn space into an attractive site to invest emotionally and fiscally. The following quote is a sample of a narrative intersection that tourism makes available to itself:

> A story of the Caribbean can begin as follows: some 100 million years ago in the late Cretaceous period (when dinosaurs became extinct), volcanoes erupted deep in the Caribbean seabed. . . . A few million years of undersea volcanic activity passed like this. The slow thickening of lava flows coincided with an overall decrease in water depth and an uplift of the entire Caribbean areas. . . . It is the period of earth building favored by moviemakers, with a fiery horizon and boulders glowing sky high. . . . During the passage of thousands of years of hellfire and brimstone land building—a period politely called subaerial volcanism—the slopes of the explosive cone weathered and the sediments were deposited in the surrounding seas. . . . Continuing changes, due to active earth movements along faults, resulted in the Caribbean's valley systems and deep bays.[1]

The inbreeding of narratives present in Columbus's confusion, and in this case of geology, geography, and history, creates the sensation of the picturesque, that which can be frozen by framing an object and contemplating it as in a picture: the Caribbean, a picture to be enjoyed from the comfort of our living rooms. The Caribbean is the solicitous place from which we practice ethno- and geophagy, the consumption of culture and world. Making it small, manageable, bite-size reminds us of Rabasa's "exoticism," now turned into Spurr's sense of aesthetics and Pratt's ideas of investments. Epistemic mixtures also permit geology to feed us knowledge in the form of romance. Would it not be just too picturesque, and so thoroughly romantic, to imagine a different geological formation, when Jamaica was perhaps united to Nicaragua, Cuba part of Florida, when Trinidad was alongside the Orinoco River, and Puerto Rico and the Virgin Islands were probably a single landmass? Would it not be exciting to picture the geological violence that gave rise to the splintering islands and made them look like pebbles forming a passageway connecting one mass of continental land to another?

In addition to providing pertinent and useful enframed information, tourist guides do very well to use new technologies such as condensing and reducing to make the Caribbean islands attractive. Size in square miles is an important category used to measure societies. Their size, epitomized in what literature has called a "small place," is puny, ranging from single digits (the 5 to 8 square miles of Saba and Saint Barts), to double digits (30 to 35 for Grenada and Anguilla, respectively), to the largest—Jamaica, Puerto Rico, Hispaniola (Haiti and the Dominican Republic), Cuba—4,200, 3,339, 29,389, and 42,804 square miles, respectively. Some of the islands are so tiny that one can easily walk the entire periphery by foot; they could almost be transformed into jogging trails. In fact, tininess is a poeticized aspect, as can be seen in Simone Schwarz-Bart's *Ti Jean L'Horizon* (1981), as well as in Jamaica Kincaid's *A Small Place* (1988).[2] There is not much difference between their images. Schwarz-Bart speaks about Guadeloupe as a tiny spot. Sweetly caught up between hyperbole and the supermimetic machinery of the West, the Caribbean is one of the most spectacular textual places in the world, a Hollywood paradise backdrop set, where, as one of my favorite tourist billboards reads, "Your pleasure is our business."

As in Columbus's descriptions, people in tourist guides are conveniently bracketed, subsumed either into the category of servants in a picture of luxurious apartheid hotel complexes, or placed within minuscule traditions and written off as amusing anecdotes. Their history is the *grand récit* of geology, the prestigious narratives of colonialism, or a series of anecdotal references reduced to a couple of pages organized as holidays. Caribbean peoples, narrated by tourist books, keep on regulating their lives according to premodern parameters, Christianity, subsistence agriculture, or the solar system. For the biggest ones (Cuba, for example), history is also monuments, architecture, and museums, such as Hemingway's residence in San Francisco de Paula, in the poor municipality of San Miguel del Padrón, or the in vitro museum of a bygone failed social project known as socialism.

But the best job of describing the islands is done by the *petit récit*, the short report that presents the traveler with important pragmatic information, a brief and succinct narrative about the culture of the everyday, what is useful and profitable, as well as functional. Cultural history is once more statistics, numbers: area, population, communication systems, customs regulations, time zone, type of currency and exchange rates, taxes and tips, type of electricity. These are the listings to which Margarita Zamora points as characteristics of *roteiros* (rutters), now applied to an overview comprising things to see and do—historic sites, fishing villages, beaches, nightlife, shopping, hotels, food, sports (tennis, fishing, boating, diving), whereabouts, capital cities, language, religion, government, location, health, clothing. These lists are usually small, and they indicate just how uneventful and ahistorical the islands are.

Caribbean islands, classified as tourist resorts, natural sanctuaries, or "satanic" islands, remain the epistemological site of an old paradox that makes of them inferno or paradise. For scholars, the landscaping of islands by tourism constitutes a double bind. The paradox between beaches and plains, between cities and hotel networks and compounds, basically establishes the difference between people—imperial discoverer/indigenous person, master/slave, mulatto/black, tourist/local people. In the lingua franca of the Cuban people, beaches, that is, the natural elements of sun, sand, sea, and sailing, are dividing lines spoken more quietly, a linguistic apartheid.

In a stream of consciousness, a hotel employee in Jamaica supplied the following narrative to me: Jamaica's most exclusive resorts are large collections of villas and clusters of rooms. Some of them, like the Trident Hotel in Port Antonio, include among the amenities roaming peacocks and priceless antiques. The Half Moon Hotel at Montego Bay, the Trident at Port Antonio, and the Round Hill at Trelawny belong to a group called Elegant Hotels and Resorts. They cater to a very upscale clientele such as

Hollywood stars—Goldie Hawn, Warren Beatty, Tom Cruise, Eddie Murphy—and Japanese industrial barons. They are controlled by one family, the Rousseaus, and generally managed by Europeans. The greatest tourism success has arguably been Butch Steward, who started the "all-inclusive package" craze that has taken over the industry. He owns the Sandals chain, which in about ten years has expanded throughout the Caribbean, to Antigua, Saint Kitts, and the Bahamas. His style of management approaches Leona Helmsley's. Good management minimizes capital risks. One price includes everything, from meals to drinks to sports activities. People love it! The average Joe on the East Coast or in Middle America knows somebody going to, or who is planning to go to, Sandals. A big thing to do is to get married or to honeymoon there. Because the economy is small, most major businesspeople in Jamaica have more than one interest, but the overall interest is in land for tourism, in the form of beaches, real estate, food, entertainment, and insurance. Rousseau, Steward, and Issa are the Big Three, visionaries in terms of pioneering fearless international marketing; Stewart and Issa are worth multiple millions in any currency. They are in "dog-eat-dog" competition, and don't speak to each other, except through the press.

Exclusivity comes with the rating. The hotels rate with the George V and the Savoy. Physically, and in terms of relationship to the community, they are just as exclusive—walled and guarded. To move from the Third/Fourth World environment of Jamaica's infrastructure, through the gates and into one of the island's resorts, is to experience the kind of mind-bending contrast that would make for great movie scripts. Hotels shield their guests from the realities of what lies between resorts and the attractions (waterfalls, farms, parks, etc.) by building large walls and fences and planting many a bush. This also keeps the unfortunate outside and prevents them from encroaching upon the inner reality. Where security has been lax, the result is violence, death, all the scandal one hears about. No comment necessary about the catch-22 of this dynamic. All-"inclusive" packages and communities have been criticized for excluding the outside economy from the benefits of the thousands of tourists they pull in each year (indeed, all-inclusive complexes are almost solely responsible for the survival and continued strength of the country's tourism industry). Obviously, if guests don't need to come out for anything, they won't.

Originally located against the backdrop of Columbus's narratives of

paradise, it is evident that today the Caribbean is a place south of Henry
Miller's *Tropic of Cancer*, between the novels of Ernest Hemingway and
his dreams of freedom in Cuba, and the extravaganza of Hollywood, *The
Return to Fantasy Island*, the popular television show with Ricardo Mon-
talbán, of building an earthly paradise in Jamaica.[3] It is also a place located
within what Fredric Jameson calls the twin forms of the postmodern: con-
spiracy and allegory.[4] Looking at it from this viewpoint, the Caribbean lies
at a crossroads between an espionage and Mafia thriller, such as *Havana*
(Sydney Pollack, 1990); playing insurgency and counterinsurgency in the
Blue Mountains of Jamaica, as in Michelle Cliff's *No Telephone to Heaven*;[5]
a spot to hide a psychosexual killer like Hannibal Lector in *The Silence of
the Lambs* (Jonathan Demme, 1991); the site of a Mafia gathering, as in
The Godfather (Francis Ford Coppola, 1972), or the KGB meets the CIA
in Castro's mystery-clouded regime, or William F. Buckley's espionage
novels; all the way to politically correct films about homosexuality and
politics such as *Fresa y Chocolate* (Tomás Gutiérrez Alea, 1994) or *Azúcar
Amargo* (León Ichaso, 1996). With the exception of Fidel Castro's Cuba
and possibly Michael Manley's Jamaica, in all these islands imagination
has the rite of passage. Novels such as Ernest Hemingway's *The Old Man
and the Sea* and Jean Rhys's *Wide Sargasso Sea* can provide the language
and setting for those transnational, vacation-oriented imaginaries—one
for fishing, sailing, and having a drink paid in dollars at Hemingway's
landmark restaurant Floridita in Havana, the other for romance and
falling in love.[6] Cuba is thought of as a safe haven for criminals such as
Robert Vesco, or fugitive ex-presidents such as Carlos Salinas de Gortari.
This is to say that these islands are seen from afar, from above, from outside; they are the islands of explorers, planters, tourists.

In *Caribbean Style*, a picture book of houses and landscapes, colossal
mansions are set inside splendid natural seascapes. *Caribbean Style* has borrowed its mode from *Good Housekeeping* and *House and Garden*, juxtaposing the learning of journals on architecture with city builders' and planners'
manuals and the work of photographers. Poverty is totally absent from
these pictures. Only here and there, next to a peasant house in miniature
rendered quaint, might we see the small figure of a man or a woman standing. Otherwise, the few pictures of people, taken from above, show them
small and crowding the space—beach or marketplace. Are they made to
represent the servants of estates? Whites are not in sight. Absent owners

could not be photographed. Occasionally their guard dogs and uniformed servants serve as scenery and props. Big, small, whole or in ruins, in the mountains, or by the seaside, the pictures' message is that good planning and heavy investment will render this land a paradise. Echoes of cocktail party chitchat tell stories that melt the drama of slavery into the anecdote of gentility and good manners: "millions of Africans were *convoyed* to the islands. . . . All were forced to *reeducate* themselves in order to survive. . . . Native Amerindians *tried to help* the foreigners, even though the new-comers were anxious to *exterminate* them. . . . Nothing remains of these Amerindians except a few tools and some of their savoir faire."[7] Nothing remains except a poignant light blue picture book, and the ongoing debate of postcolonial studies.

PART II

THE GUATEMALAN HIGHLANDS

chapter 4

CULTURAL GEOGRAPHIES

Stories of Bloodlust and Land

> Mesoamericans, past and present, have lived their lives suspended in webs of significance which they themselves have spun.
>
> —GARY GOSSEN, ed., *Symbol and Meaning beyond the Closed Community*

THE LAYOUT OF THE LAND

In this chapter, I examine the geographic layout of the Guatemalan highlands at the time of the Conquest and how it was redrawn by Spanish colonialism. My point of departure is Pedro de Alvarado's "Cartas de relación." These are two letters in which he informs Hernán Cortés about his military incursions (*avanzadas*) through what is today Guatemalan territory.[1] I am awestruck not only by the enormous confusion generated by his description of the layout of the land but also by the critical tradition it has produced for the study of Guatemalan cultures. The degree to which colonial texts repeat verbatim the information provided by this foundational document encumbers the study of the confrontation between the Spanish and the indigenous worlds. In tracing the genealogy of this confusion, I intend to underscore the concurrence of narratives of war, settlement, and investments. The story begins with the perplexities of two cultures at odds with each other, and ends with the tourist project of investments created by neoliberalism. Land, land titles, and land jurisdictions constitute the main tropes of the history of colonialism in the

79

Guatemalan highlands, and, by extension, in the whole area of Central America. Geography and geographic location are the main markers of this history.

Language plays a key role in the development of my argument. Misperceived phonemes led to the misunderstanding of not only subsequent depositions and debriefings, the writing and rewriting of land titles, the transformation of history into literature, of geography into politics, but, most important, the designing and redesigning of the topographies of conquest to which Alvarado's texts give rise. Scholars' first interest in following Alvarado's course is militaristic, involving questions pertaining to war and conquest, but as researchers unravel the data, they hit the crucial point—the organization of colonialism and colonial rule, which is settlement, the reorganization of the land, and the establishment of a different jurisdictional system.

Throughout the colonial period, all bibliographies rely on this confusing data. Beginning in the nineteenth century there is an epistemological shift. With the advent of positivism and the prevalence of pragmatic reason, the layout of the land suffers a drastic reconsideration in the work of geographers and naturalists. Settlement yields to investment. The Spanish tradition is superseded by North American pragmatism and positivist geography takes over the work of friars. All previous indigenous knowledge is declared obsolete and relegated to the realm of fiction. The first part of the chapter takes on the Spanish and indigenous, and the Spanish and criollo confrontations; the second, the relationship between criollos and North Americans. Thus this narrative moves from the narratives of war to those of settlement and investment.

Initially, the geographies of the Guatemalan highlands were no better mapped than those of the Amazon jungle. This fact cannot be explained by invoking the absence of a nomenclature or an ordering and classifying system. In the Guatemalan highlands, the Europeans encountered well-developed societies that had given meaning and order to their physical, mental, and social universe. Spaniards entered the highlands as conquerors, and as conquerors they disregarded the previous order and renamed the indigenous topographies, with the aim of disrupting and controlling. It is clear that the purpose of the geographies was not only informational but political. As we see in Pedro de Alvarado and repeatedly in Francisco Antonio de Fuentes y Guzmán and Domingo Juarros, what matters is whether the roads Alvarado is crossing help or hinder the passing of cavalry and infantry; whether the area is an open plain, closed mountain, ravine or valley; whether "Indians" are "of peace" or "of war," obedient and governable or insubordinate and ready for combat. The Spaniards were eager to document "Indian" tactics of war and their intelligent strategies. What mattered to the Spaniards was to fight, to win, and to conquer, because the aim was to settle and to rule. Therefore, battles were just the first step of the confrontation; the second step was the foundation of towns and the administration of "justice," and the third step the exploitation of natural and human resources. Hence, war, urbanism, administration, and agriculture were all played out in the initial descriptions of the land. As the army crossed over mountains, gorges, ravines, rivers, and lakes, the environment reproduced a habitat incorporating the extended settlement of milpas, ceremonial grounds, and urban centers. It is therefore important to understand the nature of the terrain the *avanzada* traversed as an aspect of the urban planning of the Quiché-Maya social formation.

My interest is in the legacy this massive narrative confusion has produced. To properly address the production of the new colonial jurisdictions, the Spaniards must come to grasp the previous formation, its singularities and continuities. Therefore, reaching an understanding of the Quiché-Maya cultures was a necessity. As J. Eric S. Thompson pointed out, no understanding of the new discursive colonial formation is possible without the singularization of Quiché discourse.[2] The production of this knowledge already occupied the minds of the sixteenth-century administrators and scholars, who were entrusted with the task of understanding and managing this universe, and no solid governance could be achieved without it.

THE TOPOGRAPHIES OF WAR

In the history of the Guatemalan highlands, Pedro de Alvarado's "Cartas de relación" (April and July 1524) mark an uncontestable epistemic break. They were written in Utatlán and Santiago de Guatemala and directed to Hernán Cortés. Although there is no original version—they were published by Gaspar de Ávila in 1525 in Toledo—these letters are the only report of the Conquest by a direct Spanish witness. They reveal how the leader of the expedition saw the Conquest. In his first and second "Cartas de relación," Alvarado describes the cardinal points of his journey.[3] The first letter speaks about the conquest of Utatlán and the death of the Quiché rulers. The second letter refers to the city of Iximché, the conquest of the Zutujils, and the founding of the city of Santiago. In contrast, the indigenous texts *El Memorial de Sololá* and *The Ixquín-Nehaib Title* tell the same story from an altogether different point of view. They speak about the arrival of the Castellanos. *El Memorial* relates their arrival to Xetulul and speaks about the Cakchiquel people. This text gives an account of the resistance to the Spaniards and it offers a correct chronology of the events. At moments it even provides more information about the foundation of the first Spanish city. The *Ixquín-Nehaib Title* is one of the most extensive accounts of the Conquest. It was probably gathered as a testimonial during the sixteenth century and served as a document in territorial disputes. It is also useful in gauging the impact of the Conquest on the indigenes.

The important point for my study is that regarding the route the Spaniards followed in their entry into the Guatemalan highlands, the "Cartas de relación" and the *Ixquín-Nehaib Title* plot a different one.[4] Who is right and who is wrong cannot be verified, but all subsequent historiography is intent in finding this out. In this work of repetition or reconstruction, the real questions are whom to believe and to find out where we are. What is certain is that the map of Alvarado's military incursion blurs all the former borders. In his altogether bewildering construction of the terrain, Quiché-Maya geographies become tangled and mangled. His lack of precision is the starting point for a scholarly tradition predicated on ignorance, forgetfulness, and erasure, a liminal position that redefines both the Quiché-Maya and the Spanish epistemic fields.

On the borders of Alvarado's discourse, new rules of engagement come into play. All former options within each of the two contending fields are interdicted, and processes of severe confrontation can be said to begin. This fact alone explains why Alvarado's account is so perplexing and why disorientation is the clearest sign of an incipient cross-culturation observable in the new superimposed geographical layout of the land. But what is most important is that his obvious bewilderment impels in the nineteenth and twentieth centuries a scholarly tradition whose purpose is the historical reconstruction of this past.

Language constitutes the clearest sign of a threshold.[5] As Alvarado's *avanzada* crossed the Quiché-Maya territory, the misheard, misunderstood, and mispronounced indigenous words are warning signs of distress. As his account moves from one language to another, from Quiché-Maya to Hispanicized Quiché and then to Spanish in a series of successive displacements, the Quiché-Maya hegemony was drastically displaced. I read the phonetic traces of languages and dialects as the unequivocal signs of a war-marked discourse, as sets of differentiated subject positions and functions. The new mode of localization and circulation of these altered phonemes is defined by the military actions depicted in the discourse of war. War itself sets the limits and forms of discourse. My argument thus hinges on sounds, sounds not heard, sounds kept, sounds discarded. To take over signs is to take over lands, although the Quiché-Maya names lingering in their Hispanicized versions are specific remnants that subtend the power of the indigenous epistemes to this date.

The real problem is that most of the sixteenth-century chroniclers and the seventeenth- and eighteenth-century historians repeat the original documents verbatim. They reproduce the same events and values, compounding the original historical quagmire. For instance, Bernal Díaz repeats verbatim from his sources.[6] And although at times he edits and sorts out data, his text is already greatly informed and underwritten by a colonial cultural legislation that lays bare the networks of power, denoting the latitude of knowledge provided by settlement. Through Díaz, the colonial administrative apparatus speaks. In the seventeenth century, the famous criollo writer Francisco Antonio de Fuentes y Guzmán returns to the sources to repeat Alvarado's journey; and in the nineteenth century, Guatemalan historian Domingo Juarros rehearses again the new and well-established divisions of the Spanish empire, while still keeping the old indigenous names that serve as a backdrop to his palimpsest.[7]

Vested with a more pro-indigenist mentality, early-twentieth-century social scientists engage this same question of reconstruction. For instance, José Antonio Villacorta meticulously fills Alvarado's discursive gaps concerning Quiché-Maya topographies.[8] He establishes the dates and places of Alvarado's incursions, the days of the battles, and the correspondence between the Julian and the Quiché calendars.[9] Villacorta says that there were roads from Mexico to Central America; that these roads extended along the present Mexican republic and came into Central America "via the provinces of Chiapas, Retalhuleu, Suchitepequez; and from Cuyote-nango a branch went up into the Guatemalan highlands, which was the same road which Spaniards crossed during the first months of 1524, to the cities of Utatlán and Iximché" (295). And finally, Robert Carmack has Alvarado's *avanzada* traveling via Soconusco to Xetulul, Pinal, Xelaju, Salcaja, Chuwi Mik'ina, Utatlán, and Iximché (see Figure 6).

However, Alvarado's disorientation and the prismatic effect that it produces in scholarly research, as well as in the constitution of research fields, does not end with the factual unraveling of his route. His confused empirical observations of the topographies of the highlands are further aggravated by other absences that war narratives simultaneously reveal and occlude, such as his glossing over of the events of everyday life. As we can gather from the documents, his invading army is not just crossing over physical geographies, "empty lands," but lands inhabited by people who live in accordance with an ordered universe of meaning, and who follow

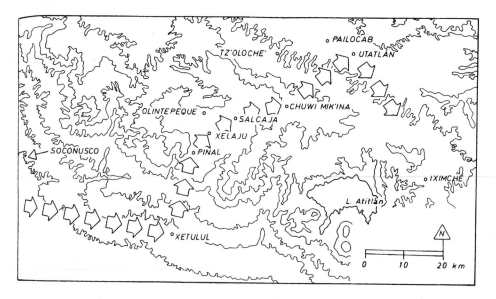

Figure 6. The Spanish conquest of the Quichés. Based on a map by the Instituto Geográfico Nacional, Guatemala. From Robert M. Carmack, *The Quiché Mayas of Utatlán: The Evolution of a Highland Guatemala Kingdom* (Norman: University of Oklahoma Press, 1981); copyright 1981 by the University of Oklahoma Press; reprinted by permission.

a routine that is also disrupted. A look at Villacorta's carefully reconstructed topographies permits us to see that this is a densely populated
land. Alvarado himself recognizes this, saying that "there [Quecaltenango]
I lodged and was recuperating and passing through the land which is as
populated as Tescaltepeque with its average farmland and is most exces-
sively cold" (Luján, *Inicios del dominio español,* 82). Settlements are scattered throughout the physical space, and Alvarado's arrival during the
month of April coincides with one of their agricultural production cycles.
Ruth Bunzel's agricultural worktable slates April as the period for the
planting of potatoes and the farming of early white corn. In May, early
yellow corn is cultivated. Alvarado wrote his letter to Cortés during April
1524. One can assume that by the time of the letter's composition the land
had been subdued and all forms of life and agricultural production had
been disrupted. In addition, all the symbolic rituals and festivities related
to food production, as described by Father Francisco Ximénez, must also
have come to a halt. Furthermore, Villacorta says that Alvarado's exploration stops because the rainy season had started, and he returns to Iximché
at the beginning of July 1524.

It is pertinent at this point to remember Alfred Crosby's perspective
on winning or losing wars.[10] As he argues in the case of the Canary Islands,
victory also depends on food production, on the localization of the terrain
of war. In the terrain or location where war is fought, food production is
disrupted because all the able bodies are engaged in the war effort, not to
mention the fact that the entire population is subjected to the traumatic
effects and emotional distress a protracted war brings with it. All these
daily events are glossed over in Alvarado's war narrative, as are other
important matters, such as the coping mechanism of the indigenous people and the processes of confrontation that must have immediately
ensued—among them the burning of the Quiché-Maya Lords, the setting
of their texts on fire, and the torturing of their scribes, their mass bap-
tisms, and the practices surrounding their immediate conversion. A set of
discursive activities has thrived in these gaps.

Reconstruction of this information has promoted further investigation
in agricultural and folk-culture research in the fields of ethnohistory,
archaeology, and linguistics, which constitute the vast field of Maya studies. But at the moment it was written, Alvarado's discourse was concerned
only with the nature of the terrain; consequently, he focuses on the

topographies, meticulously recording the names of places, towns, and peoples that mark where his army was passing through, and carefully annotating the physical aspects and conditions of the land. His main interest lies in the topographical nature of the terrain, finding those flat surfaces that will maximize the advantages of the Spanish war machine, specifically of the horses. Composite views of indigenous towns, sites, monuments, war strategies, symbolic dress, and tactics constitute a foundation that binds the scenery to the battles that will later lead to settlements. The epic-heroic, which is later reproduced, stressed, and enhanced, mainly in Díaz del Castillo, in order to serve the construction of identities such as that of the dignified enemy, is born in the interrelation between scenery and dexterity in war. Any data referring to daily life is eschewed. What matters here is to plot the advance of the cavalry, the action of the army, the nature of the weapons, and war rituals. The speed of construction and destruction runs fast-forward. At this moment, geography is just a maze of information in which to get lost. Given that Alvarado's letters are fundamentally narratives of war and conquest, they begin by describing his route of entry into Quiché-Maya territory, and reach a climax in the burning of the city of Utatlán, the destruction of the enemy's center of power. All in all, what we are referring to is a very small geography made large by an abundance of names and by the mutual crisscrossing and enormous juxtaposition of traditions, languages, and interests.

DAY 1 GANEL: FEBRUARY 20, 1524

If my point of departure is Pedro de Alvarado, my points of contrast are the indigenous documents—*El Memorial de Sololá, The Ixquín-Nehaib Title*, the *Popol Vuh*.[11] In these books, the Quiché topographies introduce other taxonomies, further complicating the real geographical location of the Quiché-Maya. The element that the indigenous texts bring to bear in the discussion adds two important dimensions: the structure of feeling predominant in the indigenous world as the result of the confrontation, and the effort in trying to cope with the forced acculturation. In the confusion created by the narrative intersections of cross-culturation, indigenous documents contribute a consistent obscuring of referents. This obscurity can be interpreted according to different epistemological frames as an impossibility, an unwillingness, or both.

It is simple common sense to presume that, even with the assistance of interpreters, during the first moments of the Spanish–Quiché-Maya confrontation, it was impossible to fully and competently translate both languages and ways of thinking to inform one another. It is not difficult to imagine that translation is the most precious object of desire. Truly, writing indigenous cultures and epistemologies, in a precariously known and unmastered Spanish, under the vigilance of authority, is a quite maddening proposition. To the technical impossibility must be added the indigenous reluctance to speak about themselves, given the overbearing and obscure presence of the threatening Christian context. Obscurity, then, is simultaneously a technology and its effect; it is a way for indigenes to renegotiate the continuation of their culture by submerging it. Again, if knowledge is power, the denial of knowledge constitutes a denial of power.

However, there are other markers that make indigenous documents appear quite trustworthy—for one, the strong presence of their coerced biculturalism, noticeable in the giving of the double patronymic to "Indians" as they become baptized (e.g., Don Francisco Izquín Ahpalotz Uzakilbalha, Don Francisco Calel Atzih Uinac Tieran, Don Noxorio Cortés Galel Atzih Uinac Rokche). The ambivalent literacy, visible in the enjoining of names that indicate a mixture of words, the misunderstanding of where one word ends and the other begins, such as in calling Alvarado Tonatiúh (or Tonadiú) Avilantaro (Alvarado + Adelantado), gives us access to a world in which at least two epistemes are being interwoven. And important as a sign of defense and preservation is the placing of events within indigenous chronologies such as Day 1 Ganel (February 20, 1524) (Luján, *Inicios del dominio español*, 75), the day the Quiché-Mayas were defeated by the Spaniards; likewise, the presence of indigenous terms such as *calpulli*, and the plotting of indigenous visions and symbols within the indigenes' own core belief system, or in the same sense blending the flying wings of Tecúm with the appearance of a white girl/dove that protected Tonadiu. The heroic narrative about Tecúm, a hero who could fly, because wings were part of his body, and the belief that Tecúm was so beautiful that Alvarado himself went to defend him from the dogs that were about to tear him apart, offers another sign of the persistence of their belief system.

In this regard, the anonymous *Isagoge* serves as a cross-reference to *The Ixquin-Nehaib Title* when it reports: "They say the Quiché king, Tecúm Umám, was a great warlock and that he flew over all the armies in the form of a bird they call Quetzal, of long and very fancy, green feathers, and that with an emerald wand in hand, he went about giving orders to his captains and encouraging his soldiers."[12] The realm of "magic," as the bibliographies have chosen to label this interpretation, is what highlights the absolute impact of the hegemonic discourse into the indigenous lives, and, conversely, of indigenous discourse into the hegemonic. Perhaps the feathers on Tecúm's body, and the birds they came from, quetzals—to this day a symbol of value in Guatemala—gave the place the name of Quetzaltenango. It is not clear whether the feathers were from the quetzal, or the indigenous cacique was himself viewed or represented as a quetzal, or both, because *The Ixquín-Nehaib Title*'s informant reports that the Adelantado called all his soldiers to come see the beauty of this "Indian" quetzal. The truth is that a flying-like figure, a beautiful fleeting image, represents the courage of a warrior in the full performance of the defense of his land. After that, "the Adelantado told his soldiers that he had never seen another Indian as handsome and as commanding (cacique)" (ibid., 73).

A drawing of the remnants of a mural at Utatlán provides a representation that not only approximates the literary description of Tecúm's war gear as it is recorded by *The Ixquín-Nehaib Title* but, together with the reconstruction of the figure of the monkey, pinpoints the convergence of religious, governmental, and defense functions stated in the *Isagoge* as follows: "They also say that he [Tecúm Umám] had the same ability of the warlocks, several other caciques that roamed about in form of lions, eagles and other animals. . . . it has been recorded in the same histories of the Indians that the Quiché-Maya kings were great warlocks and that this cursed pact with the devil perseveres among some Indians; it is not incredible that this king Tecúm Umám was a warlock and that he did transform himself into a quetzal bird" (186). To get an idea of the indigenous war gear, see Figure 7.

A feeling of a disrupted everyday life bleeds through each syllable of this emotive historiography. The heterogeneous comes out in the glaring contrast between the obscurity of the indigenous document that speaks of grief and the pragmatism of Alvarado that speaks of neglect. Whereas the broken syntax of the native documents denotes an oppressive and crushing pain, Alvarado's ellipsis registers indifference. The first impact of submission is that of a gruesomely forced acculturation. Ancient and dear habits must be shed overnight! The witnesses cannot hide their agony;

they bemoan the great affliction caused by the defeat. In the gaps left by this intermittent and mixed syntax, indigenous organization and the commitment to indigenous culture are underscored by the memory of the military organization of Tecúm, commanding ten thousand Quiché-Mayas armed with bows, arrows, spears, and slingshots. The counterposed heroic establishes a tension within the defeated and is a place of retention, of hope and pride, where cultural legacies can be retrieved and maintained. Tecúm's warrior introjects the symbolic in his gear, which makes him look like a bird, makes him into a bird—quetzal.

Figure 7. Reconstruction of painted mural from Cawek palace showing Quiché warrior. Drawing by María Gabriela Patocchi; reproduced with permission of the artist.

But, equally important is that the broken and interfered syntax also denotes a speaker caught up in the dilemma of saying and of silencing. The testimonial betrays these doubts of adjacency. What to say—and how—is the question. There is a process of second-guessing being suggested. The Quiché-Maya informants must guess what the Spanish compilers want. They must be careful with their words. Are they to trust these foreigners? What should they keep to themselves? How do they keep their culture and simultaneously give it away, rendering a testimonial amenable to the interrogating and prosecuting Christian epistemes? Assuring these evangelists that their religious teachings have taken hold is a principal concern in these narratives, but so is the simultaneous preservation of what is their own. The informant's own Quiché-Maya history of resistance and heroism and the Spanish religion are mixed within his own troubled consciousness, all amalgamated with grief. The consciousness of negotiation—that is, politics mixed with sorrow—is, then, the context of testimonial production. The lack of a common language to communicate and the presence of cultural parameters overwhelmingly at odds with each other add trouble to what is already an untenable situation, namely, that of what to say and not say, or whether to say simply what they want to hear, to express oneself properly, or simply to hide it all away. Theories of transculturation thrive on these intersections.

In *El Memorial* the Indian markers of time—1 Ganel, 4 Qat, 1 Hunahpu—have not been edited out. The names pull us back to a preserved Quiché-Maya legacy. Time is a comforting feature because, in time, Quiché-Maya predictions may come true, and the world the Spaniards are constructing will inevitably come to pass. According to their predictions, it must come to an end on 4 Ahau, 3 K'ank'in, Sunday, December 23, 2012. In fact, the recurrence of cyclical conceptions of time, a culturally ingrained epistemological flexibility, and the transferability of signs are established hypotheses in readings of the Quiché-Maya field.

Additionally, the following statements in *The Ixquin-Nehaib Title* can be imagined to be indigenous markers: the narrative relative to the presence of a very white girl, or a very white dove, which is perhaps the encoding of the Virgin and the Holy Spirit, or, rather, what is understood by the Quiché-Maya as the Virgin and the Holy Spirit. The Quiché-Maya seem to interpret these figures as sources of empowerment—the white girl/dove enables the Spaniards to win the battles, according to the Quiché-Maya reinscription. In their interpretation, the power of this image resides in making their own people incapable of getting off the ground—perhaps the metaphorical encoding of the lethal effect of gunpowder.

Alongside the narrative of this vision and its interpretation, we have the plotting of the indigenous leader Tecúm as a person who can fly, a winged flying body that can be compared to lightning. The symbolic warrior gear, feathers, used as a specially coded sign, are endowed with the power to intimidate. A flying Tecúm-bird and a flying dove/girl are working synergies of a budding cross-culturated mentality combining the attributes of both worlds as a sign of compromise that braids two distinct and heterogeneous discourses. The transposition of courage, valor, and defense with that of the symbolism of a bird's feathers again provides a flexible space for simultaneous interpretation, discrepancy, and compliance. The informants clearly understand that the dramatic costume and performance is part of their display of strength and determination to fight. Feathers prove economic-cum-military superiority. The figure of Tecúm is well endowed with the power of aesthetics.

Another example of contesting powers is provided by the incident of an indigenous sorcerer sacrificing a dog, which is interpreted by the Spaniards as *brujería*, an action that when performed is believed to empower the indigenous agent. What is it in this performance that elicits so much concern? On what type of dramatic surface does it act to draw out such a daunting effect on the conquering armies? That is hard to know. I can only suggest that *brujería* names that particular moment of indigenous power described in a colonial document as an exorcism—the sign of an agency shaking up the ground of deep-seated beliefs. Disregarded by most of the chroniclers, the story of this *bruja* is picked up by seventeenth-century criollo historian Fuentes y Guzmán (whose work will be studied further on), who explains the incident by juxtaposing the two examples, that of Tecúm/bird/eagle and that of the *bruja*. The *bruja* and the dog serve to explain the power of "Indians," or, even more so, the power of the indigenous tradition demonized, the persistence or survival of coded signs, or of sudden code switching, which become carriers of culture in the form of culturally accumulated and reinvested capital.

The force of the testimonial is visible in the Spanish chroniclers, in that the indigenous war gear and *brujería* fall within the category of a narratable war incident. By the time they all reproduce it, this type of incident has transcended the real and been fully endowed with the power of the symbolic and preserved in the aesthetic. In the Quiché-Maya field, history is more powerfully encoded and preserved in the aesthetic. For would it not be logical to think that at this point in history, the Quiché-Maya have in all probability already been forbidden from honoring this warrior-leader-warlock, and more so, from making much ado about his war gear? Mixing war tactics with superstition, and defense with *brujería*, is, then, the Spanish way of dislocating epistemes and rewriting histories. For the indigenous informant, to preserve Tecúm as a military hero is deemed inconvenient; hence, they can simply register this presence as just another war incident.

The main tendency of indigenous documents to obscure the referent, or our modern inability to decode their original intent, hopefully keeps the reader on guard and leads her or him in the direction of a tradition equally characterized by encores, that is, a recalcitrant repetition of the initial events and their reinterpretations. I call these incidents stocks, that is, capital investments of culture on culture, ones that assist the reification and calcification of profiles. Nevertheless, a caveat is in order. The Spaniards are establishing a dominant tradition. They had already conquered and dominated the Mexican highlands, and, having covered the terrain all the way to Yucatán and now the Guatemalan highlands, their prose is very assertive. It displays a sense of direction and aim that is lacking in the indigenous documents, which, while still being much more knowledgeable and authoritative with regard to their own cultural matters, are tentative and have already started the process of obscuring culture so that it could live clandestinely, so to speak. Assertive ignorance and intentional obscurity, then, set the foundational rhetorical moods that document the traversed physical and cultural geographies that plotted the first confrontations. This tradition is initiated by Alvarado himself, and by the Quiché-Maya and Cakchiquel vanquished lords who write the early chronicles and titles. After them, the territories are physically, politically, historically, and academically cross-fertilized, and the story is repeated by all the major Spanish chroniclers, by criollos fighting for independence, and by postcolonial historians, until it becomes the province of contemporary fiction in the works of Miguel Ángel Asturias, Luis Cardoza y Aragón, Mario Monteforte Toledo, Arturo Arias, and Mario Roberto Morales, to mention just a few.

RECONSTRUCTING THE QUICHÉ-MAYA CULTURES:
THE PRODUCTION OF BOOKS

The disconcerting topographies I have outlined constitute only a minute, yet significant, sample of one single body of literature on the pre-Hispanic societies inhabiting the Guatemalan highlands. The great divide is Alvarado's "Cartas de relación." From then on, two different historiographies emerge, one clandestine, esoteric, and scarce, the other creating a superimposed cultural tradition, which at best twists and misconstrues and at worst conceals the previous one. The first tradition embraces the indigenous documents, texts such as the *Popol Vuh*, the *Rabinal Achi*, the *Titles*; the second is made up by the bulk of Hispanic texts—histories, relations, reports, and petitions. The works of archaeologists and ethnohistorians studying the Quiché-Maya world invest in the indigenous tradition, and try to reconstruct the indigenous world. What follows is a brief review of some aspects that contribute to the unraveling of topographies through a lens interested in the indigenous.

Mayanist archaeologists and ethnohistorians plainly state that the rendering of Quiché-Maya societies by Spanish documents is sketchy. Scholars of the Quiché-Maya expect little from them. Mayanists have proven that most of the groups referred to by the colonial documents have been erratically documented, some thoroughly, some not at all.[13] For them, the Spanish interest in Quiché-Maya societies was limited to matters of government and the extraction of wealth; hence, it paid attention to political geographies and trade networks. The net result is the running of parallel histories, ones that only rarely mention even the existence of the other. It is accurate to say that the feeling one gets from the Spanish documents is that of a truncated culture, one without sense or continuity, or the sensation of a culture that was on the verge of, if not already in, crisis. By contrast, the abundance of data on domestic and quotidian matters concerning the building of the city of Antigua is highly disproportionate and truly overbearing.[14] The result is that the indigenous populations of today seem to have no relation to their forefathers.

Reading against the grain of these Hispanic texts and into the stone documents that form part of the indigenous culture, an opposite tradition is established by anthropological work, which tries to prove cultural continuities and bridge the gap between ancient and modern and postmodern indigenous societies. It is through the studies of sites, agricultural patterns, and religious rituals, as well as through the reading and deciphering of glyphs and reconstruction of monuments, that archaeologists try to reconstruct a "lost" world. One of Mayan archaeology's main purposes is to bridge the gap between indigenous peoples across time through the theories of crisis and migrations as related to food production and social exploitation.[15] Mayanists divide the area chronologically and geographically. Chronologically, there are three major periods, the preclassic, the classic, and the postclassic. Geographically, the Mayan area is divided into the highlands, and the southern central and northern lowlands. I am concerned with the Guatemalan highlands during the postclassic period. It is in the postclassic that all the controversies we have been engaging here are situated.

The story begins with the subjugation of the Quiché-Maya people. The construction of the new habits, a process that is studied under the rubric of acculturation, begins with the second generation of newly Hispanicized indigenes who are put in charge of writing their own histories using the Roman alphabet. Writing indigenous history is, from the very beginning, tied to Spanish governance, and governance to the political reorganization of the land. The most important source for the reconstruction of the past is the *Popol Vuh*, a text of lineages and migrations where the Utatlán lords try to keep their records straight. For Carmack, this book is largely the work of the descendants of the Cawek rulers of Utatlán. It was apparently written after the *Totonicapán Title*, signed by Don Cristóbal, a Nijaib chief, in 1554. By the time the *Popol Vuh* was written in 1560, the original Utatlán was a heap of ruins, and even the newly constructed Santa Cruz de Utatlán had already been depopulated.

My point of entry into this labyrinth has been the cultural geographies of the land that support the jurisdictional divisions among the ruling Quiché-Maya elite. My main question is related to boundaries. Spanish administration was assisted on these matters by local informants. Hard data was provided by the former rulers. We can read indigenous literature in terms of these services. This is a reason why one of the most productive and polemical aspects of Quiché-Maya reconstruction is located in the relationship between author and scribe, text and cultural tradition. Who wrote what, when, and under what circumstances brings us directly into the social organization of people, and hence into questions of rights, legalities, and legitimacies. That writing was an aristocratic privilege, transmitted through patrilineage, has been very well documented. Books were symbols of power, to understand them the labor of specialists. After the Conquest, all these functions were carried over into the new system, although converted to suit the needs of the new ruling elite.

The first forty years of Quiché-Maya–Spanish confrontation were difficult. Books and book writing were part of this confrontation, while also becoming the instances of an early cross-culturation. Thus, the new books are a cross between traditional elite historiography and legal documents serving the rights of the recently oppressed rulers. All the *Titles* are clear examples of it. History, as a sadly remembered and reluctantly translated apocryphal association between land, land boundaries, and social groups, constitutes the grounds for indigenous elite defense. Spaniards based their land-grant petitions on their narratives of conquest, and so did the native lords. Land (understood as former political jurisdictions) and lineage became one and the same thing. Special documents proved it. Titles and insignia were sent to the Spanish courts, but the document itself constituted proof. Literacy was selective, and only the sons of lords were targeted for instruction. Writing was, then, a passport to distinction. It indicated that the writer had been duly indoctrinated and lettered, that he had been chosen. But language instruction was also the key to acculturation and collaboration, to *ladinización*. All native documents bear witness to this, for instance, the inclusion of legitimate Spanish motifs such as the use of biblical references as a legal strategy.[16] Literacy is the marker of the move from war to administration. Soldiers are needed to create borders, but only clerks are required to maintain them.

The new question is the changes in the function of cultural artifacts. If, within Quiché-Maya historiography, books served the function of counsel and divination, constituting the political records of the hegemonic lords, and unequivocal signs of their government and governance (the *Popol Vuh*, for instance, served the functions of spiritual guidance and counseling, which was later lost), during Spanish rule they became exhibits that constituted the legal records of destitute lords, lords who, in order to partially preserve their status, wrote them to prove they were the *señores naturales*.[17] Students of indigenous documents have long speculated about these changes. From counselors, readers, and writers of the calendar, and parts of the governing body, the writers became informants, the carriers of a subjugated tradition, intellectual historians and legal advocates, ironically reclaiming their former privileged status from a position of subalternity. From governing political documents, books became the political documents of the governed and books of counseling (*consejo*), *Títulos*, while still constituting the basis for public policy.

The foundation of books and book writing, then, shifts from establishing hegemony to garnering counterhegemony. Based on their past privileges, Quiché lords claim their civic rights and thus inscribe their historiography into the history of colonialism. How these books came to represent the generic indigenous, or "the traditional" as authentically popular, is probably obtained through another conversion, which promotes the production of books as instances of the popular by equalizing all defeated, putting lords on the same level with *maceguales*—the common people. Yet elite historiography is the vehicle that represents pre-Hispanic Quiché-Maya society as a whole. The indigenous texts make clear how previous hegemonies become the seedbeds of the traditional, the privileges of lords, the generalized rights of the masses. Is tradition, then, a way of defending past elite cultures? And were the *maceguales* any better off or worse under either regime?

Such a change in function does not respond to the question of who is writing. We are told that a second generation of Hispanicized Quiché-Maya is in charge, but are the books written by one person, or are they the product of a collective? The hypothetical book of counsel, a book of *consejos* and "divination," a primary source of which, according to Carmack, the *Popol Vuh* is just a summary, paraphrase, or memory, establishes a continuum in and of Quiché-Maya culture, linking at least two generations of writers, several—or one—Hispanicized second-generation Quiché-Maya, in collaboration with several elders.

Another unanswered question in the writing of these books is that they seem to respond to one and the same questionnaire set up by the Spanish administrator. They read as if they were providing answers to the following questions: What are the lines of descent? What are the lines demarcating territorial divisions and jurisdiction? What are the main parameters of their belief systems? Thus, the new books provide information on lineage, territorialities, and cultural, ideological, and religious habits. But here is where all hell breaks loose because buried within this information is a voice speaking of a clandestine cultural authority and from a totally different frame of mind. The proverbial obscurity of the books refers to the intersections between open and covered codes, between translatable and untranslatable data, which the random inscription of phonetic alterations betrays. Spelling exposes the conditions of indigenous production and strategic acculturation. Clendinnen has observed this obscurity effect in the books of *Chilám Balám*, some of which are simply unreadable. Carmack is of the opinion that this obscurity resides in words and terms that are no longer in use, of things we do not know. In some documents—for instance, in the *Totonicapán Title*—if Spanish equivalents are not given, the story line is confusing and the information is rendered meaningless. There are cases when the name of a ruler (e.g., Quik'ab Mina Yax) has become a synecdoche; it is used today as an equivalent of the word *authority*.

From this information it follows that the uncanny intersections between war and administration are located in the meaning of the written word. Now the question is that whereas for the Maya, or Quiché-Maya, writing books in Quiché means governance, for the Spaniard it constitutes legality and information, or paganism, idolatry, and divination. The truth is that books at this time are simultaneously narratives of administration, public policy documents, records of social pacts or struggles between elites. Spaniards understood well that the indigenous books were carriers of indigenous ideologies, and worse, signs of the preservation of their cultures. As a consequence, the writing of the indigenous tradition is simultaneously suppressed and encouraged, or rather, restricted to family trees and jurisdictional data.

Documents, then, cross all kinds of narrative intersections; they act not only as testimonies, but also as reproductions of pre-Hispanic codices, as transculturated legal and religious documents, and as the preservers of traditions. In the documents' inscription of several legacies resides their perdurability and cultural power, their historicity. The texts' trajectory registers a series of cultural conversions: from public sacred books to land titles; from openly sanctioned and even requested information to the inscription of clandestine cultural data. Their basic themes, though, enable us to reconfigure Quiché political territorial jurisdictions; to reconstruct their social institutions; to gauge their usefulness to the colonial administration. Eventually, the creation of the new pueblos and the resettlement of populations splintered the culture and diluted the power of a dominance that has since become tradition and stories of origins, if not folklore. Disengaged from state and policy affairs, or related to other types of political behaviors, the books of counseling and "divination" became self-referential, representing nothing more than themselves, and, with time, their rhetoricized autotropism could be understood only as literature.

THE LAYERING OF MEANING: TRANSLATIONS AND JURISDICTIONS

Like any topography remodeled by conquest, those of the sixteenth-century Guatemalan highlands are deeply disfigured by the legacy of invasion.[18] Given the enormous layering of meaning, interpretation became the business of knowledge and of politics, and hermeneutics the first scholarly colonial task at hand. Father Antonio Remesal, a contemporary to the events, commented on the tiring, fatiguing, and unpleasant truth of this enterprise. So difficult was it to untangle the data that it was "the same to transcribe [it] from the memoirs or the books of the natives or from those that the [Spanish] authors had written."[19] The legacy of colonial documents to scholarship has been the unraveling of this incredible mess. Thus, if the historiographies of confrontation produced the confusion and those of colonialism the compilation of data to resignify it, today's agenda is to retrieve all the past cultural topographies in order to validate the indigenous knowledges that subtend the data. To that end, present-day research goes to the root of the problem and begins by examining the phonetic displacements involved in the mixture of languages in use in the process of recording the foundational documents. It looks for the different ways of spelling the same word. It is in sounds that it identifies meanings and their shifts. Translation is one of its keenest interests because in translation, in the sliding from one language system to the next, or in the extrapolation of systems, the epistemic borders of the Quiché-Maya and Spanish worldviews can be distinguished.

To the basic languages involved in the early stages of the conquest of the Guatemalan highlands, namely, Quiché and Spanish, we must add the mediation of Nahuatl introduced by the Nahuatl-Quiché-Spanish speaking Tlaxcalan warriors turned translators who accompanied Alvarado to Guatemala. Moreover, the number of languages spoken in the Guatemala highlands at the time of the Conquest is large. Among them, Mercedes de la Garza lists Huasteca, Chol, Tzeltal, Chuj, Kanjobal, Motocintl,

Mameano, Quiché, Kekchiano, and Maya. The diagram in Figure 8 maps the number of spoken languages and their regional distribution.

The indigenous colonial texts were written in many of, or a mixture of, these languages. The work of Spanish missionaries was to adapt all these languages and their sounds to Latin characters. For that, the friars had to invent "special symbols to represent non-existent consonants in Spanish such as CH', DZ', and P'. In addition to creating the system of graphic representation . . . they studied diverse elements of the language, elaborating a good number of grammars and vocabularies in the process."[20] Linda Schele reports that contrasting sounds of many Maya languages do not exist in Spanish and therefore cannot be heard, repeated, or written. And Quetzil Castañeda explains it more clearly, speaking about glottalization as the crux of different spellings:

> While the glottalization of some consonants ("p," "ch") has been represented by a duplication ("pp," "chh"), others ("tz") are changed altogether ("dz"). The hard "c" or "k" is more complicated in that if a "c" is used for the k-sound, then a "k" may be used for glottalization of that value; otherwise the contrast is made between a "K" and glottal "K'"; but often both graphic forms are used and may not actually represent the difference of the glottal in any given word depending on the text. The "c" in the Yucatec Spanish words "cenote" and "cenotillo" is soft, or an s-sound.
>
> The current tendency has been to use the apostrophe after the vowel to represent the glottal (e.g., "p'," "ch'," "k'," "tz'").[21]

Inconsistencies in the spelling of these sounds (e.g., "Cucúlcan," "Kukulcan," and "K'uk'ulkan," which is the name of "Quetzalcoatl," the English "Feathered Serpent" in Nahuatl; or *ahaw, ahau, ajau, ajaw,* or *axaw,* the word for lord) was the result, as is the multiple writing of grammars, and the sets of new orthographies added having as a consequence "as many ways of spelling Maya words as there are Maya languages and researchers."[22] Besieged by doubts produced by a multilingual universe, the diverse ways of spelling the names, and what this brings to interpretation and reconstruction, David Freidel states that "[o]ne of the most confusing problems facing students of the Maya, especially those new to the field, is how to make sense of the many different ways the same word can be

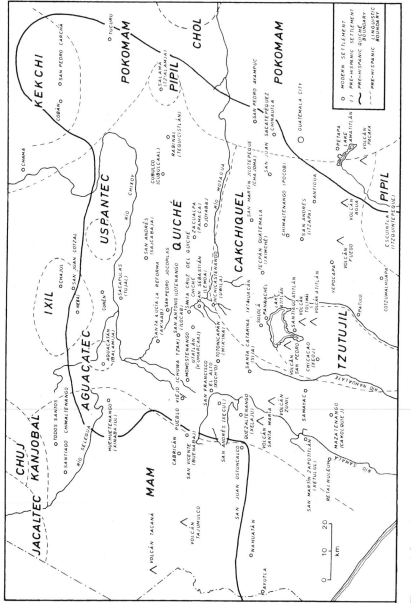

Figure 8. The political and linguistic boundaries of the pre-Hispanic Quiché state, c. 1450. From Carmack, *The Quiché Mayas of Utatlán;* copyright 1981 by the University of Oklahoma Press; reprinted by permission.

spelled."[23] One of my favorite instances is Dennis Tedlock's play with the schizophrenic trope of hearing voices. He brings up the problem of how the misperceived sounds of words change not only the range of semantic possibilities, but also the genres in which information is narrated. In other words, a sound can produce a protuberance in the whole area of the cross-culturated. "The net result," he says, "is that one word in the *Popol Vuh* text may have many different readings, all equally allowable if the reader's sole purpose were to establish a phonologically and syntactically correct text, without regard to meaning."[24] But if meaning is the issue, that is, if hearing the voices correctly and not schizophrenically is the purpose, then Tedlock gives a series of instances that change everything. For example, the word *uchacatahic* (which has one "ch" and two "c"'s) "would permit a total of thirty-two possible readings" (144), but even if they were reduced to its minimalist expression, slight variations in the word spelling would obtain the following range of meanings: "his getting disillusioned," "his getting cooked," "his getting defeated," "his getting hung up to dry." Ted-lock observes, "we know that we are about to hear a story in which a croc-odilian character will come to be stood up on all fours, disillusioned, cooked, defeated, or hung up to dry, in some combination with arriving or dying" (142).[25] The net result is the transformation of "an anthropo-morphic and primarily beneficent Quiché deity into a poisonous reptile and a Christian symbol of evil" (144).

Faced with examples like this, Mayanists either compare textual evi-dences among themselves, rely on contemporary informants, or are left with absurdities bordering on "Dadaism." In keeping with his idea of hearing the voices of an old text correctly, that is, in hearing the culture or the dead correctly, Tedlock presents a case in which he studies intonation and pace, the poetics of orality, rhetoric, verse measurements, punctua-tion, Quiché's paradigmatic verticality, and a syntagmatic horizontality, the balance between prose and verse. He deploys a stunning array of tech-nologies of all kinds to demonstrate the absences, hiatuses, misunder-standings, and general problems of cross-cultural communication.

In bringing problem and method to the attention of the reader, my point is to illustrate all the negotiations that cultural geographies presup-pose if we are to consider them from the point of view of cross-culturation, together with all the interferences, aporias, and obstacles found in cultural hybridity, among them linguistic ignorance, which is the real condition of the colonial production. Tedlock eloquently proves how this condition leads the interlocutors to ambiguities, some of which undergird the demonization of indigenous peoples. However, there is a point at which the method of inquiry becomes so engrossing that we can lose sight of what is being unraveled when attention is given only to the technologies of information retrieval. When this occurs, we have come fully into the modern era.

We can move now to the consideration of jurisdictions. Concerning indigenous jurisdictions, there is the fact not only of the Christianization and Hispanicization of names (how Utatlán becomes Santa Cruz de Utatlán and later Santa Cruz del Quiché, Iximché becomes Santiago, Sapotitlán becomes San Antonio), but also that Spaniards do not understand the language or the indigenous jurisdictional layout. Thus, a phonetic misunderstanding found in the multiple spellings of the same word (e.g., Guatemala is spelled as Juitemal, Quauhtlemallan, Goathemala, Quanhtelalia) becomes a hermeneutical disorientation not only about the geographical whereabouts of these sites and the size of the land, but also about the perimeter of the jurisdiction and the hegemonies ruling it. In this regard, not only phonetic alteration but also the crisscrossing of nomenclatures constitutes a big stumbling block in interpretations. Father Francisco Ximénez, a witness to and participant in the events, offers a good example of this process. Trying to grasp the essence of the social organization, in one paragraph he speaks about kingdom as synonymous with region, province, and royal court—a place that is high in the mountain: "Among the very extensive kingdoms in New Spain, there was that of Guatemala. This region has another title among them, and is called Utatlán, which is in the same province of Guatemala, high in the mountains. . . . Utatlán is called Santa Cruz del Quiché, which is the royal court of this kingdom; today it is called Guatemala, since this city is the seat of the kingdom, and it is called Quiché, which means many trees or mountains."[26] Figure 9 offers the crisscrossing of Quiché-Maya and Spanish jurisdictions. Notice that what used to be *calpules* (indigenous divisions of land) are now haciendas, and what was governed by Quiché-Maya lords is now the province of missionaries and their religious orders.

In an effort to elucidate part of this confusion, in his annotations to the *Popol Vuh*, twentieth-century anthropologist Adrián Recinos comes back to the descriptive categories and explains that the word *Quiché* (*varal*

Quiché ubi) was the name of the region; that cities were called *Quiché tinamit*; and people or nations, *r'amag Quiché vinac.* In this manner, he straightens out the Spanish juxtaposition of "place," "city," "region," and "nation," which is incommensurable with the indigenous categories.[27]

Although considerable research has been invested in reconstructing the original sites, it has opened a Pandora's box. It has taken considerable effort on the part of archaeologists, ethnohistorians, and anthropologists to produce working hypotheses that attempt to understand the nature of the overlapping jurisdictions. In their works, they rename and remap the past. Concepts such as pueblos, cities, and people are used to resignify milpas, *calpules*, and ceremonial centers, thereby making it unclear whether the Spaniards are traveling through actual urban centers or just passing through territories where the "Indians," who call themselves by their different names, exerted their particular hegemonies. To call a place a province might imply government, hegemony, or control of territory.

Modern anthropology has tried to clean up the clutter. In her study of Chichicastenango, Ruth Bunzel tells how the basic contemporary social structure that divides town, as the center of civic and economic life, and *cantón*, is not very different from the ancient structures. For her, Utatlán "was unquestionably a great center of population."[28] Her description of the topographical aspects of the terrain follows the tradition. Utatlán was "surrounded on all sides by deep *barrancos*," and it contained "large public buildings and spacious courtyards" (6). But it was not a modern city where large numbers of people lived. People, it is assumed, lived in dispersed farms, in milpas, as they live today. In all appearance, cities like Utatlán were places assigned to public activities and functions such as those of governing. They "comprised the court, the temple, and the marketplace, the setting for public activities" (ibid.).

The social organization of the land reveals a dispersion of farms, which draws the figure of an immense patched quilt, an image formed by the scattering of fields throughout the land. Ximénez explains this dispersion in the function of the ruling elites and their respective hegemonic areas of control:

> they say that first there were the three lords, the great ones of the kingdom, who were Conache, Beleheb-queh, and Calel-ahn, and, growing much in number, it was when they divided the kingdom into twenty-four great ones;

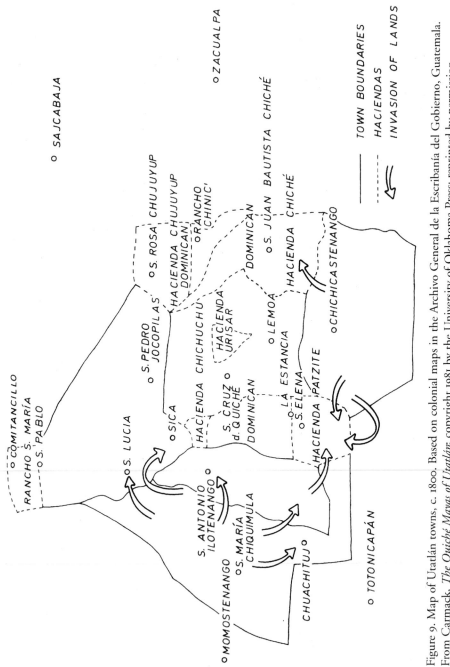

Figure 9. Map of Utatlán towns, c. 1800. Based on colonial maps in the Archivo General de la Escribanía del Gobierno, Guatemala. From Carmack, *The Quiché Mayas of Utatlán*, copyright 1981 by the University of Oklahoma Press; reprinted by permission.

which is what they mean by twenty-four great houses; because in the palaces and shrines of the idol, each one of these lords had their houses where they lived, when they gathered together for their festivities; that the rest of the time they were in their houses that each one had in their family lots, which was the way in which the Indians had to live in their lands and milpas, which only in very rare parts had a formal population as a town, but in community where they found good land opportunities; that it was regularly in the *bajíos* and *quebradas*, where lived one family or *chinamital*, not all together, but each one in its milpa. And these had a head of all that family, as they have it today, and these were subject to the lords or caciques, which were the great ones, and that is why this time of populations was called Amac, which means like a spider's leg, or that which extended as does a spider leg. (163)

Inga Clendinnen reinforces the description of the milpa as a social formation: "Maya towns strike strangers as very spread out . . . each house was surrounded by a substantial house-yard, big enough to allow for the raising of animals, vegetables, and fruit trees, and often enough a handy supply of maize."[29] Clendinnen believes that it "is possible to glimpse the Maya conceptualization of the generic features of their landscape through which they were able to recreate their traditional social worlds within the physically restructured villages imposed on them by the friars."[30] The Maya are horticulturists, producing cornfields anywhere possible, even on the steep sides of barrancos, where land is scarce. Laborers come from the ranks of the disinherited—those without land or a trade.

Jurisdictions and their boundaries are therefore an argument that runs through the bibliographies of confrontation in the Guatemalan highlands. It is only in the eighteenth century, when the political division of the land is already Spanish, that we know we have come to a settlement of the jurisdictional boundaries. In the topographies drawn by Pedro Cortés y Larraz, there are sixty-six detailed maps of his route and an ordering system relating geographies, demographies, and government.[31] Cortés y Larraz is a visiting archbishop with a doctorate in theology, who took the trouble of visiting the 113 curates, from Chiapas to the Gulf of Fonseca, traveling on mule back for two years. He is interested in finding out the languages spoken, how spiritual duties are fulfilled, if rents are paid, what kinds of schools and books are in use, what sort of scandals and abuses, punishments, and superstitions and idolatries occur. He finds that the *reinos* are "in a deplorable state, drowned in all kinds of vices, sunk in all kinds of iniquity and placed in so much disorder. . . . Lying is so dominant that one can see the truth neither in conversations nor in reports, not even in trials" (11–12).

Cortés y Larraz's opinions are based on many sources: a poll (the prelates' answers to a questionnaire Cortés y Larraz sent them ahead of his visit); his conversations with the prelates; and the memoirs submitted by the indigenous people. The author insists that his work is rushed, unfinished, rough, and at times erroneous, but it is difficult to know if this is not just a protective rhetorical strategy. The report, however, produces the effect of the real, and he seems to be telling the truth, because his only stated interest is to know and to inform. Truth is to be found in geography, because here geography tells about the distribution of people and their social, cultural, and productive living conditions. His intention is good government: "To come to know that which will lead to the spiritual and temporal well-being of the parishes" (15). A parish is a basic unit of government, the religious equivalent of a district or municipality, constituting the basis for census and population control. Hence the parameters are punctual assistance to doctrine, punishments, distances between towns, distance between town and the curate, scandals and abuses, schools for children, families, haciendas, idolatries and superstitions, spoken languages, sugar mills, the number of leagues the parochial district comprises, books, *pajuides* [hamlets], persons, precepts for confession and communion, towns annexed to the curates, remedies applied, and rents.

It is valuable to know that in those years the diocese is divided into 10 provinces as follows: (1) the city of Goathemala Valley: 2 large mayorships: Chimaltenango (11 curates) and Amatitanes (10 curates); (2) Sonsonate: a mayor and 9 curates; (3) San Salvador: 5 mayorships (that of San Salvador, 9 curates), the rest consisting of 4, 6, 5, and 2 curates, respectively; (4) Chiquimula: a mayor, 10 curates; (5) Guasacapán: a mayor, 11 curates; (6) San Antonio Suchitepeques: a mayor, 7 curates; (7) Tzololá: a mayor, 8 curates; (8) Totonicapá: a mayor, 11 curates; (9) Quetzaltenango: a mayor, 4 curates; (10) Verapaz: a mayor, 4 curates.

Cortés y Larraz takes the trouble to outline geographies: towns, mountains and rivers, trails, and distances: "with distances . . . there can be some and even many errors; because in this kingdom leagues have not been measured, nor does anyone know how many are enumerated . . . each one would count the leagues according to the rush with which they walked them" (13). One important cluster of the data gathered refers to groupings of peoples, which underscores the coincidence between productive units and towns. For instance, estates (*haciendas*), herds or huts (*hatos*), sugar mills (*trapiches*), salt-producing areas, sown fields (*sementeras, sitios*), farms (*estancias, rancherías*), and ranches (or *pajuides*) are commensurate with houses, valleys, hills, cities, hamlets, towns. A second type of valuable information he provides is the distance between each population and/or productive unit. On average, they are located between three and thirteen leagues from each other. The types of roads communicating the towns are also signaled: "good roads, sharp climbs," "labyrinths of mountains and hills," "very long plains from east to west," "very rough mountains" (59).

In Cortés y Larraz's document, we learn the numbers of families, the type of people inhabiting each site, the language they speak, the taxes collected, and the problems they face. We know that most people do not speak Spanish, while others are bilingual; that there are some people whom nobody is in charge of, "families and people from the ranch hands' quarters . . . vagrants . . . who are now here and then go someplace else and of whom nobody takes notice" (ibid.). The demographic maps display abundant vagrancy, a rejection of government, internal migration, evasion of regulations, becoming maroons. People walk around naked and most claim to be very poor. The relaxation of customs and habits is the result of the indifference of the prelates, who are negligent and "of little talent" (ibid.). Cortés y Larraz also reports what is produced: salt, cattle, corn, beans, and sugarcane. Geographers and naturalists will incorporate all these themes in the nineteenth century in recognition of the fact that they are problems yet to be solved.

FROM THE NARRATIVES OF WAR TO THE NARRATIVES OF AGRICULTURE

The founding text that establishes the shift from the narratives of war to those of agriculture is Francisco Antonio Fuentes de y Guzmán's *Recordación Florida*. Fuentes y Guzmán (1643–1700) was born in Antigua, Guatemala, of Spanish descent. He was the great-grandson of Bernal Díaz del Castillo and the first criollo historian to write about Guatemala as his patrimony and fatherland. As a criollo, he was considered a man of lineage and at the age of eighteen he was already a *regidor* (alderman). During his lifetime he held the posts of mayor of Totonicapán, Santiago de Guatemala, and Sonsonate. Fuentes y Guzmán was a poet and a historian, a soldier and a politician. He wrote *La cinosura política o ceremonial de Guatemala*, and *El norte político*; both pieces were lost. The latter was on administration and judiciary procedures that gathered the experience of his long years of service.

Fuentes y Guzmán's most important work is *La Recordación Florida, discurso historial y demostración natural, material, militar y política del Reino de Guatemala*, known simply as *Recordación Florida*.[32] *Recordación Florida* was first published in Madrid in 1882, 187 years after he finished it. He had solicited permission from the king to write an official history of Guatemala and to be appointment official chronicler of the kingdom. We are told that the manuscript was lost in the Archives of the Council of the Indies and that in spite of the fact that Fuentes y Guzmán requested it, he never got it back. Besides the fact that a criollo had the pretension of being appointed official historian of the Kingdom of Guatemala, what is of interest today is that Fuentes y Guzmán had all the information he needed at his fingertips. He had access to the official archives containing all the histories of his predecessors, many of whom had been living witnesses to the Conquest, and he could bring together the secular history written by Bernal Díaz and the sacred history of Las Casas and Remesal, as he in fact did. In addition, the fact that he had lived for some time in the Totonicapán region gave him access to the indigenous knowledge of the aborigines, whom he must have interrogated and from whom he drew out many of their secrets. *Recordación Florida* covers the history of the Kingdom of Guatemala from the Conquest to the end of the seventeenth century and is, to borrow Antony Higgins's phrase, the founder of the criollo archive.

Recordación Florida is an encyclopedia of things Guatemalan. It is a mixture of natural geography (orography and topography, containing one of the most complete descriptions of the extension of valleys, mountains, jungles, their products and climate, flora and fauna), ethnohistory (containing detailed aspects of the population, their rites, costumes, indigenous traditions, arts and crafts, festivities), political and military history (detailing uprisings and the subjugation of people), art history (with the description of buildings and their construction), and a dictionary containing the data about governors, captains, bishops and archbishops, principal *señores*, dates of services, biographical data of the principals—a kind of dictionary of products, people, and knowledge. Fuentes y Guzmán's work is encyclopedic in nature, a reason for which it was criticized by all subsequent positivist writers, who considered it as imperfect and inaccurate as it was excessive in the use of adjectives and very partial to the Spaniards. The book was published for the first time in Guatemala in 1932 (first volume) and 1933 (second volume).[33] In this section I analyze the work of Fuentes y Guzmán in reference to the criollo constitution of his fatherland.

Writing 150 years after Alvarado's events, and only a century before Pedro Cortés y Larraz, Antonio Fuentes y Guzmán observes the same topographies from the perspective of a sugar planter interested in agriculture and natural wealth. By this time, all territorial disputes seem to have been settled, all phonetic battles surmounted. The writing subject is now a landholder, lord and ruler of a new colonial world order that he is to document and legalize. In full possession of the land, the criollo author prides himself in being knowledgeable about the territorial and jurisdictional divisions, the natural conditions of the soil, and the nature of the roads. His prose is idyllic, albeit still weary of war, uprisings, and disobedience. Looked at from our moment in time, *Recordación Florida* is the text of the reconversion of the topographical Quiché-Maya patrimony into the criollo's fatherland, that is, it is a text that speaks to the subject of how the criollo constituted a place for himself, his citizenship, his patria. In anticipation of political independence, agricultural narratives refurbish the relationship between "Indians" and criollos, their entitlements and different political profiles.

Fuentes y Guzmán's impassioned observations offer an outline of the economic conditions of his properties. Although he is a military man—the reader is constantly made aware that a captain is narrating—his eye is that of a landowner calculating the fat of the land and its political and cultural topographies. In pondering the realm of nature—valleys, rivers, and mountains—enthusiasm impels him. Adjectives are precisely located, their range and variety forming a parataxis that heightens the property value of nature, the "Indian" heroic past, and the justification of conquest. Hyperbolic rhetoric serves equally to magnify landscapes and to devalue

Amerindian cultures. The division between "yours" and "mine," "mine" and "not mine," "mine" and "not yet mine" is neatly traced. The narrative ambition here is hampered by a dilemma located between productive land and scarcity of people, between fecundity and barrenness, which in turn joins people, *gentío* (multitude), villages, culture, and colonialism with scattered territorialities, which he calls vicinities, communities (*vecindad, vecinos*), namely, the localization of *gentíos* within their past cultural milieus—milpas.

The result is a fracture in which two types of tracking of agriculture, and of the lives of laborers, are located adjacently. This is what Severo Martínez Pelaez, rewriting the works of Fuentes y Guzmán three centuries later, calls "la patria del criollo" (the criollo's homeland), a concept counteropposed to Amerindian lands—the administrative strategies regarding Amerindians expressed in terms of the size, type, and location of lands assigned: *ejidos*, grasslands, mountains, and pastures and the seeding and planting of communal lands and private lands.[34] Civic or territorial divisions of land mark the boundaries of human and civic rights, the distinction between hegemony and domination, agricultural and labor systems. What is really at issue in Fuentes y Guzmán's florid prose is the transition between the criollo's fatherland and the unfathered land of the indigenous lands. Measurements and writing are the technology for dispossessing some and repossessing others. Mathematics and grammar hold sovereignty over all types of localizations, territory assigned, community-held farmland (*ejidos*), pasture, mountains, communal and private lands.

Fuentes y Guzmán is a man who seems to be writing elegies, constantly interested in adding pertinent information on the subject of the nature of the terrain. The criollos' interest in agriculture makes them perceive the topographies as sites of cultivation, very much in the same fashion Englishmen would assess plains in the Caribbean at the end of the slave era. In fact, one point that carries over from Fuentes y Guzmán to Richard Madden, and from him to Wilson Harris, is measurement and gauging. Land has become private property and profitable business. But what is new is that unlike the English chargé d'affaires, Fuentes y Guzmán is interested in engaging and romanticizing his past. Property is the product of a historical genealogy, and Fuentes y Guzmán acknowledges this debt to his forefathers by restaging and aggrandizing the struggle on both sides, claiming heroism for both parties, "Indians" and Spaniards, while making

it evident that what he is consecrating is the terrain itself, the Kingdom of
Guatemala, his private property and land-tenure rights. The rhetoric and
style of Romanticism serving the politics of a preindependent cause are in
full swing.

A new factor that Fuentes y Guzmán adds to the cross between agriculture and history in his prose, and one that connotes an important
transition, is that in reenacting the wars of conquest, the criollos take
the position of Spaniards, referring to them as "ours," or our side. However, a crack is already discernible. He already writes that some Spaniards
refer to him as a "foreigner." An inversion highlights the semantics of
a sign that is temporarily defined by the Spaniards versus the criollos, and
then reversed. In this disjunction between noun and pronoun, Fuentes y
Guzmán's writings denote an early spirit of disengagement, which will
fully come out in the open in the prose of independentist Domingo Juarros, whose work will be examined subsequently. In the struggle between
criollos and *peninsulares* (Spaniards born in Spain), "Indians" have been
ruled out of the game, and their status as the principal opposing force has
been superseded, radically altering the nature of the cultural contention.

However, there are other scores to be settled, and one of them is the
frustration Fuentes y Guzmán feels with some criollos for their nearsight-
edness, lack of initiative, patriotic fervor, passion, enthusiasm, and spirit
of enterprise. He does not much relish arguing this point, but there are
already a number of *aindiados*, Spaniards who have adopted Amerindian
culture and who live in their houses and "*milperías* . . . and there they are
without justice. . . . not only do they not have mayors . . . [to] restrain
their passions . . ." Fuentes y Guzmán leaves the sentence incomplete for
"to have to write what in this place and in others is executed, the discourse
would be prolific, taking up the majority of this work" (21–22). We have
a glimpse of the politics of *mestizaje* that divide Spanish born in Spain
(*peninsulares*) and Spanish born in the colonies (criollos), Spanish *aindiados*, and *"Indios" latinizados* (Ladinos).

Overall, the structural matrix of Fuentes y Guzmán's work is geographic—
valleys, towns, rivers, mountains, forests. Geography relates to the property of land and land-tenure systems. Ethnography refers to labor, products,
population, hacienda, milpa—in other words, it is economic ethnography. Vast country, fecund, abundant, and excellent pastures, thick and rich
forests, precious woods, famous valleys, fertile wheat fields and cornfields—

abundance is immediately coupled to battles, defense, embattlements, conquest, colonization, colonialism. Long-standing scores had not been settled between the contenders, and hence a return to the original sites of conquest and a rerun of its topics. Once more we come back to the geographies of the Guatemalan highlands, to the valleys of Canales, las Vacas, Panchoy, Mixco, Jilotepeques, Chimaltenango, Alotenango, Sacattepeques, plus the mountains of Petapa, and San Diego, the river of la Chorrera, and Pancacoya, and the city of Guatemala, the village of Tecpángoathemala. Old positions are rehashed, and the decisive moments of conquests, where Spanish and Indian places were won and lost, are reenacted.

The problem is that an ideal landscape, while being so strenuous, so highly exalted, is described with a second or a simultaneous agenda in mind, namely, the intent to demean contemporary Amerindians. The adjectives used to depict Amerindians reveal a double bind. They are of two varieties. The first reads as follows: superstitious, ignorant, unhappy, dull-witted, brutish and indomitable, heretical, or even *brujos*; the second as brave, cunning, embattled, calculating, of good judgment, and nobly treacherous. As will be the case of the description of rebels in Matthew Gregory Lewis's prose at the time of the abolition of slavery, so is it now in the case of the criollo prose. Here, dissimulation and dishonesty are as central to the Amerindian character assassination as they will be later on for the "negro character" in the Caribbean. The ambivalence of the dominant subject in contemplating the dominated is a point that carries over from one imperial legacy to the next. The old notion of peace and of war (which will be examined in the next chapter) used in reference to Amerindians is now revealed in the discrepancy between the "Indian" as warrior, the "Indian" as a laborer—*Indios laborios*—and the "Indians" as ungovernable subjects, between the "Indian" as friend and the "Indian" as enemy, between old and new "Indians." "Indian" warriors are, then, preeminent, and perennially tied to the property of land. Hence, Fuentes y Guzmán's definition, and the description of battles, is still prescriptive. The difference between good versus bad or old versus new "Indians" can be obtained by examining handicrafts, rituals, and festivities—such as *El Palo*, and *El Volador*. The glossaries of terms that Fuentes y Guzmán adds at the end of his two volumes, listing kings, lords, governors, captains, geographical points of interest, biographical data and vocabulary further clear up the matter.

In these divisions and distinctions between types of "Indians," one thing is clear: there is no trust. Disbelief in Fuentes y Guzmán (as with doubt in Lewis) mars the relationship on both sides and prompts a theory of knowledge irremediably based on testimonials and depositions. Hearing and seeing are no longer the providers of clean criteria and must always be passed through the Cartesian sieve. Criollos are always careful to note who speaks, what or how the seeing eye sees, what the questioning mouth asks. All the senses become disjointed, and sense perception and empirical evidence are no longer the sole criteria of the true. In Fuentes y Guzmán, we access the same questions besieging students of testimonial literature today, namely, the relationship between empirical vision, reliability on oral informants, learned epistemologies, Western frames.[35] Nonetheless, the distinction between old and new "Indians" is rendered profitable in that it gives access to cross-examination and mutual rebuttal among the two, or more, narrative subjects/voices. *Patriae/tierras* relate to habits and cultures, and also delimit the terrain of caution.

Being close to the events of the conquests, when not talking directly to a friend or a relative of the actors directly invested in the conquest, Fuentes y Guzmán is able to trace his own genealogy of knowledge. He obtains reliable information through his access to *cabildo* archives and the "papers of his elders" (73). As a *corregidor* (major), and war captain of the Totonicapán and Gueguetenango districts (75), he is able to peruse the documents, having the frozen world of archives directly at his fingertips. He writes: "And although my meticulous care has been able to find out . . . other curious particularities . . . I have not acquired nor obtained them because they all recur to sterility and arid territory; being true that it is not due to my lack of diligence. . . . But further on I hope God will open the roads so that the secrets of some archives that today deny my prayers will be open and forthright" (55). There is in Fuentes y Guzmán still the need to justify and legalize the violation of and violence inflicted upon Amerindians, and he trusts that he will find in his elders, such as his uncle, Pater Fray Jacinto del Castillo, a provincial of the region, and in "his Castillo" (Bernal Díaz), answers to his questions. But what are his real questions? And do they concern criollos and "Indians," or rather criollos and *peninsulares*? His real questions perhaps refer to what side the Amerindians might take in the war of independence. Will they fight on the side of the criollos or on the side of the *peninsulares*?

Fuentes y Guzmán's research method to solve his problems is that of an *oidor*, a hearer, and that of a surveyor, a seer. He hears/sees the landscape—culture and nature are paired together and no disengagement between the two is rendered negotiable. Both methods are empirical. As a caballero-captain, he enjoys mobility, and can directly inspect the fields—cultivating grounds and battlefields. However, as an *oidor* he confronts the same problems baffling earlier *oidores*. Fuentes y Guzmán, like Lewis in the Caribbean centuries later, cannot discern how much of the telling is mere mimicry, playacting, performance. What is hidden can be physical, like Mixco's cave; epistemic, like what Amerindians don't tell; historical, like what has not been, or has been erroneously recorded. An infinite process of interpretation ensues, which often regresses to the very naming of sites, people, and habits with which this chapter began.

This is the reason the topographies of the highlands are often revisited. The problem is that what to Amerindians is customs, culture, and preservation, to *peninsulares* and criollos is superstition, stupidity, and obstinate resistance—the ungovernable. In order to distinguish what is accurate from what is not, Fuentes y Guzmán conceives the ideal informant: educated, religious, experienced "in the subject I undertake, firmly and legally instructed by religious people, learned and experienced, or by Christian caballeros of certified credibility and certain about those things" (57). He also tries using his knowledge of Amerindian languages and grammar to trace the etymological roots of words, sometimes to no avail. Although he can trace some etymologies and genealogies with a certain degree of accuracy, he is forever suspicious of "Indians" who, in his opinion, do not entirely tell everything, who never completely surrender. This type of distrust will echo in R. R. Madden's feelings about slaves when he says that "unless a negro has an interest in telling the truth, he always lies" (Madden, *A Twelve Month's Residence*, 129). The result is to write deep distrust into Fuentes y Guzmán's narrative plot and to produce segregation.

But where does doubt come from? I suggest that it comes from the fact that Amerindians' cultures are still not subdued. Fuentes y Guzmán feels that his cities are besieged, that Spaniards live in perpetual misgivings. Fear fattens the notion of the Amerindian as warrior, rebel, resister. On the flip side of dumbness lies cunning. The cross-fertilization between cultural and war topographies forms a continuum. To cast the indigenous groups in the mold of excellency or the moronic simply underwrites the moments and types of resistance. What is observed as a war stratagem carries into the second moment of resistance: secrecy, guarded counsel, mystery, reunions—the occult. Here is one example of the battle of Sacattepeques, which Fuentes y Guzmán describes lavishly:

> All among them was meetings, discussions, council, and intrigue, and all doubts on the part of our men, until, arriving at the end of the third day, their secretive and repeated conventicle burst forth in anger . . . with raucous shouting, they arrived to our first group of guards . . . fighting like beasts, they had taken the tremor to signify the anger of their god Camanelón . . . appearing very angry and sad because the Sacattepeques faithful had distrusted his power and rendered all his lands to those of Castile, who came to subdue their freedom. (81)

In sum, it is clear that by the time *Recordación Florida* is written, the cultural struggle has not been settled, and everything concerning populations and the interrelation between the contending groups is viewed as issues affecting the relationship between agriculture and labor. Cultural warfare hampers the organization of labor and curtails production.[36]

A note on Antony Higgins's outstanding book *Constructing the Criollo Archive: Subjects of Knowledge in the Bibliotheca Mexicana and the Rusticatio Mexicana* is in order to close this section. In his work on the criollo archive, Higgins touches some issues that are pertinent to my work. Particularly relevant is his reconstruction of the social and political atmosphere surrounding the production of Rafael Landívar's *Rusticatio Mexicana*, as well as his discussion on the sublime that serves Higgins as the formal ground to construct his argument on the relationship between modernity and the criollo self.

Higgins argues that at the time Landívar writes his poem, the dominant episteme of scholasticism is giving way to a more practical mode of thought. In Higgins's view, Landívar represents "the most outstanding example of the fusion of these different forms of practical and theoretical knowledge" (112), which aims at the production of knowledge "within the framework of the emerging scientific disciplines, especially natural history and economy" (113). Thus *Rusticatio Mexicana* "offers a totalizing picture of the geography, nature, and agricultural and industrial production of the viceroyalty in the second half of the eighteenth century" (ibid.). The shifts

and mutations from one dominant to an emergent episteme is what constitute the clearest sign of the construction of a criollo archive, one that
points to a rearticulation of the relationship between knowledge and the
exploitation of the materialities of the land, whose investigation, observation, and linguistic representation is thereby refurbished.

In contrast to Higgins's, my argument is that the criollo archive truly
begins with the work of Fuentes y Guzmán, about whom the same observations Higgins claims for Landívar could be applied. The difference is
that in Landívar the tensions have been sharpened and are, so to speak,
ready to snap, as they were in Juarros. This does not mean that I am
making unequals equal. I am aware of the changes between early and late
forms of colonialism. My sole point is that it is on the tenure and productivity of the land as the criollo fatherland and *patria* that the criollo
archive is, from the very outset, predicated. Having said that, the point of
convergence between Higgins's study of Landívar and my study of Fuentes
y Guzmán and Juarros refers to the utilitarian side of arts and letters that
Higgins's discussion on the sublime enables. The point of divergence is
that my interest does not lie in a discussion of aesthetics per se. It lies
rather in the examination of how cultural narratives—not yet arts and letters but a mixture of history, ethnology, and natural history—are the
founding works that constitute the genealogy of the narratives of research
and development; how these narratives plot the social struggles over land-
tenure systems and pit the different ethnic groups and epistemes against
each other, turning the representation of society into a representation of
nature. In this respect, Higgins's take on aesthetics is very pertinent. He
argues that in his work, Landívar blends "the concern to produce an aesthetic that might transcend the world of economic utilitarianism with
modes of knowledge that developed over the course of two centuries during which the Jesuits had exploited agricultural and mineral resources in
Mexico according to principles of efficiency" (118).

Thus viewed, the criollo is the product of a double articulation: on the
one hand, the subject of aesthetics; on the other, the producer of sys-
tematic and practical knowledge. And here is where the discussion on aesthetics paradoxically provides the ground for a detailed empirical depiction
of the key areas of economic production, the range and breadth of geographical scenarios that underscore not only the centrality that agriculture

plays in the criollo's conception of identity and his anxiety for emphasizing the documentary character of his writing, but his capacity for scientific knowledge. What is for purchase is that empirical-cum-scientific knowledge that the criollo possesses about his lands and his lands' productivity. This is in essence the nature of the criollo sublime. Higgins's argument is that the vastness of this empirical knowledge could not be contained within the strict parameters of neoclassicism because it transgressed the norms that neoclassicism had set up for the representation of beauty. It is thus that the argument of aesthetics dovetails the argument on productivity and where art and letters come to play a role in the discussion of politics. In the same manner, a discussion of the picturesque enables the representation of the transition between plantation and subsistence economies in the Caribbean islands and in the highlands of Guatemala; the sublime is the register that opens the door to the representation of the unrepresentable that has to be theorized through its medium. The sublime, Higgins argues, "served to accommodate the very tendencies towards excess and disruption that did not fit comfortably into that aesthetic system [neoclassicism] with its emphasis on a neat, harmonious sense of beauty and order" (124). Hence the move to accommodate the unbridled, immeasurable forces of nature alongside the creative power of genius was the perfect conjunction for the formation of a criollo self and his fatherland. Hence, the difference between Fuentes y Guzmán and Landívar is the difference between an early and a full-blown consciousness; the similarity is the use of the land and its riches to claim legitimate possession and ownership. In both cases, the knowledge of agricultural data and the topographies of productivity are what serve as the basis for self-formation.

GENEALOGY OF TOWNS AND ARCHAEOLOGY OF URBANISM: NAMING THE CITIES, CHOOSING THE SITE

Fray Domingo Juarros (1752–1820), whose work I analyze in this section, was born in Antigua, Guatemala. He is one of the best-known Guatemalan historians and his work enjoyed great reputation. His *Compendio de la Historia de la ciudad de Guatemala* (written as three notebooks) was published in 1808, 1809, and 1810, and the second volume, titled *Cronicón del Reino de Guatemala,* was published in 1818. A second printing came out in 1857. The English version translated by John Baily is from 1823.[37]

Like Fuentes y Guzmán's, Juarros's text is encyclopedic in nature and follows the same format as that of his predecessor. The first volume is a geographical description of the Kingdom of Guatemala with an index of the principals of the city of Guatemala; the second volume is divided into four parts, dealing with the general history of the kingdom, the provinces, the conquest of Salamanca, and an appendix referring to the Metropolitan Church of Guatemala. It has been said that Juarros's work is simply an edited version of Fuentes y Guzmán's text, but this assertion can simply mean that he made use of the bibliographical archive at his disposal. What is most interesting is the purpose the text serves for English investments. In the Preface to the English edition, translator John Baily notes that Spanish America soon will be open to British capital and industry, that the continent will prove a propitious terrain for the various branches of English manufacture and commerce, and that Juarros's book gives English capital the opportunity to know portions of Guatemala. Baily notes that Juarros has access to good government records as well as those gathered in convents and that he has himself visited the country directly; that is, he can be trusted because he possesses firsthand genealogical archival, as well as direct empirical, information, and "his materials have been drawn from sources that stamp upon them the character of authenticity" (vi).[38] In this section I read Juarros's text to understand his layout of the land and how he proposes to portray the settlement of scores between the new contenders.

My claim is that Don Domingo Juarros's text is a tale of two cities, Utatlán and Santiago de Guatemala. Juarros undertakes the reconstruction of the topographies of the highlands once the scores between the two contending ethnicities, Spaniards and Quiché-Maya Amerindians, have been settled and new social conflicts, mainly between criollos and peninsular Spanish, have emerged. The first title of the text, "Succinct Notices of the Natural and Political History of the Principal Places," clearly proves his intentions and concerns. His opening statement reads as follows:

> A discovery of so much importance required that those who had made it,
> should immediately communicate their good fortune to all the world with

the most scrupulous exactness; but although three centuries have elapsed, we see . . . that provinces, and even whole kingdoms, on this spacious continent, are at this time as little known to the world in general, as if they had but just been discovered. . . . where towns are mentioned, it is scarcely more than to record their names: the few that are described in any detail, are represented under so many circumstances of error and falsehood, as to remain as much unknown . . . as they ever were. (5)

Juarros then makes it his task to fill the gap, composing a text in which geography is closely intertwined with agriculture. His road map, like R. R. Madden's in the West Indies, is made up of nouns such as *yields, species, grains, production, commerce, woods, medicinal plants, animals, mines, watered terrains,* and *streams.* These nouns provide an inventory of products, an economic fact sheet reporting yields and net worth. Geographically, he begins by dividing areas by districts (such as Petén), and provinces (such as Chiquimula)—north and southwest—but often the names of provinces and districts overlap, and in this respect his text, rather than clarifying the issue, further obscures it. A drawing would have greatly helped to comprehend the locations, which, simply written down, do not come across as clear as he believes.

After dividing the geographies into districts and provinces, Juarros mentions five middle provinces—Totonicapán, San Miguel Totonicapán (or Gueguetenango)—to the northeast—Santa María Nebah, Malacatán, and Jalatenango. Then he adds other kinds of jurisdictional categories that disturb his original order; and to complicate the issue further, he provides the reader with extra information, such as the languages spoken by the natives, types of militia used to control them, numbers and type of government, and which religious orders—Franciscans, Dominicans, Mercedarians— were assigned to each region. Soon to become past and present, sixteenth- and nineteenth-century information is cross-referenced and merged. The reader is left to decide whether this is a syntactical or a strategic tangle.

After layering the information one layer on top of the other and trying to give precise data about these provinces, Juarros moves on to describe the provinces of Quezaltenango, Sololá (or Atitán), Chimaltenango, and Sacatepeques, until reaching "The Topographical Description of the City of Old Guatemala" (104). The foundation of the new center of power, the Spanish city of Old Guatemala, is going to supplant the indigenous city of Utatlán and become the new hegemonic center. The Spanish city is to be a migrant city for many years and to have many different names. The foundation of the city is an obsession throughout Juarros's text, and this obsession is rendered evident in his disorderly prose. There is no scholarly discipline in his work, and his text is in dire need of good editing. He does not conclude one theme before starting another; on the contrary, all kinds of interests, histories, and stories intersect his commercial prose. In my view, Juarros's prose style underscores self-complacent oligarchic conversational styles, which nineteenth-century geographers such as E. G. Squier, are going to find unacceptable.[39]

Juarros's themes highlight the coexistence of two parallel interests. One is to contribute to the criollo emancipation cause; the other is to attract capital. His interest in criollos' emancipation becomes evident in his revision of past Amerindian histories, historicities, and heroism. Criollos establish their hegemony over the land on the basis that they are the legitimate heirs of those who defeated the *señores naturales* or legitimate owners of the land. The entwining of civic and military accounts betrays this purpose. His interest in attracting capital becomes evident in a meticulous revision of what belongs to whom. The redrawing of the city sites constitutes a genealogy demarcating the land whose products are to be exploited and traded.

To properly lay out who owns what, this historian retraces Alvarado's steps and recounts the foundation of cities following the chronicles of Remesal and Vásquez. His strategy is to foreground the struggle for power and highlight the difficulties of settling down safely after pacifying the area. In this representation, the Quiché-Maya resistance plays an important role. Embattled and heroic "Indians" not only obtain the distinction between the "old" and the "new" "Indian," but also underscore the valor of the Spanish conquerors and enhance their enterprise. Bringing back the theme of the indigenous heroics clears the ground for the independent liberal Guatemalan intelligentsia because it is through this medium that they built their ownership rights and entitlements. At the time Juarros writes, the indigenous resistance is over and, therefore, it can be recapitulated in writing, transformed into a rhetorical trope, and used as fodder to feed their own cause. This cause is closely related to the productivity of the land and to attracting foreign investments. After all, it is England that has taken interest in this story, if not by commissioning Juarros's text, at least by making it available to English readers through translation. It is within this context that we are to read Juarros's detailed descriptions of Guatemalan history and productivity.

A serious reorganization of the topographies must return to the city of Utatlán, the Quiché-Maya center of power, to explain its past splendor and how it was conquered, destroyed, and resettled. In total concurrence with Alvarado's description, the city of Utatlán was localized in the department of Quiché, and described as "surrounded by a deep ravine that formed a natural fossae, leaving only two very narrow roads as entrances to the city" (86). It was "the court of the native kings of Quiché . . . indubitably the most sumptuous [city] that was discovered by the Spaniards in this country" (ibid.). The splendor of the royal past is captured in the following passage. Juarros writes that the city center

> was occupied by the royal palace, which was surrounded by the houses of the nobility; the extremities . . . inhabited by the plebeians. The streets were very narrow, but the place was . . . populous. . . . It contained many very sumptuous edifices, the most superb of them was a seminary, where between 5 and 6000 children were educated. . . . The castle of the Atalaya was a remarkable structure, which being raised four stories high, was capable of furnishing quarters for a very strong garrison. . . . The grand alcazar, or palace of the kings of Quiché, surpassed every other edifice, and . . . it could compete in opulence with that of Moctesuma in Mexico, or that of the Incas in Cuzco. (87)

In the diagram in Figure 10, we can visualize this structure.

Utatlán was the first city captured and destroyed by the Spanish *avanzada*. After the rulers were defeated, the population was relocated a mile or so away and the new settlement was called Santa Cruz del Quiché. Santa Cruz del Quiché is a city that can be easily spotted within the new jurisdictional map traced by the Spanish governance. It actually can be said to be the first indigenous city established by the Spaniards that serves as a showcase depicting the resettlement of populations within a nineteenth-century text. Although Utatlán is already an empty shell, it serves criollos as a point of reference and their descriptions of this urban center in an aggrandizing style have the power to re-create the greatness of the Quiché-Maya culture captive in the criollo prose of the world.

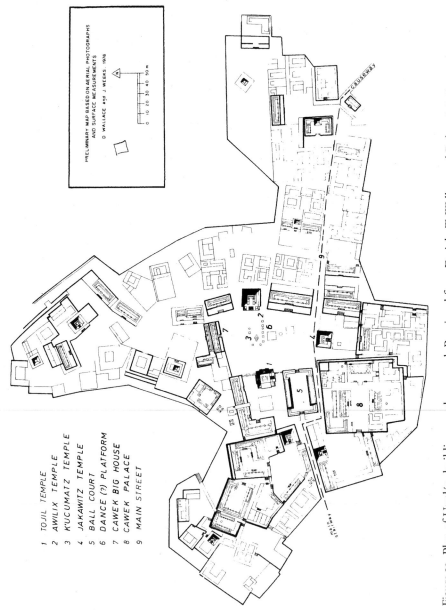

1 TOJIL TEMPLE
2 AWILIX TEMPLE
3 K'UCUMATZ TEMPLE
4 JAKAWITZ TEMPLE
5 BALL COURT
6 DANCE (?) PLATFORM
7 CAWEK BIG HOUSE
8 CAWEK PALACE
9 MAIN STREET

PRELIMINARY MAP BASED ON AERIAL PHOTOGRAPHS
AND SURFACE MEASUREMENTS

D. WALLACE and J. WEEKS, 1976

0 10 20 30 40 50 m

causeway

Figure 10. Plan of Utatlán, buildings partly restored. Reprinted from Dwight T. Wallace and Robert M. Carmack, editors, *Archaeology and Ethnohistory of the Central Quiché* (Albany: Institute for Mesoamerican Studies, 1977); reprinted with permission from the Institute for Mesoamerican Studies, University of Albany.

The literary reconstruction of the city performs all kinds of reconversions: *ajaus* become nobility, *maceguales* turn into plebeians, and buildings into seminary, castle, Atalayas, and *alcázares*. What was formerly a ceremonial center comes to life in all its magnificence in the independent imaginary and establishes an unintended sharp contrast with Santa Cruz del Quiché, which is nothing but a resettlement camp that later becomes a small town that resembles those poor towns of the Spanish countryside. As time passes, Utatlán becomes a heap of ruins. Juarros's rhetorical questions asking for all those "hewn stones of different colors," the "lodgings for numerous troops," "the accommodation of princes . . . the use of kings," and the "sumptuous magnificence" (87–88) are just his way of using the Amerindian pass as a way of aggrandizing the deeds of his Spanish ancestors. The shape and form of all those imaginary referents, the realities of the capital city of the Quiché-Maya, the life and deeds of Tecúm-Umám, are only tentatively answered today in the reconstructions provided by the works of archaeologists, ethnohistorians, linguists, and fiction writers.

Juarros's next move is to reconstruct the story of the foundation of the first Spanish city. This is a serious enterprise that requires *consejo*. The *Libro viejo* contains all the discussion corresponding to the foundation of the Spanish city in minute detail. The *cabildo* was presided by none other than Jorge de Alvarado, Pedro's brother, and the criterion for choosing the city site was twofold: security and productivity. Juarros recounts the story as follows. The first place chosen was either Tianguecillo, on the Chimaltenango plain, or Almolonga. The name of the city was San Jago. The city of San Jago was written as "the boundary of the province of Guatemala" (406). It divided "Indian" from Spanish territories.

There are, however, serious disagreements about this location, and no sooner has Juarros narrated the accord than he writes all the discrepancies concerning the case: "Authors who have written on the affairs of this kingdom, do not certainly agree in this point of its history, each relating the event according to the opinion given by him, relative to the situation of the city under its native governors" (407). Thus, some claim that the city was traced to a site to the west, at Tzacualpa, others that it was fixed in Sinacám's capital (Iximché or Tecpángoatemala), and only after the Spaniards had tried living there for a while with no satisfactory results did they move the city to the valley of Tianguecillo. Once at Tianguecillo,

Juan Bautista Antonelli, the engineer responsible for the first blueprint of the city, surveyed all the adjacent valleys (including Las Vacas, today occupied by Guatemala City) and concluded that the best place for the establishment of the city was the valley of Panchoy. The criteria used to select this valley were climate, fertility of soils, excellent pastures for flocks and herds, and quarries that provided construction material—bricks, tiles, lime, gypsum. Moreover, the large population residing in the valley provided a large labor pool for the works. Assent was given and the first Spanish capital city was relocated there. From 1541 on, the story is coherent. The year 1541 represents the end of the first and most decisive period of conquest. The war was over.

However, there is another version to Juarros's account of the migrant capital city, and this other version underscores all the troubles the Spanish endured before settling down for good. This new version states that the first site chosen for the Spanish capital city was not in Quiché-Maya but in Cakchiquel territory. The Quiché-Maya area was much too unstable. During the first moment of conquest, the Cackchiquel had befriended the Spanish and therefore they found it safe to settle next to their new allies. Thus, the first Spanish city was near Iximché and named Santiago. From Iximché, the city was moved to Xepau and called Señor Santiago; from Xepau it was moved to Tianguecillo and Almolonga and given the name of the very noble and loyal city of Santiago de Guatemala or Ciudad Vieja. From Tianguecillo and Almolonga the city was moved yet again to Panchoy and called Santiago de los Caballeros, or Antigua, and from there the city was moved to La Ermita, where the new name was Nueva Guatemala de la Asunción, known today as Guatemala City.[40] That, in a nutshell, is the story of the migrant Spanish city whose story is directly related to the story of Utatlán. While one is reduced to ruins, the other is raised from the ground to establish Spanish power and ownership over the land.

Ciudad Vieja and Antigua, the two older capital cities of the Guatemalan captaincy, are still standing in the valleys of Almolonga and Panchoy. Two spectacularly beautiful volcanoes, Agua (water) and Fuego (fire), flank the cities; each in turn has been responsible for the destruction of the city of Antigua on several occasions. Ciudad Vieja is to the north of Agua and to the west of Fuego; Antigua is in the northeast and very near Ciudad Vieja. Juarros notices that this area properly belongs to the jurisdiction of Chimaltennago, as it still does today. Almolonga is the place chosen by the Spaniards to found the first and most stable capital city of Guatemala, which lasted fourteen years before it was destroyed by Agua. That old capital city is what is now called Ciudad Vieja—not Antigua, but the city founded before Antigua. Ciudad Vieja was also called New Guatemala, not to be confused with today's Guatemala City. In Juarros, the migrant histories of the cities concur with the struggles and alliances among and between the contending groups. Within the larger map of the region, Antigua was built south of Quiché territory and near Ixhimché, in Cackchiquel territory. The roads connecting these two cities are spectacularly winding and dangerous. A look at the sensational mountainous terrain makes it difficult to imagine where the battles took place.

The point of this detour detailing the tale of these two cities is to bring together human geographies, civic chronicles, and military historiography. The migrant quality of human settlements sets culture and politics in command of topographies and often narrates military histories in civil and productive prose. It is in Juarros's interest to explain the archaeology of cities in reference to the ordering and reordering of territorialities in *alcaldías, corregimientos,* provinces, whose number waxes and wanes. At the time he writes, there are fifteen provinces. Before, there were thirty-two, divided into governments (Nicaragua, Costa Rica, Soconusco, Comayagua), *alcaldías,* and *corregimientos.* The numbers are never quite reliable and all rearrangements are contingent on numbers of people and seemingly heavy population flows, with numbers often changing the territorial divisions politically. In this particular case, Juarros's prose denotes the commercial style so dear to English observers of the time. Among the most relevant information Juarros provides his readership is that the valley of Panchoy was surrounded by no fewer than thirty villages within two leagues' distance, and this means that the reduction of Quiché-Maya into pueblos had been practically achieved, at least in that small area, and that their settlers could be employed in all kinds of trades.

Throughout Juarros's text, history and geography are closely entwined. In the section titled "Treatise the Second," Juarros dovetails one into the other. His main source is Fuentes y Guzmán, the *corregidor* of the province of Gueguetenango, who "had the opportunities of verifying many points of [this] history. . . . he had also an opportunity of seeing, and having explained to him, many of the paintings used by the Indians instead of books as records of their history" (160). But Fuentes y Guzmán, Juarros says, has also read "books, records, and other papers in the secret archives of the city. . . . Besides . . . Gonzalo de Alvarado and Bernal Díaz del Castillo, the histories compiled by caciques of the Pipil, Quiché, Kachiquel, and Pocomán Indians, who having been taught to write . . . communicated many historical fragments, which had been transmitted to them by their ancestors" (ibid.). All of these sources enable Juarros first to validate the work of his compatriot criollo Fuentes y Guzmán, and second, to reconstruct a detailed history of "Indians." As his ancestors did before him, he does his privileged readings along the royal lines of descent. He recounts and reorders indigenous lines of descent and command, main warriors, ranking order of Ahaos (caciques), heads of lineage, and the *calpules*. The sources are the testimonials of Don Juan Macario, Francisco García Calel Tzumpán, and Francisco Gómez Ahzib.

In the section titled "Some Account of the Quichés before the Arrival of the Spaniards" (167), we find again the reiteration of topographical divisions into four territorialities, and the dovetailing of geography and history. The Quiché occupied the present "districts" of Totonicapán, part of Quezaltenango, and Rabinal; the Cackchiquels, the provinces of Chimaltenango, Sacatepequez, and the "district" of Sololá—where Spaniards, considering these groups their allies, founded their first cities; the Zutugils, the "district" of Atitán, the "village" of San Antonio, Suchiltepeques; the Mams, the "district" of Gueguetenango. This territorial division corresponds to the language division and points to the multiplicity of languages spoken that originally gave rise to the confusion of data, which was later made more complex by the introduction of Spanish. Parts of Quezaltenango and the "province" of Soconusco are places where Quiché, Cackchiquel, Zutugill, Mam, and Pocomán were spoken.

Juarros's contribution to the knowledge of the layout of the land is the clarification of the indigenous and Spanish nomenclatures. His clarifications identify the localities of the first confrontation that occurred within the perimeters of the five middle provinces (Totonicapán, Quezaltenango, Sololá, Chimaltenango, and Sacatepequez). All the main Amerindian cities were located in this area. These cities were, in Juarros's view, "the most magnificent and opulent . . . of the whole kingdom of Guatemala," because of "the magnificence of its temples, the grandeur of its public buildings, . . . as well as from numerous castles and fortifications" (379).

All of them were relocated to keep people under control. The new names given to population centers, coupled with their constant relocations, create the absolute confusion that characterizes the topographies of the Guatemalan highlands. It is difficult to know who is where, and hence the convergence of narratives of war and urbanism.

The same confusion of names that takes place in the Quiché region occurs subsequently in the mapping of the perimeter occupied by the Cackchiquel and their capital city of Pitinamit (or Tecpán Guatemala, which means "the royal house") and the other groups, such as the Zutugil and their capital city Atitlán. I gather that the movement of populations from one place to another is the occasion for changing the names of the towns in such a way that if a group of people are moved from one place to another, in some instances they carry their names with it. This is what seems to happen in the case of the city of Xelahuh, a city that was supposedly taken over easily because its inhabitants abandoned it in fear of the famed Spaniards. Regarding the name of this city, Juarros states: "At the expiration of 4 years, the population of Quezaltenango was transferred to the city of Xelahuh; from which period it has exchanged its original appellation and title of city, for that of the village of Quezaltenango" (381). One can see the transition in nomenclature: first there are two separate "towns," Quezaltenango and Xelahuh, and then one becomes the other. The genealogy of names goes as follows: Quezaltenango → (Xelahuh) Quezaltenango. But what really seems to be going on, and what this constant flow of people and names indicates, is the relentless confrontation between the two groups. Most likely, these resettlements obey either the settlement of uprisings, the needs of Spanish *encomenderos* for *"Indios" laborios*—hands—or the religious orders' interference in population policies and their zeal for the custody of the new Christians. There is no clarity on any of these issues. Colonial prose has resolutely enmeshed and tangled all these stories.

It seems very possible that the first attempt was to found a Spanish city right where the old indigenous city of Utatlán was, right on top of it, as was the custom, but that indigenous resistance made this desire impossible. As a result, the Spanish moved south and settled near Iximché. When nineteenth-century criollos mention Guatemala City as a very industrious place where "Indians" and Ladinos produce wheat, maize, or work as artisans, and as a place that has more than thirty-one nearby villages, surrounded by valleys providing all kinds of goods, they could be talking about either Antigua or Guatemala City. This is also true when they thank their forefathers for the succession of villages they founded: "The present inhabitants are indebted to the original conquerors for this succession of villages as they were all desirous of forming and establishment upon the lots that fell to them, on a division of the lands in the valley" (478). In the meantime, stranded Amerindians roam their former territories as "wild Indians," and Spaniards hunt them down like beasts of prey. "Indians" have disregarded all friendly gestures and have shown little inclination to hear the preaching of the missionaries. In consequence,

> the governor gave permission to hunt them out of their retreats. . . . the officers each taking 10 or 12 soldiers, sallied forth on the darkest nights, conducted by expert guides to an Indian hovel, where they frequently seized 6, 8, or 10 Indians whom they brought home and placed on their maize plantations, and other works. . . . these excursions were repeated until 60, 80, 200, 300, or even greater numbers, were got together and formed into a village, on which was usually bestowed the name of the saint of the proprietor's peculiar devotion, with the addition of the surname of his family. (479)

This information clearly outlines the genealogy of towns and the archaeology of urbanism. In other places, there are only ruins.

CONCLUSIONS

There is so much confusion in all these stories of people, towns, and topographies told and retold by Spaniards and criollos that researchers studying the Maya universe have not been able to unravel it. That which the colonial discourse obviated can only be presumed and invented. If the reconstruction of the physical layout of the land has been painful and costly, we can surmise that more subtle questions such as understanding the ordering of the symbolic Quiché-Maya universe, the study of time, with the hosts of calendrical cycles differing in length and portent, and all other topics that constitute an essential part of the Quiché-Maya epistemic ordering of the universe, present even more insurmountable problems and are yet to be thoroughly understood. Munro Edmonson's observations on

Itzá history are pertinent in this regard. He agrees that historiographies correspond

> on numerous points, but the focus of attention is totally different. The Spaniards chronicled their *entradas*, the sequences of their officials, their laws, discoveries and conquests. They themselves appear in Itzá history, however, as an annoying but shadowy and largely irrelevant presence, alluded to by nicknames. . . . The thrust of Maya history is a concern with Indian lords and priests, with the cosmology that justified their rule, and with the Indian civil war that was perceived as the real dimension of colonial history. In effect, this is a secret history. Certainly the Spaniards remained largely oblivious to the continued existence of a traditional Maya government in Yucatán and ignorant of the ideology that supported it.[41]

In Edmonson we come across the evidence of two histories running parallel to each other. In this parallelism, we find a correlation of powers that set rules for subjects and objects, their operations, concepts, and theoretical options. The existence of this discourse proves that the indigenous epistemes are still living forces today, and that the confrontation persists, as a sign not only of the existence of discursive pluralities but also of the endurance of their currency over time; that is, the Maya subjacent power is contingent on the negotiations established between the competing technologies of knowledge operating at the moment of discourse production.

My aim has been to examine the nature of war; how war replots physical geographies, and how that replotting comes to constitute itself into a symbolic universe that determines the conditions of the future production of discursive practices, such as our own. How war and peace combine to create social-cum-epistemic formations is of interest to cultural historians, because it is in the practices of war and in politics that labor, coercion, government, and rebellion take part as particular instances of the generation of discursive pluralities. It is precisely in the practices of the daily as political that the process of identity production is rooted.

War leads to settlement, settlement to possession and dispossession of lands, the establishment (and reestablishment) of properties, and the normalization of labor routines to provide for the necessities of food, shelter, and clothing. After war comes the formalization of new jurisdictions through legislation. However, it is in war that the different factions first know each other through their own cultural practices. In this sense, wars are cultural encounters where human practices, to become known later through discourse, begin to be displayed. Among these practices, the quotidian and the symbolic come into being as one entity through the use of war gear, formations, and fighting stratagems. War is, then, not only weapons and killings; it is the cultural space in which terrains are defined and defended, and where topographies are constructed and deconstructed.

What is lacking in the earliest narratives of confrontation is the details of the everyday life of the ordinary Quiché-Mayas. Anthropological and archaeological fieldwork endeavors to supply this information. More accurate topographies are rendered only after the sixteenth century, once the Spanish colonial world order became fully operational. The most attractive topography is provided in the seventeenth century by Fuentes y Guzmán. His idyllic economic narratives serve as the basis for the nineteenth-century liberal historiography, such as Juarros's, and for the radical twentieth-century labor of reconstruction in reverse undertaken by Severo Martínez Pelaez. Because all the chroniclers base their knowledge of the terrain on the first accounts of the encounter, we are forever wedded to the testimonials of conquerors, friars, and the first Ladino "Indians."[42]

In order to further these investigations, financial solvency is required. A large part of the research activities have found their infrastructural base in the American university system (Pennsylvania, Tulane, Texas State) and research institutions (Carnegie Mellon, the Peabody Museum at Harvard). Prior to that, the research base was in the travels of explorers, geographers, and diplomats whose work I study in the next chapter.[43]

chapter 5

BANANA REPUBLICS

Nineteenth-Century Geographers and Naturalists

THE PARAMETERS OF A POSITIVE SCIENCE OF GEOGRAPHY

In this chapter, I analyze the work of E. G. Squier.[1] Squier (1821–88) was born in Bethlehem, New York. He first worked as an editor of poetry journals such as *Literary Pearl*, *Village Messenger*, and *Poet's Magazine*, and then as an editor of *New York State Mechanic*, *Hartford Journal*, and *Scioto Gazette*. He was also interested in indigenous cultures and studied the indigenous mounds and earthworks of the Scioto Valley, Ohio. The result was the publication of *Ancient Monuments of the Mississippi Valley* (1848). About the middle of the century, Squier was appointed chargé d'affaires to Central America and he is responsible for negotiating commercial treaties with the nations of El Salvador, Honduras, and Nicaragua. When he returned to the United States in the 1850s, he published *The Serpent Symbol* and *Reciprocal Principles of Nature* (1851) and *Nicaragua: Its People, Scenery, Monuments, and Proposed Interoceanic Canal* (1852). Then he traveled extensively in Europe and was introduced to the European ethnological and geographical societies. His interest in Central America was evident in his promotion of commercial treaties, his scheme for migration, and most important, his endorsement of interoceanic communications via the isthmus. In this section I analyze his critical stance toward the previous genealogies of knowledge he encounters in the indigenous and criollo archives and how he laid out the parameters for the positivistic study of geography.

Unhappy with the conjectural and imaginary geographies bequeathed by colonialism, a tradition he is for other reasons obliged to admire and ponder, in his book *The States of Central America* Squier establishes the parameters of a positivistic approach to the science of geography. As in all nineteenth-century positivistic-oriented studies, the contrast between previous and new knowledge—in this case, between the Spanish tradition and Squier's own hermeneutical practices—lies in methodology. The main parameters of the new methodology are direct observation, accuracy, and accountability. Accuracy means faith in what the eye perceives, the mind understands, and the senses quantify. Although all the previous archives, established through the collaboration of indigenous and Spanish peoples, are important, geography itself is here disengaged from history and portrayed as a science without a reliable genealogy. And although most of Squier's bibliography acknowledges the works of British captains, French naturalists, and U.S. chargés d'affaires, he still asserts that what is known about Central America has been produced by foreigners whose shallow observations, following the convention of genres such as travel and adventure, lack close and accurate research.

To achieve his purpose, Squier must first perform surgery on the previous archive, the body of ancient knowledge. His method is threefold: first, to separate the knowledge produced by conquerors from the knowledge produced by monks—the corollary of which is the disengagement of geography from archaeology; second, to convert history into physical and natural geographies—the corollary of which is the disengagement of history from ethnology; third, to drive a wedge between old and new "Indians"—the corollary of which is to move them away from geography and history and reposition them back into archaeology and ethnology. In the process, the reorganized and compartmentalized disciplines of geography, ethnography, archaeology, and history come to intersect and produce the following grand rubrics: nature (which subsumes commerce, products, and investments); politics (which displays the forms invented by the Enlightenment and how they can be reinvested to serve management and administration forms of control); and race (which subsumes the reproduction of ontologies of barbarism and the split between ancient, civilized people, and extant Amerindians). Of these three overarching rubrics, the productive ones are the first and last, with the middle mediate between them.

CONQUERORS/MONKS—
GEOGRAPHY/ARCHAEOLOGY

The first drastic incision in this body of previous knowledge is that which divides the information provided by Spanish captains from that provided by Spanish monks. By driving a wedge between these two types of knowledge, Squier erases with the stroke of a pen all the geographies of the *Popol Vuh* and all the clerical works of reconstruction of the Quiché-Maya topographies produced through the close collaboration of monks and Amerindians. From now on, Amerindian knowledge is dismissed or relegated to the dustbin of museums. The reason for this cut is that the presentation of crucial details of natural features with sufficient fullness is lacking; that is, "a clear idea of the scenery of the country and the architecture of its people" cannot rely on past knowledge, which is characterized by unfit representations, "total lack of order, gross neglect and wanton destruction . . . to confound and defeat all investigation" (xi). And although he makes use of past recorded geographical knowledge, he is of the opinion that "not only were important places wrongly located, but topographical features . . . were laid down where none existed, while others which really did exist were entirely left out. Most of the American maps executed in Europe are filled with names which are unknown in the country itself. These errors are perpetuated, and it often becomes exceedingly difficult to conjecture their origin" (ibid.).

Although the real gash that Squier establishes is one of method— empirically verifiable versus imagined data—a distinction that divides European cartographers in Europe from European cartographers in America, his point is also to reassess knowledge production in America; and, in America, to drive a wedge between the European culture transmitted by conquerors and that transmitted by monks. My contention is that the maps traced in situ by conquerors have value because, in the nineteenth century and even today, they accurately pinpointed the locations of indigenous cultures, and that it is over the surface of the cartographic space that Squier is to debate people. In contrast, the work of monks lacks value not so much because it is an immediate and haphazard recording of facts, but rather because it is a compilation of all the cultural, linguistic, and political practices of the indigenous cultures that positive sciences have no use for and therefore can throw away. The cross-cultural interaction is thus selective and the colonial legacy split asunder. Whatever of this indigenous past is considered worth preserving will be securely stored in the vaults of archaeology.

My interest in narrative intersections is precisely to identify the places where these changes occur and to discuss their implications. In this particular case, the shift from geography to archaeology helps me understand the place of the indigenous within positivistic knowledge. It serves me in discussing how cross-cultural erasures lie at the basis of the genealogy of positivistic knowledge. It also helps me understand the criteria for the transculturated, that is, the selection of that which is going to sediment as cultural wealth and serve to forge the cultural discussion of identities in Latin America, and that which is to be gotten rid of.

From all the evidence provided by Squier's text, the transculturated is the careful and deliberate grafting of colonial European culture onto U.S. culture, in particular those passages that "convey a clear idea of the scenery of the country and the architecture of its people" (ibid.). Observe how in the following passage Squier retrieves the colonial in the positivistic. Referring to the topographical knowledge that makes reference to indigenous populations, he states that "[t]he original names of places, however, have been preserved here [in Central America] with the greatest tenacity, and afford a very sure guide in defining the extent of territory over which the various aboriginal nations were spread" (319). My earlier point was *(a)* the instability of these names; and *(b)* that whatever the type of knowledge acquired, it could have never been obtained without the participation of the Quiché-Maya. Therefore, in this passage Squier is indirectly admitting the cross-cultural information provided by the indigenous peoples. He is, however, very consistent in the citation of his sources. His privileged information always comes from military reports because, in his view, they provide the most accurate information about the lay of the land, the physical terrain where past and future projects are to meet. What he establishes as normative is proper measurements, positive descriptions, accurate accounting. In his work, the measurement of a league is never determined by the nature of the terrain; it will never be one that "seldom exceeds two

English miles" in San Salvador and the plains of Honduras, while in the mountains it is less than a mile and a half. What Squier creates is a tradition in which the separation between object and agent is effected. Officially, subjectivity has no place within positivism.

For Squier, the new positivist tradition begins with Heinrich Berghaus, a Prussian geographer who drew the first accurate map of the region in 1840. This tradition is contrasted with that established by Domingo Juarros, the Guatemalan historian whose work was examined in chapter 4, and whom Squier wants to debunk because his work is simply "a transcript from the municipal and monkish chronicles of Guatemala. Reference is rarely made to the physical features of the country, and even then in an exaggerated and marveling tone, which always denotes the absence of positive knowledge" (xv). If in the early colonial period exaggeration and hyperbole are valid rhetorical forms to provide information about the "new," in the nineteenth century those forms are totally outlawed. Juarros does not cut it because he does not provide quantitative information, much less knowledge, in Squier's view. In disqualifying Juarros's information as knowledge, Squier makes a tabula rasa of the budding national Guatemalan intelligentsia as well. From now on, it is established that reliable knowledge is produced in the United States or by U.S citizens. Do we not hear similar debates today?

HISTORY/ETHNOLOGY: PHYSICAL AND NATURAL GEOGRAPHIES

Having discussed how Squier flattens out all prior historical information to make geography accountable, I will now explore how his treatment of history parallels his treatment of geography and how all policies toward Amerindians are now managed by the discipline of ethnology. Like geography, history and ethnology are made to serve the U.S. grand imperial design and manifest destiny.

In his extensive and thorough study of physically productive geographies, Squier's central concern is the possibilities Central America offers for building interoceanic, trans-isthmic, and inter-national communication shortcuts and passageways between the eastern and western coasts of the continental United States. This is a vision of history as a device to promote future projects rather than as a discipline to understand the past.

The distance drawn between past and future is political and serves to dehistoricize the present. The present is only that which makes possible the investment of the past into the future. Past history is reduced to events, two of which are privileged. One is the confrontation between Spaniards and Amerindians. The other is the diplomatic relations between the United States and England. The confrontation between Spaniards and Amerindians yields road maps leading to the locations of indigenous groups—still useful in spite of all the resettlement of populations carried out in the past centuries. The relations between the United States and England yield the (re)partition of the continent leading to Pan-Americanism, the recognition that America is for "Americans," and that Latin America is just "America's backyard" and Central America a set of Banana republics.

And what of local events? Local histories are not histories but ethnologies. A new social morphology was much in need to provide an overall grid to reorganize all types of excess knowledge, and for this purpose alone ethnology was perfect. All that matters to nineteenth-century positivistic imaginaries is numbers, the practical tools of its scholars and agents. Thus, current local political events are classified as ethnographic data and used as variables that will potentially derail investment plans. The struggles for independence are reduced to caste wars, and Amerindians are set up within a vast pan-indigenous encyclopedia whose function is to identify the exact physical location of their habitats. If the old "Indian" was to be frozen in the science of archaeology, the new "Indian" was to be neatly tucked away in the discipline of ethnology. I will come back to this later.

On the positive side of the positivistic science of geography, Squier has been able to achieve that which Michel de Certeau calls the "proper." The proper is the "triumph of place [geography] over time [history]," "a rational organization [of science/knowledge] repressing all the physical, mental and political pollutions that would compromise it."[2] That de Certeau establishes these principles as a corollary or illustration of the difference between strategy and tactics is most appropriate to our purposes, because it provides the missing link between the two overarching rubrics of nature (geography) and people (history).[3] Physical geography is that special "proper" space. Description and accountability are, then, the twin sisters delimiting the proprieties of the proper. Description and accountability are the most positive of the positive. They are that which permits the appropriation of geography as spaces of their own (America for "Americans"),

one that has been repossessed through knowledge. The positive knowledge of Central America in Central America has hardly matched, let alone
surpassed, Squier's. To the degree that his knowledge holds currency
today, it is a living sign of the heritage of the second stage of colonization,
or the second discovery of America.[4]

Let us move on now to the examination of how cartographic and
ethnic descriptions intersect to constitute a tradition that is matched only
by the literary description of geographies, how the foregrounding of the
cartographic backgrounds the ethnic, and debunks the notion of *mestizaje*
as a link between theories of race, social pacts, and development. And finally,
let us study how Central America is first represented as a metonymy,
enjoining space and time contained in the proposition of trans-isthmic
routes by Squier—an idea that in the twentieth century was recycled by
José Coronel Urtecho's metaphor of "rapid transit."[5]

I will treat physical geographies first. Insofar as identity is concerned,
physical geographies are invested with an epistemological privilege. Squier
says, for instance, that "[u]nder this aspect, as affording an avenue between the seas, the great transverse valley of Comayagua may justly be regarded as the most important physical feature of Honduras" (76). But why
is this feature the most important of Honduras and who is it important
for? Honduras's physical features are important for building a railroad, for
investment. Honduras is important because it becomes an extension of
the lands of the United States, America's backyard, part of the U.S. project of the "Far West." The U.S. national purpose and manifest destiny
can be said to constitute the subjective element of Squier's positivistic
geographies. This is a core belief system that this geographer reiterates
throughout his writing when he refers to any and all the parts of Central
America, be it the plains of Comayagua for the railroad or the rivers
Lerma and San Juan in El Salvador and Nicaragua for small steam vessels.
"The most remarkable topographical feature of the state, considered in
reference to the facilities which it offers for the grand economic purposes
of travel and commerce between the oceans" (72) are the valley of the Rio
Humuya, and the valley of the Rio Goascorán, "altogether constituting a
great transverse valley reaching from sea to sea" (ibid.).

"Puerto Caballos . . . extending thence southward . . . through the
plains of Espino and Comayagua . . . down the valley of the Rio Goascorán to the Bay of Fonseca . . . , a distance of one hundred and fifty

miles" (75), could be the site of the interoceanic railway. Squier's goal is to measure the extension of the lands and the length and width of valleys; length and width become weight, tons of steel and labor hours necessary to cover the length of the tracks. The economies of the Bay of Fonseca, Comayagua, and Puerto Caballos are tied to those of the Midwest, from the northern Minnesota iron range, passing the great furnace of Gary, Indiana, all the way down to the ports of New Orleans. The 150 miles through Honduras will be drastically reduced when they are crossed, not on foot, as many European immigrants did, but on steamboats, which will cover the distance from one ocean to the other through the Isthmus of Panama, or through the river San Juan and Lake Nicaragua, as Vanderbilt's steamliner business was to do through Nicaragua.

Topography, the physical layout of the land, is, properly speaking, the criterion for a history that projects itself toward the future in the form of U.S. modernization. Central America is just a geographical medium. It has potential because of its diverse topography, fertile valleys, elevated plains, terraced mountains, and variety of climate and soils, all "conditions favorable to nurturing and sustaining a large population, and point unerringly to the ultimate, if not the speedy development here of a rich and powerful state" (78). What is lacking is a "stable and liberal government" (ibid.), and it is at this point, once more, where the history of investments turns from geography to ethnology. The discussions on government and population, or politics, are predicated on race, on the reexamination of indigenous societies, on figuring proposals, on emigration and resettlement, on questioning *mestizaje*, as we will see further on. The "ethnic problem" resides in the fact that some of the main routes for railroad and steamboat construction are precisely the pockets of lands held by the indigenous communities. Indigenous peoples must be disposed of.

Regarding the indigenous question, the positive science of geography has no compunction in turning for help to the archives of monks. And, as in the case of Carvajal in the Amazon, whenever nature is about to be converted into industry and commerce, a synthesis between the sciences and the arts takes place, and developmentalist arcadias spring to life: "Together, these two plains, both of surpassing beauty of scenery, fertility of soil, and salubrity of climate, occupy nearly one third of the distance between the Bay of Honduras and that of Fonseca" (73). Beauty is the best ally of development. Scenery (beauty), soil (agriculture), and climate come to stand for the possibilities of civilization, the pillars of modernity. The mountains and valleys of the *Popol Vuh* are beautiful again when they produce canals, gold, or railroads.

If plains and valleys are railroad tracks, waters are navigation, irrigation, or dams. The vistas of the ports of San Juan (Nicaragua), Point Arenas (Puntarenas) (Costa Rica), and La Unión (El Salvador) produce an extended surface that contains a body of water capable of harboring all kinds of vessels, from *pangas* and canoes to frigates and transoceanic ships. The bays are foregrounded and the towns backgrounded. The contrast established between towns and vessels focuses on the thatched roofs called *mediaguas*, conical structures that speak of the legacy of Amerindian house-construction styles and materials, and of the lack of industrial ingenuity of nations and their representatives, which the image of flags and smoke make pervasive. All illustrations remind us of the West Indian ideoscapes sketched by English commissioners, discussed in chapter 2 (see Figure 11).

With steam and railroad tracks, the whole society will transform itself: mules and "Indians" will lose their function as a labor force and will be replaced by steam; volume of production will rise; technology, and a more accurate way of gauging distances and knowing specimens—mineral, vegetal, and animal—will circumvent natural obstacles such as rapids and bars. Transportation and agriculture are, then, the twin aspects of Central America's nemesis: its fertile and well-adapted savannas for the cultivation of rice, cotton, and sugar; its bays abounding in fish; its shores swarming with every variety of waterfowl—cranes, herons, pelicans, ibises, spoonbills, ducks, curlews, and darters are its damnation, what will make them today into the repositories of nonrenewable natural resources.

Naturalists and geographers know the names of all the species of animals, insects, trees, and indigenous groups. Their ordinary English or French names are often coupled with their Latinized nomenclature: "Brazil-wood (Coesalpina Echinata) . . . Copal-tree (Hedwigia Balsamifera) . . . the Avocado or Alligator Pear (Persea Gratimina); Citron (Citrus Tuberosa); Tamarind (Tamarindus Occidentalis) . . . Mango (Mangofera Domestica)" (203), "Monkeys (Simia), Raccoon (Procyon Lotor, John Hoyd or Usus Lotor, L.)" (214). Squier is in possession of all the scientific vocabulary that is wanting in John Lloyd Stephens, whose main contribution is the realm of ethnography and aesthetics. There are no bananas, except in the Atlantic Coast where Thomas Young saw "[t]hou-sands of banana-trees, loaded with fruit . . . growing spontaneously" (quoted in Squier, *The States of Central America*, 84). In view of this wealth, the Central America cornucopia with a soil of unbounded fertil-ity, any lack of accountability is unpardonable. For instance, not to know the value of direct trade between Amapala and Bremen, Liverpool, Mar-seilles, Genoa, New York, and Valparaíso, or the approximate value of cargo—type of vessel, tonnage, crews and of import and export products in wood, cattle, bullion, hides, and so on—is simply unacceptable.

Figure 11. San Juan in 1849 and 1853, and Point Arenas in 1853. From E. G. Squier, *The States of Central America* (New York: Harper and Brothers, 1858).

To illustrate matters further, alongside the series of maps, graphs, and illustrations, Squier's texts include a set of minimalist drawings "From Nature and Stone" by D. C. Hitchcock, plus an assorted group of anonymous drawings in the same minuscule style as Hitchcock's. Although Hitchcock's illustrations are intended to work in tandem with Squier's narrative, making the narrated and the depicted totally consistent with each other, sometimes they are at odds with each other, and can constitute contradictory statements. Looking at this layout from a cultural point of view, the relationship between the production of watercolor landscapes, the picturesque, and the natural sciences turns landscapes into practically profitable and symbolically manageable and governable spaces. Nevertheless, there is a contrast between these minimalist tableaux and Squier's apprehension manifested in expecting people (savages) around each turn. This fear betrays the cultural foundation of his proposal. Thus, while small scale and miniaturization render the landscape technically manageable and convey a view of the region that is minuscule, ethnology constitutes the grotesque, and archaeology the site to deposit the auratic sublime.[6] Physical landscapes are, then, a direct opposite statement to archaeological landscapes. Monuments and ruins, as they are called, are bypasses to enable the nineteenth-century ethnocentric scholar once more to bracket contemporary Amerindian populations and to lock them up in the discipline of ethnology that is to establish the divide between "new Indians" and "old Indians." Historical ancestry is part and parcel of the category of the manageable, one that sets in stone the third epistemological break, creating a wedge that separates the inhabitants of the ancient cities, clearly representatives of an advanced civilization, from present-day Amerindians. John Lloyd Stephens, considered the father of Maya studies and a contemporary of Squier, would further elaborate all that is relative to the distinction between new and old in "Indians."

OLD/NEW "INDIANS"—ARCHAEOLOGY/ETHNOLOGY MANAGEMENT OF CONTROVERSIAL IDENTITIES

In the nineteenth century, the methodologies used in the constitution of controversial identities refer us back first to that historiographical body that narrates the first moments of confrontation between Europeans and Amerindians, and then to the works of John Lloyd Stephens, whose *Incidents of Travel in Central America, Chiapas, and Yucatán* was published in 1850.[7] If Squier's text drives a wedge between conquerors and monks, Stephens's provides the basis for splitting apart present from past Amerindians. In both cases, the technology is a surgical removal used to sever and fragment. "Indian" is that whole whose parts have been forever sundered. The separation of Spaniards into conquerors and monks has the effects indicated earlier—namely, to qualify the European in the conqueror and to disqualify the indigenous in the monks. The historical partition between past and present Amerindians, simultaneously argued through several disciplinary congeries, is equally enmeshed into the ethnic. We arrive at this partition via a detour that involves a discussion of the political difference between liberal Francisco Morazán and conservative Rafael Carrera. What divides them is stretched along an ethnic-cum-cultural ideological continuum where a white Creole is set over and against a crossbreed between "Indian" and "black." Stephens categorizes Carrera as follows: "He is a native of one of the wards of Guatimala. His friends, in compliment, call him a mulatto; I, for the same reason, call him an Indian, considering that the better blood of the two" (82). The difference between conservative and liberal ideologies and projects in Central America is thus converted into a caste war and talked about through the problematic notion of *mestizaje*. The ethnic profiles of Morazán and Carrera render the differentiation between the two political ideologies opaque to a culture that polarizes color, and for whom the category of "mestizo" is disposable.

What is troublesome about Carrera is not only the visible presence of hybridity, but indeterminacy: his darkness can be either black or "Indian." Carrera is the embodiment of what Homi Bhabha calls "the mutant hybrid," a colonial subject who cannot, will not, or is prevented from reproducing the metropolitan cultural system.[8] Thus a discussion on race centered on the allegorizing of the figure of Rafael Carrera introduces the discussion on Amerindians in the text of Stevens that will mirror a whole generation of North American scholars, including Squier. But if in Carrera the indeterminacy of "race" becomes the troubled space, the site of the uncertainty principle, in the case of the distant past, of the classic "Indian," this same uncertainty principle becomes profitable. The remote past, coupled with the absence of written documentation, makes the indigenous one who can be hypothesized, discussed, stored, exhibited, and classified.

Closely related to this discussion is that concerning the civilized. Civilized is a vacant sign that can be filled with the capacity to assimilate, absorb, and enact the new hegemonic cultural values (that capacity for mimetism that Bhabha's notion of the hybrid forecloses), or not. Civilized is the capacity to be acculturated. Morazán embodies it because he is a white criollo. His capacity for acculturation is enabled by his race. But the past, ancient, and dead "Indian" is civilized too, because he is manageable. He has been made the container of both "the classic" and the modern auratic. By one of those invisible logical tours de force, the dead "Indian" signifies not so much the civilized past as a bridge to the civilized future, which here means the possibilities for investment understood as development. The positivistic mind extrapolates ancient monuments into modern transoceanic canals and railroads.

Thus, the disembodied, dead, old "Indian," another empty or vacant slot incarnated in the petrified culture, becomes one of the most fabulous investments of knowledge. He is a hermeneutical tool used to explain the unexplainable, the mysterious civilization of the "forest kings," as Linda Schele calls them: first, through the cultures of urbanism and the development of linguistics and archaeology; second, through the reconstruction of history as the cultured past through literature; and third, through the discussion of the cross between literature and legal documents in the indigenous land titles. The modern "Indian" is made profitable too, in that he is made into the object first of ethnography and then of anthropology and sociology, and now of cultural studies.

The old, dead "Indian" is what sutures the past to the future, enabling the present to stand as a transitory moment to be remodeled by development. Many fragments of texts come as props to this reinstatement of old and dead Amerindians into archaeology. The fragmented and severed is then reconstituted back into the whole through the careful reinscription of incidents, anecdotes, aboriginal names of places, cultural artifacts, and physical topographies—roads, rivers, settlements—into the new positivistic text. But the whole is severely rearranged and reinterpreted. Some of the cultural artifacts are placed under the rubric of antiquity—the ancient mythical cities, ruins—and some others under the rubric of the savage. The critical point is established by the contrast and distance between the two extremes of predication. Antiquity is the dead "Indian"; the savage is the live "Indian"—the one who has resisted. *Mestizaje*, as in Carrera the rebel, is, then, that third force that has incorporated the savage "Indian" into the white, and not the other way around. The savage Indian's nature is to resist the civilized because he disbelieves it. Amerindian history, namely, the possibility of a progression from less to more development, is absolutely foreclosed.

Located in the very distant past and severed from the present—and, what is worse, from the future—Amerindian history is transferred to archaeology and ethnology. In the present, indigenous customs decline, and indigenous people become refugees, expatriates, foreigners in their own lands. Their singularities are erased. Their towns are resettled, women repossessed, and nature reclassified. The destruction of the aboriginal is a question of the past; what is left in the present are shreds of identities, fragments of ancient culture, reminiscences of struggles in the form of anecdotes of conquered and unconquered "Indians"—in other words, the zero degree of culture in the decultured. What of the remaking of splintered and shredded identities does not fit in the ready-made categories is transferred to folklore. The past is history, but history of art. The historical reconstruction of Amerindian cultures undertaken by archaeologists and ethnohistorians is a hermeneutical exercise, an investment in knowledge, a production of fields and academicians, a way of promoting careers, like ours.

TROPICALISM

Tropicalism in Squier is a way of thematizing people within productive landscapes that have been targeted for progress. The descriptive geographies of tropicalism privilege the portrayal of people as specimens, and therefore their description is a kind of zoologized ethnology. In his work on "savages in the mirror," Roger Bartra states that primitive figures mixed animal elements with human ones, as in the case of the horse or the goat in centaurs and satyrs, and that their dangerous quality resided not only in being creatures of the forest, namely, those living on the outskirts of civility and signaling the limits of the secure and known, but in being sexually uncontrollable.[9] Nineteenth-century depictions of Amerindians echo this tradition, minus its cultural prestige. Sexuality, eating, and dressing habits, the body and its parts, pleasure and comfort constitute dangerous zones for progress and impinge on the proposals of *mestizaje*. These are the aporias of both national independence and foreign research and development narratives that have to deal directly with the management of populations.

The first encounter with people is an abstract observation, one that could be quantified in Celsius or Fahrenheit degrees, and that refers to the controlling influence of the geographical and topographical features on the character and destiny of their populations. This is the point where human and physical geographies either become complicit with each other or part ways for good. Squier rereads Spanish colonial literature:

> At the period of the discovery, it was found in the occupation of two fami-
> lies of men, presenting in respect to each other the strongest points of con-
> trast. Upon the high plateaus of the interior of the country, and upon the
> Pacific declivity of the continent . . . were found great and populous com-
> munities, far advanced in civilization, and maintaining a systematized reli-
> gious and civil organization. Upon the Atlantic declivity . . . among dense
> forests, nourished by constant rains into rank vigor, on low coasts . . . were
> found savage tribes of men, without fixed abodes, living upon the natural
> fruits of the earth. (21)

What in Stephens is a distinction between ancient and nineteenth-century indigenes, in Squier becomes an in situ distinction between highlands and lowlands. How are these distinctions thematized in one and the other? In Stephens, the difference in marked identities resided in history—in monuments, aesthetics, and symmetry, and an implicit presupposition of a missing link between the former and the latter; in Squier, the difference resides in geography—in heat, dampness, and moisture, which impedes advance. But while the former simply dismisses the question as irrelevant, the latter deepens the analysis, dooming the inhabitants for "the exuberant vitality of savage nature, which even the civilized man, with all the appliances that intelligence has gradually called to his aid, is unable to subdue" (22). Detailed temperature tables, recorded month by month, rain precipitation, the state of prevailing winds and weather, meteorological observation tables, variations offered by month and region, and tabulated average maximum and minimum temperatures are ways of telling how climate affects all living creatures—human and vegetable—cultures, character, destiny, and yields, all of which suffer the saturation of vapor and heavy dew, which wilts cultures while it enhances the beauty of vegetation. Changing the natures of people will require refrigeration and air conditioners.

With the same precision that Squier observes and measures temperatures, he also tracks many of his favorite nomenclatures, for instance, the number and names of all aboriginal groups inhabiting specific regions, that is, in the Atlantic Coasts of Guatemala, Nicaragua, Honduras and Costa Rica, the Petén Itzaes, Xicaques, Payas, Towkas, Woolwas, Ramas, Guatusos, and Talamancas. He states that their ethnographic censuses are not, and cannot be, accurate because "the ignorant [later called 'the vulgar,' then 'wild' tribes] masses of the people, and specially the Indians, avoid a census as in some way connected with military conscription or taxation" (44). Severo Martínez Pelaez's research on labor, military conscription, and taxation proves that the Amerindians were right to be so leery.[10]

Statistics are decisive for Squier's skewed thesis on *mestizaje*, registering an approximate 15,232 whites, 27,676 Ladinos, and 387,951 "Indians" and Negroes (45). His concern with marriages, deaths, and births is related to the same question. The proportions and rates of growth will determine the balance between acculturation and transculturation.[11] Humboldt's observations of the proportion and ratios of births to deaths in Mexico is extrapolated by Squier to Guatemala: "proportion of births was as 1 to 17, and of deaths as 1 to 30 . . . and that the proportion of births to deaths in the country at large was as 17 to 10" (46). Humboldt, says Squier, warns that "[t]he relative proportions of whites, mixed (Ladinos) and Indians . . . is a subject of profound interest, and to the modern student will appear of vital consequence in all speculations on the condition, capacities, and destinies of the people of those countries" (56).

What is the problem with respect to populations? The problem lies, first, in firmly believing that "in all cases where a free amalgamation takes place between two different stocks, unrestrained by what is sometimes called prejudice, but which is, in fact, a natural instinct, the result is the final and absolute absorption of one in the other" (59); and, second, that "all violations of the natural distinctions of race, or of those instincts which were designed to perpetuate the superior races in their purity, invariably entail the most deplorable results, affecting the bodies, intellects, and moral perceptions of the nations who are thus blind to the wise designs of nature, and unmindful of her laws" (60).

The order of nature, or the reordering of nature, then renders first a legitimate observation of climates, which from meteorology is extrapolated to physical and from it to human geography, and then to the cultures studied by anthropology (verging on zoology), and from there to government. This is what tropicalism is all about. From here only one step remains to fascism, apartheid, and a holocaust. At the end of the century, Squier does not feel compelled to hide, attenuate, or nuance his beliefs in superior and inferior stocks; nor does he want to repress his advice that governments for the inferior, of the inferior, and by the inferior—like Carrera's—are not advisable. What Stephens observes, Squier canonizes; what in the former is simple description of facts and prejudice, in the latter becomes policy statements, a pseudoscientific racism that lingers in the shadow of physical geographies. How Squier will bridge the gap between art and science, or more specifically between what Stephens called "ancient civilizations" and the present state of debasement of those same people three hundred years after the confrontation with Europeans, is not part of his problem. Squier does not waste time in describing internecine struggles for liberation; nor does he bother with character assassination; he simply states that, based on geography and anthropology, "[t]he Indian does not possess, still less the South Sea Islander, and least of all the negro, the capacity to comprehend the principles which enter into the higher order of civil and political organizations" (61).

It is, then, a question of intelligence, intelligence being what separates humans from animals, superior races from other zoological species. Here we are face-to-face with literary studies and the principles of naturalism that inform *costumbrismo*. I will return to this later. The parallelism of cultural statements and the continuation of a racist tradition is noticed here. But now the question turns to government and governance. By nature, these native populations are incapable of an "appreciation of the value, or a disposition to abide by the reciprocal obligations involved in a government of the people. The ideas of government, like those of the Arabs, and the nomadic hordes of Central Asia, are only consonant with the system called patriarchal" (ibid.).

But how is all this talk about "Indians" related to *mestizaje*? It is related by and through percentages and the observation and quantification of color, by the record-keeping function of the geographer-cum-governmental-agent Squier, who observes very few whites and very many undefined masses whom he is not sure whether to call "Indians" or Ladinos, those undefined people who traverse the roads, serve as guides, and sell products at markets. The absent ones are those inhabiting the cities he does not care to narrate, because they fall out of the area of inquiry.

The universal subject position extrapolated from Europe to America reiterates the place of "Indians" in the new regimes of knowledge. In Alvarado's story of conquest as reduction (surrender, extermination, concentrated resettlement into towns) of Amerindians, we can already notice that the category "Indian" is bound into the categories "of peace" and "of war." In Stephens it becomes "old" and "new." In Squier it is transformed into the categories of "culturally assimilable" or "indomitable" within the range of the targeted territories. Peace and war converted into assimilable or indomitable, docile or rebellious, is one of the descriptive elements acting upon theories of climate in reference to progress as civilization. Climate is geography, the new descriptive hegemonic mode to code the area. This hegemony becomes evident in such statements as "they [the 'Indians'] were at first intractable, and favored by the physical conditions of their country, for a long time obstinately resisted the attempts of the Spaniards to reduce them to their say" (224). Those who were not favored by their geographies became the repositories of the melancholic indolent—depicted in many of the short stories of Salvadoran *costumbrista* writer Salarrué. Those who "were not directly incorporated in the civil organization of the various states" fall under the "denomination of 'Tribus Errantes'" (53). "Nearly all of these Indians admit a qualified allegiance to the various states within which they fall, but the relationship is scarcely more than nominal" (54). The politics of people, serving as the basis for an undefined constitution of *mestizaje* and a veiled and indirect attack on mestizos is what matters the most to Squier.

I will end my analysis of Squier's work with a note on *mestizaje*. If the criterion for good investments engages physical geographies in a time–space relation, the debate on culture is caught up in the cross between transculturation, cross-culturation, and acculturation. *Mestizaje*, as the undifferentiated hybrid in between, becomes the targeted site for U.S. traveler-scholars to discuss the stumbling blocks of progress. *Mestizaje* is a living proof of unachieved acculturation and a problematic transculturation. In and through *mestizaje*, agents are to prove that when races mix, the most backward absorbs the most advanced. Like all nineteenth-century writers, Squier writes a disclaimer on ethnic mixtures, and, to argue against them, he returns to the first moments of confrontation, when exploratory narratives took care of the human condition. He then adds to that foundational moment some of the ingredients provided by nineteenth-century natural and human sciences that lend positivism and modernism their fuel to promote their policies of *blanqueamiento*. The crossing of exploratory and natural-sciences narratives is the modern way of discussing *mestizaje* and makes evident the reinvestment of culture on culture.

For Squier, the population of Central America can be divided in three types: (1) the non-"Indians," who in turn are divided between the suspicious métis, Ladinos, and criollos—*mestizaje* targets the first group; (2) the old and dead "Indians"—the ancient/classical Mayas, who being so different from present-day "Indians" are therefore non-"Indian" "Indians"; and (3) present-day, modern "Indians." I have already specified the debates in (1) and (2). Here I will address the nature of (3). Present-day, modern "Indians" are easily discerned and classifiable: they are either servants, scouts, guides, beasts of burden, or specimens—the irreducible whose status as human beings is encoded in biological terms. Present-day, modern "Indians," "aboriginal inhabitants," "native tribes"—Xicaques, Payas, Guatusos, Miskitus, Sambos, Caribs, Lempas, Itzaes—"the roving fisher-tribes who dwelt on the low shores of the Caribbean, now called the Mosquito Coast" (224), are found far below the old "Indians," the "Quichés, Kachiquels, and Nahuals," who inhabited the highlands at the time of conquest.

In describing these groups, it is important to address two questions: first, their exact physical location on the terrain, to find out whether or not they are within the range of territories targeted for progress; and second, whether they are mixed, assimilated, reduced, acculturated, or retain their "original modes of life" (223). Both questions render information as to how they contribute to the general composition of society, whether they have assimilated the whites or have been assimilated by the whites— the two types of cross-cultural interaction studied by Fernando Ortiz, and after him by Ángel Rama, to refer to transculturation and acculturation. Here we are already in the murky waters of *mestizaje*. There is always something that escapes the gauging, measuring, and classifying eye. "In some districts of the state it is difficult to say if the whites have assimilated most to the Indians in habits of life, or the Indians most to the whites" (ibid.)—the specter of the *aindidados* that criollos such as Fuentes y Guzmán were so leery about. This doubt is to be assuaged by the answers given to the questions. These answers in turn contextualize acculturation and transculturation, and document the nature and degree of the heterogeneous.[12]

Customs, the daily habits of people—where they sleep, whether they go dressed or naked, whether they drink alcohol or not, what they eat, their phenotype—is the place where *mestizaje* is discerned and where natural sciences are useful to distinguish old from modern "Indians." The description of bodies and features becomes most biological, and the line between humans and animals is blurred. For instance, the Toacas, Towkas, Thuacos, or Juacos (the exact name being only an approximate mixture of English, Spanish, and aboriginal phonemes) are described by Young "as having long black hair hanging over their shoulders, very broad faces, small eyes, with a peculiar expression of sadness and docility, which predisposes the beholder in their favor" (Squier, *The States of Central America*, 22). Docility is the telling adjective, a characteristic of domesticated animals and one of the possible adjectives of acculturation. This type of description does not come as a surprise, for nineteenth-century writers are enamored with the methods and practices of modern science. In another part of continental America, Roberto González Echeverría has documented how the classical Latin American writers described their characters. For Domingo Faustino Sarmiento, the gaucho is "like a species of vegetable or animal life," and for Euclides da Cuhna Antonio Conselheiro "the central specimen of his herbarium . . . Like Facundo Quiroga [and Carrera], is a kind of monster, a mutant, an accident."[13]

That the narrative of indigenous peoples and their culture constitutes the antinarrative of development is self-evident in the passages quoted above. The science of ethnology lends itself ideally to the compilation of human data that is to bring the "instincts" of native Americans under the dominion of reason, and control the self-contained subsistence communities by disrupting, displacing, and reorganizing peoples. Ethnology thus parallels the science of geography in the closer authentication of the facts on which it proceeds. Ethnographers are the ones to hunt down the ghost of *mestizaje* to pinpoint the problems subtending transculturation.

In retaining some Amerindian customs, the hybrid becomes hubris. The following passage is illustrative of the riddles of *mestizaje* even for the well-trained ethnologist. In San Salvador, for instance, in the Costa del Balsimo or Balsam Coast, which is

> about fifty miles in length by twenty to twenty-five in breadth, lying between La Libertad, the port of the city of San Salvador, and the roadstead of Cajutla, near Sonsonate the district is entirely occupied by Indians who have retained their habits and have changed little from what they were at the period of the conquest. This coast is only traversed by foot-paths so intricate and difficult as to baffle the efforts of the stranger to penetrate its recesses. The difficulty of intercourse is enhanced, if not by the absolute hostility of the Amerindians themselves, then from their dislike to any intrusion on the part of the whites, be they Spaniards or foreigners. (319–20)

Because the area where they live is in between the most productive areas targeted for development and because they are reluctant to mix or to move out, the question is to figure out if they are "Indians" or not. Where does the difficulty in classifying them lie? It lies in the mixture. Their houses are thatched, but their churches are covered with tiles. They presumably read and write Spanish; however, they understand few mechanical arts and they practice them even less. They profess the Catholic religion and cultivate music, but their necessities are few and they go naked from the waist up. They get married, but their ceremonies are "peculiar." Coupling and mating are "strange." They practice incest and daughters become wives. They have a dual notion of governance, respecting the civil authority alongside the authority of age in their "ahuales" (chieftains). They obey the state, but do not consult it in their internal civil and criminal conflicts. They only cultivate maize; their sole wealth is balsam; they have little or no commerce. In their features "they are not symmetrical in form, and are darker in color; more taciturn, and apparently less intelligent. Their women are much smaller than those of the other Indian nations, are generally ugly, and, when old, little short of hideous" (322). Here it is not the place or the occasion to discuss Squier's perplexity but is it not legitimate to wonder whether he is here selecting that phenotype which will be more advantageous to *mestizaje*, or solely pointing out one of the aporias of *mestizaje*?

THE NATURALIST MOMENT: FLORA AND FAUNA
AS COMMERCE AND INDUSTRY

Geographies are everything: from what is potentially navigable—rivers, lakes, lagoons, bays—to ports, harbors, and islands. Geography is anything and everything that is extractable—minerals, precious woods, vegetable products, animals. Geography is everything that helps the understanding of valleys, mountains, general and specific climatic conditions, altitude, extension. Political boundaries and civic organization—religion, industries, revenues, currency—are of minor importance. Unlike the work of naturalists that foregrounds the collection of specimens and the cultures of people, the nature and type of industry and commerce, the state of the roads, the work of geographers is one that curiously overlooks all the impediments encountered. Their aim is the accuracy of description of a landscape whose beauty resides more in its future possibilities than in the existing ones. In this, nineteenth-century geographers are the best representatives of developmentalist utopias, ones who scan the topographies and keep an accurate record of the untapped wealth. The prose is clear and the purpose well stated.

The counterpart of geographic narratives is provided by those of naturalists. Speaking about research guidelines and normative principles provided by the founding institutions, perhaps a perplexing aspect of the more than four hundred pages of Arthur Morelet's *Travels in Central America, Including Accounts of Some Regions Unexplored since the Conquest,* published in 1871, is his précis, delivered as "A Memoir" to the French Academy of Sciences.[14] This is the textual place where he claims to have undertaken his "explorations under the sole incitement of [his] love for natural history, and with . . . an honorable spirit of national emulation" (418). I say this text is perplexing because in it Morelet shows his capacity to synthesize in a couple of pages all the experiences of his travels through the region. The text intrigues also because with it Morelet introduces the notion and practices of what will come to constitute a scientific abstract. Like Sir Walter Raleigh's *The Discoverie of the Large, Rich and Bewtiful Empyre of Guiana,* which will be examined in chapter 6, the contrast between extensive and synthesized narratives makes us wonder about forms and audiences, as well as think of the relevance of rhetoric in relation to the scientific abstract. What brings together the two forms? What sense of audience and purpose do they underscore? Whose formation of identities do they serve?

On first reading, the brief form explains what the larger neglects, namely, Morelet's proposal to carry on research "in a part of the American continent which had never been explored by naturalists" (415), and his implicit contract to surrender the products obtained upon completion of the mission to the Museum of Natural History. In other words, the scientific abstract speaks about telos and protocols, about financial support and the approval of projects. It speaks about originality of research too, research that explores the yet-to-be-explored; and it also specifies the form of payment. For the Academy, perhaps, the memoir is the formal presentation, part of the protocol of completion; and the text is the extensive report written to propagandize for further funding and research, as well as to promote auctions. But the real interests of the Academy, which in his brief format the document reveals, are the transformation of scientific facts into concrete products. For Morelet himself, perhaps, rhetoric, as memoir, is the extended text where he expands upon some of the relevant data presented, and the space where the "I" (of "national emulation") comes to be constituted as a transnational scientific, superior, and civilized public French eye.

A reading of the memoir offers the parameters of the Academy, which I presume is funding the construction of the images of overseas countries as geographical and natural localities. The intent is very similar to ours today, to denationalize by discrediting processes of national formation— theirs in terms of development, ours in terms of the reluctance of nation-states to represent the people. The first parameter converts those countries, societies, and cultures into physical geographies—a road map, a listing of the principal names of towns, rivers, and cities, the physical characteristics of the terrain and of the soil, natural production, climate, natural conditions. Reduced to its geography and to its specimens and looked upon from afar, the region becomes a relatively good museum of natural history, whose collection contains minerals, plants and animals, some of which are not to be found in the French museum. Mineralogical samples, as well as samples of cryptograms and phanerograms, some grains and shrubs, resins, wood specimens, some sea specimens—sponges, starfishes, crustaceans, mollusks—in addition to vertebrates, reptiles, saurians, birds, and mammals; in sum, the results of his journey and explorations are, after the research trip is over, "in the hands of competent professors, who will make a just use of the materials [he has] given them for the benefit of science" (418).

The love for natural history, coupled with Morelet's honorable scientific spirit and a sense of national emulation, are the subjective reasons for undertaking a project that produces more than what the researcher purposefully intends. Equally as important as his collection of natural specimens are his collections of social data, and the conversion of this data into topographies and physical geographies. As with Squier, nature (geographies) becomes a warehouse storing the rich products that will come to satiate the cravings for investments—what in Morelet's narrative is called industry and commerce—in the regions overseas where the research has been undertaken.

The disadjustment between the extensive and the reduced narrative pointed to above is what stands out as the principle of rhetorical construction. Morelet meanders through narrative spaces that are apparently disconnected. The factual, such as events, things observed, scenery, or what Stephens called incidents, and even specimens come to him as if asking to be narrated. But what is the connecting thread constituting his logic? Or, more properly, of what type of logic is his narrative a sample? In the appendix, he explains that he is doing research for a natural history museum. But the space dedicated to other matters is as extensive, if not more so, than that dedicated to the museum. In that case, can Morelet's reporting on other cultural matters, his unseemly actions as an agent, his promotions of other products such as ancient cultures and American antiquities (the museums of the dead), alongside other natural products (the museum of the living), his detailing of transportation and communication routes, habits, and inhabitants, all be considered industry and commerce? The answer is in the affirmative. Morelet is a collector, acting as actuary, and his being there is representative of something else. He is there to serve as a vehicle and conduit, as a propagandist or censor. Through him, what is expressed is not the objectivity of objects but that of the subjective ruling. He is reproducing the socially prevalent categories of positivism, filling up the blanks with new raw data. He is adding to the inventory that upholds the status quo. In his travel narrative can be discerned all the elements of that cultural criticism characterized as immanent, positivistic, and subjective.

Morelet is a naturalist who carries on the extra duty of cultural criticism. He is as perplexed at the incivility of Central America—that is, at the lack of fit between the materiality observed (in situ facts and events) and the general concepts he brings from Europe to describe them—as he is charmed by the primitive tableaux, the utopian picturesque that provides solace, peace, and charm to his already harried professionalism. As Adorno will put it, Morelet "speaks as if he represented either unadulterated nature or a higher historical stage. Yet he is necessarily of the same essence as that to which he fancies himself superior."[15]

Perplexity and enchantment—Greenblatt's horror and wonder—are the twin moods ordering a positivistic narrative of everything observed, "facts," which he registers in an unarticulated manner and then gathers in chapters resembling each other. As in Stephens's incidents, here facts and events are passed through the European sorting machine to be properly classified according to their usefulness. Greenblatt has observed that travelers organize their narrative through the telling of anecdotes in which the interest in the particular serves to reinforce the general order or telos toward which all the events converge. Pragmatism and profitability are the means by which the gathering of data, or information, is transformed into knowledge, into scientific propositions carrying general truth-contents that conform to the identities of Central America. Yet, Morelet's aspirations to the scientific in the area of culture blatantly put in evidence a lack of fit. He is constantly disrupted. His attention span is brief. That is why his rhetorical organization, which consists of small fragments, constitutes an interrupted narrative. Minutiae perennially intercept the story line, warning the readers that the story itself, the incident, event, and fact narrated are, after all, not all that important; what is important is the general picture. A disqualifier of perception (or doubting at the center of the imperial imaginary) is built into the structure of perception itself, perception being the essential component of the methodologies of positive sciences. How far have we moved from the empirical dreams of accuracy described by Gonzalo Fernández de Oviedo?

In Morelet's series of small fragments, nothing is all that important. He finds refuge in his collection of specimens. There is, however, a pre-text, a proposal that is to constitute the central organizing principle of his narrative, his telos. This is dictated by the needs and demands of his trade as a naturalist, by the stage of data collection and description that is to feed the sciences of biology, zoology, agronomy, areas still without well-articulated discourses and therefore situated at the stage of mere description. Morelet collects samples of specimens to be displayed at the Parisian museum of natural history. But alongside his collection of natural data, he collects cultural data. The conceptual storehouse of positivism is a ready-made functional space with vacant slots to accommodate all data.

Morelet's observations of culture follow the same principles of natural data collection. Societies are reduced to observed facts, incidents, and events, which are in turn classified and stored under general concepts, the most important of which are industry and commerce. These two containers are set over and against his two other containers, flora and fauna, and these four categories fall squarely within the ideoscapes, that is, that which politicizes the data. The gathering enterprise veils the major object-concept (its telos), which is that of progress.

In Morelet's text, the categories form clusters that are not linearly and coherently organized; rather, they are loosely and casually interwoven, according to the circumstances of his travel and business. Yet, the articulation displays a pattern. The clusters of meaning can be reorganized so that they make up a professional profile of the naturalists and their needs. Interlaced nuclei of interest constitute controversial identities, not the least of which is his own subjectivity as separate from those of the narrated foreign. Morelet's self is located at the center of a forest, in the midst of a Romantic landscape, enhanced by the Maya "ruins," a self surrounded by the beauties of a recently built classicism. The focus of his attention is the collection of natural data, yet he simultaneously engages the production of meaning over cultural arrangements and artifacts, and evaluates his own materials in terms of eventual commerce and trade. Although the local political and cultural history is subordinated to the needs and interests of universal natural history, one of the real concerns is not natural but human science, not natural history but anthropology, or rather, their articulations, intersections, and interceptings. For instance, although the illustrations he includes in his text can be considered to be contingent, perhaps gathered post facto and with no other purpose than to convey a visual image consistent with the written, they display interest in a nomenclature that is urban, geographic, and archaeological. There are cities, maps, ruins, wood carvings, hieroglyphics, and theaters. The iconography itself grafts a museum into the museum. For instance, the representation of the island of Petén and town of Flores organizes the Spanish architecture and religious structure on top and what in Squier will become the houses of the undetermined mestizo-"Indians" at the bottom (see Figure 12).

If we compare the boats on the bay with the ships in the harbors depicted in Puntarenas, we can easily draw the contrast between modern industry and commerce and (pre)modern subsistence economies and barterings.

CONCLUSIONS

For centuries, wealth was, for the Europeans, America's main signifier; to become rich, the possibility of making fast and hard bullion, which so much beguiled their imaginaries, was the main attraction. However, what

Figure 12. The island of Petén and town of Flores. From Arthur Morelet, *Reisen in Central-Amerika* (Jena: Costenoble, 1872).

was in store for the newcomer in the nineteenth century was, in the words of their commanding officers, captains, traders, settlers, and immigrants, something altogether different. Arthur Morelet puts it as follows:

> The unfortunate Europeans who reside there [in Guatemala], seduced to the spot by exaggerated accounts of its wealth and facilities for enterprise . . . after having exhausted their resources in an expensive voyage, find, too late, all their illusions dispelled, and themselves reduced to the condition of abject dependence on the caprices of a suspicious and unsympathizing race. (380)

Race, "a suspicious and unsympathizing" one, is perhaps the central component of disillusionment, the place where what Walter Benjamin called the auratic—America as wealth—shriveled. Local culture is, then, all but attractive. In the cities,

> an air of solitude and abandonment pervades its environs; there are no gardens, no plantations, no country houses, nor any of those industrial establishments, which throng the approaches to our capitals. The houses of the suburbs are mere huts, covered with thatch, and separated from each other by hedges or open spaces of ground. (381)

The monuments are simply "heavy in style, and altogether in bad taste" (382). It is true that the seventeenth- and eighteenth-century cathedrals depicted in the drawings included in Morelet's text contrast with the more nineteenth-century neoclassic style of republican buildings, but the small towns must have more properly stood for those "exaggerated accounts of [American] wealth" of which he speaks. The pictures included in Morelet's text certainly highlight the contrast between the massive cathedral on the background and the mud and pole huts in the foreground. These small, single-room, single-story houses with thatched roofs and dirt floors, which were depicted so frequently in Stephens's narrative, rather speak about the poverty of the region and energize the same representational tropes.

The reproduction and reinforcement of unfamiliar identities that fortify previous imaginaries emplotting the continent are one of the main undertakings of nineteenth-century geographic-cum-naturalist narratives. Strangeness is the commodity produced by the recording eye. The main ethnic offensive of naturalists is launched against mestizos and Amerindians, who, in the European mind, are one and the same thing. The strangeness of race and buildings contrasts with the beauty of the grandiose landscapes, and with the transcendent, unclassifiable, and unique auratic or Mayan urban remains that produce the sublime. John Lloyd Stephens and Desiré Charnay see, describe, measure, and then locate this sublime within Orientalisms, by comparing it to Egypt and Mesopotamia, thus repeating and recycling what Spaniards invented. In 1530, Licenciado Palacios had already said that Copán was "a great city, such, it may well be presumed, as could never have been built by a people so rude as the natives of this country" (Stephens, *Incidents of Travel in Central America*, 242). The reason natives could not have constructed it is that it is "sculptured with much skill"; that "it is paved with beautiful stones, all square, and well worked"; that "it appears to have been constructed with the greatest care, for throughout we find the stones excellently well worked" (ibid., 242–43)—that is, technology coupled with beauty is what makes these works unworthy of Amerindian imagination and labor.

Beauty, as something distinct from the grandiose and the monumental, is emplotted as the picturesque, captured almost as in a watercolor portrait, light and airy, in the style of the illustration in Squier's text. The beautiful, or the picturesque, refers usually to a manageable portion of the landscape, or the representation and illustration of what can be easily manageable, to which other blissful aspects of nature, such as good weather, abundant natural specimens, and good topographies for transportation, trade, and extraction are added. A nineteenth-century *locus amoenus* is predicated on the collapsing of the categories of the manageable and the profitable, those fragments of the socius that can be captured within the type of miniaturization of the landscapes included in the reproductions that illustrate their texts. Graphs and production tables serve as a companion to this beautifully manageable picturesque. Here we can notice how conflicts between empirical vision and entrepreneurial expectations immediately ensue.

If to succeed during the colonial era means to take over the land and settle, to reduce and resettle populations, and to build cities; in the early postindependence or neocolonial era it means to draw accurately the physical and economic maps that serve projects of investments, to organize collections of natural, social, and cultural specimens, to fatten the historiographic body, and to produce information—and a new and more comprehensive and exhaustive catalog. Travel books and military reports are the most accountable narratives made in the service of this purpose. The researched societies are laboratories. The local societies themselves do not seem able to compete in the production of their own representation. Julio Ramos writes that the distance between the (colonial) subject and industry, utility, railroads, colonization of lands, all emblems of modernization, is notable—a conspicuous distinction if we remember that this is a history produced by the same intellectual bureaucracy. But local intellectual bureaucracies can collaborate with the project, and some do. The Economic Society of Friends of the Country, a group of rich liberal criollos, in conjunction with the Royal Geographic Society of London, for instance, produced documents that acted as road maps into the country. Such is the case of Juarros in Guatemala, later discredited by Squier, whose work is commissioned by England and published in that country.

Already in the eighteenth century, Fuentes y Guzmán had set the native basis for a tradition in which description of lands meant possession of lands, a way of inscribing within the register of intellectual properties, criollos' agricultural properties, certifying that they were the owners of the physical and of the symbolic land(scapes). If the production of narratives of research and development incorporated the exploratory moments of a literature of war, thus making a profitable transaction in reinvesting culture into culture and in creating the cultural trust fund (patrimony/tradition) so that it would accrue value, the narratives on race reinvested the narratives of the missionaries in order to devalue the indigenous. Racist narratives only credited Stephens and Fredrick Catherwood by the inclusion of their passages and drawings, thus enabling the distinction between ethnology and archaeology. The recycling of these narratives, whose place and selected passages must be theorized, also furthers the effect of accountability in the repetition of incidents, events, and facts, which reaches the observed objective.

As in the case of R. R. Madden in the West Indies, the set of illustrations included in Morelet's texts presents two alternative views of his disillusionment. Perspective is used in the case of the city of Guatemala to portray types of people who could be either indigenous or mestizos with a city whose streets can really be thought of as muddy but not asymmetrical, and where the absence of gardens is conspicuous. As usual, the Spanish elements constituted by religious buildings are located in the background. The illustration of the hills of Tierra Templada follows the same principle in counterposition with the close-ups of Depilto, a mining town in Nueva Segovia, and of Granada, Nicaragua. The cathedral of Comayagua in Honduras, and that of San Miguel in San Salvador, present alternative styles of buildings. In the case of San Miguel and in contrast with the portrayals of ports, what is foregrounded is oxcarts and canvases protecting what looks like the selling of products in a small marketplace. The size of the human figures does not allow one to distinguish the dressing styles, which can be easily confused with indigenous garb, but does allow one to see the way in which people carry objects on their heads. The theater of Guatemala has already moved from the "heavy style" of the baroque to the most appreciated straight lines of the neoclassic, a style more congenial with the counting and accountable styles of the epoch, with symmetry, one that makes Europeans feel at ease, possibly because it erases the presence of the indigenous.

To sum up, the work of nineteenth-century geographers and naturalists, the positivistic representation of Central America, is more accurate and better measured than the colonial narratives of friars, *oidores*, and court administrators. The new prose of the world is the prose of research and development, the prose of investments. Antigua, the old Spanish capital city, was the beneficiary of those investments in the twentieth century. Declared patrimony of humanity by UNESCO, it graciously displays its Spanish architecture. Old buildings, reconstructed or in ruins, serve as a romantic backdrop to the students and tourists who come to visit it every year. One of Antigua's buildings is Casa Santo Domingo, the Dominican convent that once housed the first Quiché-Maya scholars—friars Bartolomé de Las Casas, Antonio de Remesal, and Francisco Ximénez. It is now a five-star hotel that, having been partially reconstructed, uses the destroyed convent walls and all the colonial church images as decoration. The blending of historical moments brings about memories of the destroyed city of Utatlán. Situated to the north of Antigua, Utatlán, the egregious indigenous center of power, is a mute witness of a protracted warfare. The long period of militarization of the Guatemalan highlands and the massacres of the descendants of the old Quiché-Maya bring echoes of a story that began many centuries ago with the battle over Utatlán. Ruins, horses, helicopters, and submachine guns, coupled with research on cultural topographies, bear witness to the intimate relation between past and present histories and historiographies whose purpose is the object of this study.

PART III

THE AMAZON JUNGLE

c h a p t e r   6

THE VOID

The "barbarian" has not been that creature just coming out of the animal condition still abandoned to the empire of the senses and instincts which one could very often imagine, and neither is he that consciousness dominated by affectivity and drowned within confusion and participation.

—CLAUDE LÉVI-STRAUSS, *La Pensée Sauvage*

PHYSICAL AND IMAGINARY EXPERIENCES OF PLACE

In his famous text *Um paraiso perdido* (1976), Euclides da Cunha states, "in facing the real Amazon, we see it as inferior to the subjective image a long time prefigured."[1] In this chapter I make use of da Cunha's idea to explore the problem of the epistemological gap between the physical and the imaginary experience of place.[2] I argue that throughout the centuries, jungle has been explicitly thematized as that which is beyond grasp, as a resiliency that sets restrictions to the dominant discourse from within.[3] The net result is a genealogy that, in constructing jungle, extrapolates the aesthetics of landscaping to the production of primary needs, the supplying of raw materials for development projects, and the mapping of the hideouts of people. My interest lies in reconfiguring this extrapolation to underscore the correlations between aesthetic and material production, development projects, and the rights of Amerindian people. I begin with the work of Friar Gaspar de Carvajal (1541), and subsequently read Sir Walter Raleigh (1596), António Vieira (1650), Francisco Xavier de

Mendonça Furtado (1751), as well as the fictions of Mario Vargas Llosa, Alejo Carpentier, and Wilson Harris. I also draw on films on the Amazon jungle as counterpoint.

The representation of Amazonia as a humongous ungovernable void, or that which rends empirical vision and subjective understanding or imagination apart, is a colonial legacy.[4] The first text written on the subject, Father Gaspar de Carvajal's, already raises the question of how to bridge the gap between the physical and the imaginary representation of place. How to render one reality visible to another; how to change the substance of one, making it appear as the other; how to merge the rhetorical technologies of the "old" with the unrepresentable presence of the "new." In the seventeenth and eighteenth centuries, António Vieira and Francisco Xavier de Mendonça Furtado express similar anxieties. They write about the obduracy of Amazonian Amerindian languages in relation to conversion, and the government of "Indians." In the nineteenth century, Alexander von Humboldt comments on the unsignifying capacity or opacity of European languages when trying to describe the unfamiliar new.[5] In the twentieth century, Claude Lévi-Strauss reinforces Humboldt's concerns and, in defining Mato Grosso, he clarifies that it does not mean "great forest" but "great bush."[6] Latin American fiction writers such as Vargas Llosa, Carpentier, and Harris have also fallen prey to the same colonial dilemmas. But my favorite quote regarding this question is Werner Herzog's. For him, Amazonia is

> Prehistorical. The only thing lacking is dinosaurs. It is like a curse weighing into an entire landscape and whoever goes deep into this has his share of this course. It is a land that God . . . created in anger. It is the only land where creation is unfinished yet. . . . There is a sort of harmony. It is the harmony of overwhelming and collective murder. And we, in comparison to the articulated vileness and fallness and obscenity of all this jungle . . . , we only sound and look like badly pronounced and half-finished sentences of a stupid suburban novel. . . . We have to become humble in front of this overwhelming misery, and overwhelming fornication, overwhelming growth. . . . Even the stars up here in the sky look like a mess. There is no harmony in the universe. . . . There is no real harmony as we have conceived it. But when I say this, I say it all in full admiration to the jungle. It is not that I hate it. I love it. I love it very much. But I love it against my better judgement.[7]

If we take jungle to mean that which eludes, is intractable, or breaks the system from within, jungle is first and foremost constituted as a liminal border, an *orilla*. Written as forest, wood, or wilderness, jungle is a divider, and specifically refers to a ne plus ultra, a frontier, or empty signifier, at times lacking all but generic natural referentiality. The truth is that the terminology is overburdened by a certain exploratory sensibility that would come to bear on the representation of nature in the texts of geographers and naturalists trying to contain it. Even though in recent literature of Amazonia forests, woods and wilderness have been used interchangeably to represent jungle, each word actually pertains to separate paradigms of nature and consequently functions within different cultural economies.

Just to set a contrast, in nineteenth-century U.S. literature, for example, wood and forest are types of wilderness that share some of the attributes of jungle and could be considered its cognate. In the U.S. colonies, wilderness also marked *orillas* and signaled the void, a territory off limits, upon which, as Humboldt put it poetically, "man has never laid his destroying hand" (193). Annette Kolodny states that this off-limits nature poses a contrast with prairies as manageable and visible expanses of land easily transformed into gardens—that is, productive areas. Woods, she argues, are the sites of maleness, à la Daniel Boone; prairies, sites of women. Wilderness is thus on one side, un- or not-yet developed nature, and, on the other, an available emptiness. In Spanish, the terms for jungle belong to an altogether semantic field, whose expressions have no exact equivalents in English. *Manigua* and *selva*, for example, connote absolute limits and could be roughly translated as bush, shrub—*mato grosso*. Thus, although jungle and wilderness are related and both might signify *orillas*, the English words never fully embody the culturally encoded Spanish meaning.[8] *Manigua* could be wilderness, as *selva* could be forest or thicket, but neither of them ever achieves the overwhelming plenitude of jungle, which is impassable and intractable. Linguistic frustration is fundamentally an indicator that jungle resists containment, that is, it could never be completely appropriated. Thus, jungle articulates barriers to development. But there is something much more important inherent to this discussion, and that is that jungle is also home to Amerindian people, and therefore that all discussions about it are closely entwined with matters relative to colonialism, politics, policy, and human rights. In this regard, jungle also brings up questions relative to governability and administration.

THE AGRARIAN UTOPIAN DISCOURSE

The first written account of a voyage up the Amazon River is *The Discovery of the Amazon according to the Account of Friar Gaspar de Carvajal*, published in 1541.[9] Carvajal narrates the troubled voyage of Francisco de Orellana, "a captain and lieutenant-governor of the city of Santiago . . . which is in the province of Peru" and his crew across the Amazon River, "[i]n order that there may be a better understanding of the whole progress of events in connection with this voyage" (167). On the surface, the explicit purpose of this incursion is uniquely exploratory. What is at stake is nothing less than the establishment of the geographic and cartographic coordinates of the "new" territories. However, two themes arise: one is the rights of Amerindian peoples, the other, the resiliency of their languages and cultures. The difficulties of the grasping and rendering of jungle are unavoidably entwined with these two themes.

Carvajal begins describing jungle as a generic geography: rapids, forkings, whirlpools, and torrents. The reader knows about the speed of currents, depth of the river, direction, and confluence. Jungle is nature and at most geography. Yet, Carvajal's natural geography is immediately snarled in a web of European codes. Caught up between the precepts of medieval and Renaissance rhetoric, he now renders a vision of jungle as a landscape of symbols, now emphasizes commerce and underlines the usefulness of wealth and possessions. Thus Carvajal's geographies take the form and shape of what Kenneth Clark calls "Renaissance agrarian landscapes."[10] At best they organize utopian visions, and at worst form the backdrop for an encyclopedia of generic and allegorical elements in the style of the herbalists or calendar illustrators.

There is thus a structure of feelings intercepting Carvajal's geographical description of the Amazonian jungle. This sensibility expresses itself as the pleasure of the senses, which takes off from the nature of the jungle itself, and empties in the agricultural and horticultural utopian imaginaries of food production and commerce. After all, the pretext of the journey is spices—"and because of the numerous reports which circulated regarding a country where cinnamon existed, out of a desire to serve His Majesty in exploring for the said cinnamon . . . [Orellana] went to the town of Quito, where the said Gonzalo Pizarro was, to see him and put him in possession of the said territory" (167). And this search for spices produces the encounter with "the new," in this case, the river and the riverine people.

The logic of this construction is clear: what begins in a natural description of the local geographies ends in the desire for its appropriation for production. In his prose, Carvajal encourages the contemplation and vision of landscapes as profitable, lands to be developed. This country, he says, "is very rich in silver . . . [it] is very pleasing and attractive and very plentifully supplied with all kinds of food and fruit . . . pineapples and pears, which in the language of New Spain are called 'aguacates' . . . and many other kinds of fruit and of very good quality" (203). He has a keen eye for identifying the fertility of the soil, made available through the traces of burned fields. Breeding livestock is foreordained because grass grows just as in Spain. The Amazon is thus imagined in terms of agrarian productivity. The imaginary of cities closes the circle begun with the reconfiguration of the wild frontier into fields, orchards, and meadows mirrored in discourse. To the early European explorers and the late U.S. developers, the jungle, projected into the future, should look like a place of fair cities, good roads, burgeoning villages, and huge fields, where once only wilderness stood.[11] Planting, harvesting, breeding livestock, fishing, plus abundance of woods of evergreen and hard oak, compose a cornucopia of the beautiful rolling savannas and woodlands. This is, in essence, the agrarian utopian dicourse.

Yet, the agrarian utopian discourse is interrupted at the moment the specter of Amerindians comes into the scene and drives a wedge at the heart of the imperial self. The story begins with the sounds of drums followed by the sounds of words. The first thing to occur is that the imperial subject, Carvajal, is forced to shift the organs of perception from the eyes (which up to this point have freely roamed about the natural landscape of jungles imagining utopias) to the ear, which must make do with the sounds he hears. Sounds make Carvajal's story veer in a radically opposite direction. The exploratory text becomes undone and agrarian utopias turn into war narratives. Sounds interrupt the steady and otherwise unwavering gesture toward settlement. Sounds intercept the concurrence of aesthetics and productivity and put on hold all imagined agrarian communities. Sounds immediately write the confrontation with the Amazonian people into the exploratory text. If the natural geographic narratives of jungle bring with them the imaginaries of agrarian utopias and a subjective pleasure written in a cross between Renaissance and medieval aesthetics, the presence of people will open up to two critical intersections, one with ethnography and the other with politics. Both are deeply implicated in each other.

THE ETHNOGRAPHIC AND POLITICAL DISCOURSES: "INDIANS" "OF PEACE" AND "OF WAR"

The ethnographic discourse takes charge of descriptions, and works on the cultural profiles of people. The political discourse feeds on the ethnographic discourse and tries to come up with policies regarding the distinctions in "Indians" between "Indians of peace" and "Indians of war." Thus, from the very outset, the two discourses are closely intertwined. While the ethnographic discourse sets the conditions for conforming and containing the ontologies of the indigenous and provides a secure and safe grid to grapple with them, the political discourse supplies all the methodological cues for spinning the concepts, turning confrontations into encounters, oppression and domination into Christian teachings, and colonialism into the pursuit of knowledge. "Indians of peace" and "Indians of war" are the formulas that serve as a pivot between ethnography and politics, but also between geography, ethnography, and the aesthetic sublime. The same formulas explain how European and Amerindian subjectivities inform one another.

In the early days of the ethnographic discipline, when ethnography was still a subset of Christianity and priests were in charge of the management of people, the descriptive and organizing structure of the ethnographic discourse stopped short of its object. There was not much description, except of war; of dress, except when gold was involved; of everyday life, except when it referred to religious functions. Ironically enough, the two most salient cultural traits of ethnic groups recorded were generosity ("Indians of peace," noble savages) and combativeness ("Indians of war," cannibals).[12] Therefore, from the beginning, the ethnographic and political discourses are directly linked to the management of populations or to population control. Politics is discussed through the multiple implications of the categorization of Amerindian people as people "of peace" and people "of war." The discrepancy between one type of "Indian" and another bears the marks of a call for a different conceptual understanding of the jungle. As it stands, it is the Amerindian peoples who bring the imaginaries of *terra nullius* to a close, and scratch the veneer of aesthetics, leaving the politics of colonialism oozing through the wound. Their agency subverts the imperial text from within, forcing the distinctions between nature and polis, nature and society, *terra nullius* and inhabited lands.

The real service rendered by ethnography to the future of dominant discourse is not solely the gathering of data to depict aboriginal societies but locking into place the system of thinking and writing these societies as the reverse or negation of the European. And the biggest service rendered by ethnography to politics is first and foremost the grounding of the concept "Indian" as a unified and uniform political category. To reach this definition, ethnography first isolates and underscores the traits unifying those human groups, works in detail their numerical strength and subsequently their types in accord with their social organization and technological dexterity—weapons and their uses are the main topics implicated in this representation. Community classification, enumeration, censuses, and negation are the technologies that produce the anatomical and visceral organism of "Indians." "Indian" is an ethnographic concept because it classifies; but it becomes a political concept because, in discussing questions relative to rights and entitlements, it disenfranchises.[13] As we had the opportunity to learn in the discussion of islands and highlands, all these perceptions run through the works of nineteenth-century geographers and commissioners whose voices are fastened to these anchoring previous thinkers.

"Indians of peace" is an easy category to understand, because it is essentially constituted as a service category—"Indians" that make "the Captain . . . delighted at their having turned back" (Carvajal, *The Discovery of the Amazon*, 228). "Indians of war" are harder to classify. But both types of "Indians" are construed in terms of the invention of agricultural arcadias and predicated on settlement and food production. Thus, if "Indians of peace" produce food, "Indians of war" disrupt it. Food and hunger are tropes endowed with rhetorical virtues. Food lies at the basis of the discourse on agriculture; hunger makes the exploratory discourse swing from the epic to the grotesque, from the sublime to the visceral, from the cultural imaginary to the empirical nitty-gritty, and, most important, from "Indians of peace" to "Indians of war."

In Carvajal's expedition, hunger is the trope overwhelming the narrative.

The protagonists are always looking for food, not finding enough food, lacking food, being provided with food, tasting new food, or going hungry.[14] Hunger accounts for the production of cross-cultural interactions from which a categorization of people will ensue. Hunger also produces cultural adjustments—Jean de Léry writes that he learned that by boiling raw hides, the members of the French expedition to Brazil could survive. Furthermore, hunger humanizes the encounter for the Spaniards and changes the heroic high-mimetic into the low-mimetic grotesque.[15] Carvajal writes:

> [A]nd when the said Cristobal Maldonado saw the Indians coming back, he rallied his companions and attacked the enemy, and here they . . . were held in check for a long time, because there were more than two thousand Indians and of the companions who were with Critical . . . there were only ten. . . . In the end such superior skill was displayed that they [the Amerindians] were routed, and they [Maldonado's men] again started to collect the food. (193)

For the topic we are treating, the most conspicuous word in this passage is *enemy*—the "Indian of war" in action. It is most extraordinary that this enemy has the power to turn ten Spanish men into sixteenth-century clones of postmodern Rambos and cyborgs. They fight and rout two thousand "Indians" and report only two wounded. In a second skirmish, Carvajal reported six wounded—no casualties. Is this not an action that neatly ties war and the "Indians" that enable it to rhetoric, in particular to the high-mimetic heroic, and the high-mimetic to the much less heroic necessity of eating? Is it not the "Indian of war" who in turn enhances the value of the imperial self, narrated in a hyperbolic tone, and constructed as heroic when utterly dispossessed and starving superhuman beings confront unedited danger? What is really at issue in this stylistic crisscrossing of high and low mimesis, ethnography and geography, is certainly not aesthetics but the symbiotic relation of peace and of war with ethnicity and services.[16]

Now, let us examine the relationship between peace and war in the writing of Amerindians by the colonial text from another angle. Carvajal writes:

> At the end of two leagues of advancing down the river we saw coming up the river to look over and reconnoiter the land four canoes filled with Indians,

and, when they saw us, they turned about at great speed, giving the alarm, in such a manner that in less than a quarter of an hour we heard in the villages many drums from very far off and are so well attuned that they have their bass and tenor and treble. (173)

In this quote, two groups catch a glimpse of each other. In eyeing each other, "we saw . . . they saw," the "Indians" spot danger and run away beating the signs of alarm. These "Indians" are men of peace just reconnoitering the land, navigating the river. What suggests that they are men of war is the post facto sound of drums. What makes very little sense in this quote and reveals the irony of the situation is that whereas the Amerindians take flight in fear, Carvajal (as later on de Letéry) turns to aesthetics and focuses on the rhythmic nature of the percussion instruments. If what is really being suggested is that these "Indians" have given a sign of alarm, why are the Spaniards playing it so cool? Are we not to deduce they are also afraid and ready for combat? My answer is that in this passage, as in many others, in addition to the use of aesthetics to cover up the real purposes and methods of colonialism, we face an ellipsis. Something is being skipped, edited, or chipped away, and that is, on the one hand, fear and, on the other, the Spanish readiness for combat. Fear is the only possible explanation for the destabilization of the narrative. And it stands to reason that fear, the fear of Amerindians, triggers self-defense and self-defense immediately turns an "Indian of peace" into an "Indian of war." It also leads us to surmise that the absence of Amerindians produces joy, because all obstacles for a "very pretty land" and a "very fruitful land" to reemerge are removed, and that empty lands (as in the United States) are paradoxically the condition for the production of the utopian agrarian narratives of conquest.[17] The zero degree of Amerindians brings aesthetics back into the text as the medium that enables the transformation of nature into wealth, food, and spices.

There are other problems with this classification "of peace" and "of war," such as the equalization of subjectivities. In war, both warriors are of equal value, and therefore it is safe to state that there is no distinction between a European man and an Amerindian man. Remember the case of Tecúm Umám and Alvarado in the Guatemalan highlands? However, the problem here is twofold: that Europeans do not want to write themselves as equals to Amerindians, either in peace or at war; and that colonialism does not write itself as an attack. It writes itself as knowledge (geographic, ethno-graphic, and political) or as teaching (Christianity, languages, and cultures). In this sense, there is no logical connection, no way of truly unraveling the dichotomy "of peace" and "of war," unless we turn the tables and call the colonizers liars, as Stephen Greenblatt does, or predators, as Jay Appleton does.[18]

Furthermore, if predator is an appropriate metaphor for the European explorer, the metaphor is appropriate for reading the strategies of his discourse, which swings widely between the aesthetic sublime encoding agrarian utopias, and war encoding the ethnographies of peaceful and warlike Amerindians. The circularity of the argument is fully expressed in the wide oscillation between the two. The intuition of a human settlement instantaneously triggers the swing. As soon as the aesthetic sublime comes up against the wall of Amazonian people, agrarian utopias become bat-tlefields. As a result, all kinds of contradictory and confused feelings ensue. Thus, what begins as an inability to grasp and render turns into the fantasy of imagining designs for the erection of cities and the reorganiza-tion of the socius, which is interrupted by people. We have already seen (in chapter 4) how the social organization is accessed through an ample gamut of jurisdictional divisions. The distinction between "Indians of peace" and "Indians of war" underscores now the recognition that, after all, the wild frontier needs to be governed.

As we have noticed in other instances of construction of topographies, warfare is the best technology to resolve conflicts over jurisdictions. In the invention of America, we can safely conclude, one of the strongest tropes is war. War is the ideal medium to insert aboriginal human agency into the narratives of exploration. War is a type of writing with weapons. War brings into being the necessities of disciplinary displacements visible in narrative intersections. War is the device that swings the information on people back and forth from ethnography to history, from geography to politics, from the projects of civilization to those of barbarism. War writes the story with blood and it is with blood and in blood that the colonial text is written. Blood speaks of territorialities and jurisdictions, and sub-tly effects the idea of the indigenous jungle blank space, the void. And ultimately, war, contrary to what Tzvetan Todorov wants to believe, is what introduces Amerindians into the symbolic debate. War tilts the scale in favor of Cornejo Polar and de Certeau, who remind us that war is at the

beginning and at the end of the story of writing, as we can read it in all
the documents, beginning with the anchoring documents of exploration
and continuing up to narratives of research and development and environmental movements.[19] War is the untold story, the story of Amerindians as residual agencies, the leftovers that subtend the ethnographic
impulse that supports all types of narratives, from the sixteenth century to
today.

Related to this question is the exacerbation of the "Indian of war" in the
figure of the cannibal.[20] But this is neither the time nor the place to speak
about it. Suffice it to say that cannibal is another ready-made ethnographic category. This category hovers at the margins to express that feature which makes possible the perception of "Indians" as people "of war."
On its flip side, this very same category permits one to speak about the
colonizer as a beast of prey.[21] What is important is that the attributes "of
peace" and "of war" bear the signs of early managerial techniques that
serve to rend the narrated Amerindians for good, while simultaneously
writing the inseparable unit between primary interlocutors, "Indians" and
the colonial self. The corollaries are, first, that not one but at least two
divides are created; and, second, that colonizer and colonized are subjectivities constituted back-to-back. Aesthetics constitutes the former, and
ethnography takes charge of the latter.

WORDS AND WEAPONS

A few words on words is necessary to round out the analysis of Carvajal's
narrative. As already stated, in Carvajal's narrative the rhetorical turning
point between productive and war narratives occurs when the imperial self
changes organs of perception from eyes to ears, from seeing to hearing to
narrate his story. Let us begin by acknowledging that, in colonial writing,
ellipsis is a moment of silence in which words speaking about the real
terms of the encounter/confrontation are omitted.[22] Subtracting Spanish
fear from the encounter is one example of such elliptical strategy. In the
"contact zone," or in the "space of interaction," Spaniards are carrying on
an all-out offensive against the populations, and the contending groups do
not approach each other through words.[23] If words are enunciated, they
are merely empty sounds, air, noises, wind.[24] The meeting of the groups
can never be reduced to a mere exchange of words.

In Cornejo Polar's reading of the encounter between Amerindians and Spaniards, there is only "mutual strangeness and . . . reciprocal and aggressive repulsion" (26), a point of "total friction," "a clash between orality . . . [and] writing" (27). Total lack of understanding between the parties is what is being historically staged. During the eighteenth century, Vieira and de Mendonça amply testify to this problem. Jean de Léry states that when they arrived in the Amazon, he found himself "surrounded by savages, who were asking [him] 'Marapé-derere, marapéderere?' meaning 'What is your name? What is your name?' (which at that time [he] understood no better than High German)."[25] And Francisco de Figueroa observes: "On the way up the river it was not possible for the armada to be certain of anything they found, because they never spoke directly with the inhabitants, and if the Portuguese understood anything, it was through signs that were so uncertain that the meanings applied to them varied with what each Portuguese had in his thoughts."[26]

Echoing de Mendonça and Figueroa, Greenblatt explains how absurd the phrase that they understood each other is, and makes us reflect on the use of signs and sign language. He observes that sign language is not necessarily transcultural, and illustrates how, in certain instances, an act of friendliness—such as staging a dance—is immediately transcoded as a declaration of war. Greenblatt's poignant thesis is that the chroniclers were liars, and lying the principle of discourse formation. How, then, in the face of such evidence, can the documents talk about encounter rather than confrontation? Would it not be more accurate to talk about weapons rather than about words? Addressing this issue, Alfred Métreaux asserts that warlike relations between Europeans and Amerindians explain why weapons "are the only aspects of native culture known to us. Travelers have always shown a particular interest in weapons."[27] In the contemporary world, several films have contributed to the discussion of words versus weapons. In *Aguirre: The Wrath of God* (1972), a film by Werner Herzog based on the incursion of Lope de Aguirre down the Amazon, the language of Amerindians is signified by all kinds and sizes of spears, always piercing a vital organ, the jugular, the heart, the kidneys. In *The Emerald Forest* (1985), a film by John Boorman, arrows, darts, spears, and the colors of feathers are the only identity card to differentiate "fierce people," "bat people," and "invisible people" from "termite people"—people "who come down into the world and chew down all the grandfather trees just like termites."

In Carvajal, however, there is no abundance of weapons. In fact, the incident of losing a bolt that is subsequently found inside a fish they caught downstream—an incident that will surprisingly reemerge in the ironic rewriting of Spanish narratives by English literary-oriented planters such as Monk Lewis in the nineteenth-century Caribbean—is used as a sign of their shortage of weapons, the scarcity of iron needed to make nails to build boats, or rafts (poetically filmed in technicolor by Herzog in *Aguirre*). Furthermore, Carvajal makes one wonder if Spaniards are supposed to report that they were not heavily armed when in fact they were—or to report that they were when in fact they were not. The question is, are they really lying or simply caught up in the aporias of their own narrow and local paradigms? The type of weapons in reference to their courage serves as support to Rambo-like encounters.

On this question, in his book on the Canary Islands, Crosby plots hundreds of Europeans with "few inaccurate, slow-firing, often misfiring guns, a larger number of crossbows, and lots of metal swords, axes, and lances versus . . . thousands of courageous warriors armed with weapons that, though made of mere wood and stone, were murderous enough" (84). In Crosby's narrative, the indigenous populations "hurled their stones . . . with the velocity and accuracy of crossbows, breaking a shield in pieces, and the arm behind it" (85). De Léry is of the same opinion when he argues against harquebuses in favor of arrows: "the harquebus makes a much bigger hole [but] . . . our savages, strong and robust, shoot so straight that they will pierce through the body of a man as easily with an arrow as another will do with a harquebus shot" (115).

These are arguments in favor of a more balanced picture of the colonial confrontation. Numbers and weapons are war arguments that substitute for the voice and the writings of Amerindians. In the description of battles, de Léry mentions them assembled in groups of "eight or ten thousand men" (ibid.). In Cristóbal de Acuña, the names of places and of Amerindian groups inscribed in his work are so numerous as to cause a confusion very similar to Pedro de Alvarado's mappings of the Guatemalan highlands.[28] The real question is why, despite their numbers, Amerindians lost the battle to colonization, and the answer is yet to be found. Stories about internecine disputes and language differences only partially explain this big defeat. Perhaps Crosby is right when he writes that fear and allure, their metals, gear, and gods, "tended to sap [the Amerindian] resolve to

reject utterly—and violently, if necessary—all contact with these dangerous aliens" (88). Inga Clendinnen had convincingly argued that the Mayas
lacked the idea of a total war and when they had succeeded in expelling
the Spaniards from what Amerindians considered their territories, they set
them loose. Raleigh reports incidents along identical lines as Clendinnen.
This permitted the Spaniards to regroup and come back again and fight
until the aborigines were defeated. However, the fact is that in the narratives of the Amazonian jungle, neither America nor Amerindians are written as something that resists.[29] American topographies are written as the
"projection of sameness": "a cover-up."[30] In the layering of codes and the
cross-weaving of the empirical and the subjective, Europeans begin "to
invent their own image and similitude [*semejanza*]" (Dussel, *1492*, 35).

ON SPYING: DESCRIPTION AS HEARING— INTELLIGENCE, INTELLEGERE, INFORMATION

More than half a century after Orellana's trip down the Amazon River, in
1596 Sir Walter Raleigh published *The Discoverie of the Large, Rich and
Bewtiful Empyre of Guiana*, which narrates his incursion into Amazonia
via the Atlantic.[31] The title fulfills the commercial, administrative, and governmental narrative protocols of the epoch, and furnishes the proof that
the expedition has reached its destiny. Furthermore, it summarizes and
contains the main attributes of the object to be narrated. "Large, Rich and
Bewtiful" are features in consonance with the summary statement, a kind
of bill of sale or briefing that an entrepreneur must give after a military-
cum-business expedition.

We are here in the presence of a different mentality in the discursive
apparatus of continental literature on Amazonia. The English expedition
arrived in Trinidad on March 22, 1595, and ventured into mainland territories one year later, in 1596, escorted by Amerindians. The narrative itself
presents a confusion of data similar to that narrated by Wilson Harris four
centuries later. Harris maps the same obstructive geographies in his
Guyana Quartet, which situates us again in the "generic beyond." The
ledge of high and impassable mountains, the innumerable branches of
rivers emptying into other innumerable rivers, the presence of gold and
Amerindians, rapids, shallowness or fullness of currents, protracted state
of warfare—are all symptomatic of the period as well as of tropes of the

rhetoric of empires. They provide the anecdotes of a narrative that, as Greenblatt argues, "gestures toward what is not in fact expressed, to create the illusion of presences that are in reality absent" (*Marvelous Possessions*, 61). But what is novel in Raleigh, which is not in the Spanish or Portuguese geographic narratives, is a display of the system of information on which the English empire relies to make its *avanzadas* (forays).

Intelligence (*intelligere*) and information shift organs of knowledge from seeing to hearing. To hear and be heard are the paradigmatic gestures of discourse; so too is the criterion for sifting information. Raleigh's narrative relies on being informed, or "on spying" and intelligence. For him, intelligence mediates the political and military discourse and makes possible the conflation of the narratives of exploration, war, and the extraction of wealth. But who informs him? He is being informed by the main protagonists of the moment, by Amerindians, Spaniards, and the English. What do they inform him about? The evidence shows that what is privileged in hearing relates to military and geographic data. Amerindians inform him on alliances, history, and geography. Spaniards inform him on geography, on Amerindians and their forays, division, and skirmishes. The backdrop is always the climactic encounters in Peru and Mexico, which interweave military and exploratory geography with wealth. This system of cross-information permits the comparison between the two sets of data recorded by the English, who inform on the Spanish and "Indians" as well as on geography and geology. All this information is kept duly compartmentalized.

In the area of what he calls Guiana, later to become Maranhão in the writings of de Mendonça and Vieira, and today Amazonia, other minor but equally intensive and relentless skirmishes are being waged. What in the language of nations will be called wars, or military intervention, here is outlined as exploration, a term that subsumes, subdues, and sublates the Amerindian struggles for their territory. At the same time, this type of discourse foregrounds European accomplishments as the foundation of disciplines—cartographies as the landscaping of raw natural resources. But, because Amerindians are the protagonists of these struggles to settle scores over the land and its possession and repossession, they are called caciques or rulers, "Lords of the people" (4), or "Lords or Kings of the borders" (30). Borders is a shifting concept of limits related to jurisdiction and entitlements—simply put, the right to a habitat, the freedom of the performance of choice. Borders in Raleigh, like *terras* and *nações* in Vieira, are empty slots that house disparate and often paradoxical concepts related to limits and jurisdictions. But in this passing on of information we also hear what for me is Raleigh's true concern, namely, the geology of a terrain, which is yet to be taken away from the naturals—a nature not yet, but about to be, classified, stored in disciplines, and thus expropriated. Raleigh's discourse is both text and pre-text, the very condition of a discourse on mineralogy. His motto is "I have anatomized" (A5). He is anatomizing the continent, beginning with the Empire of Guyana. In his nominalization we can trace the skeleton of a territory that depicts his route and all the key locations of his journey. We know that he has taken a reconnaissance trip. He has traveled across the coast of the entire Caribbean continental mainland and, as in the Guatemalan highlands, military history records the genealogy and routes of conquerors and conquered.

The facsimile I am reading is divided into three parts. The first part is for the government official, "Lord and kinsman Charles Howard, night of the Garter, Barron, and Counceller, and of the Admirals of England the most renowned: And to the Right Honorable Sr. Robert Cecyll Knight, Councelor in her Highness privie Councels" (A2). Like Arthur Morelet's précis, which was analyzed in chapter 5, this is the part of the document that can—or cannot—be made public, in which Raleigh states his own troubles. The first part is constituted as the space of subjectivity and narrated in the prose of sentimentalism. It allows the tropes of disgrace, disadvantage, poverty, and difficulties to be stated in a style reminiscent of Christopher Columbus. The reader is privy to an intimate conversation between subject and government official. The rhetoric of sentimentalism, in this case, has the force of a plea. It is an appeal that presumes compassion and cultural understanding. At the same time, it asks for recognition of the moral principle that to oppress others is to oppress oneself, begging to recognize our own human condition by recognizing the human conditions of others. Thus, the first part of Raleigh's facsimile is a disrobing, the discursive surface where the English subject permits him to uncover himself rhetorically to his superiors, and where he honorably and deservedly "begs" for favors. "Sorrows, labor, hunger, heat, sickness, & peril" (A3), which have been followed by slander and insinuations of treason, are now settled, for he has "returned a beggar" (A4). This part briefly outlines the topographies he visited, the main ports of entry, the genealogy of the

Spanish conquest of Peru, a startlingly accurate profile of the coast from Trinidad all the way to "Iucata" to the north, to Peru to the west, and to Manoa (the locus of El Dorado) traveling inland westward.

The second part, titled "To the Reader," is a précis, a section that may have been released and circulated after the document was approved and considered advantageous to disseminate. This section is brief, only six pages in length, but contains an appraisal of the mineralogical wealth of the area explored, with some concise references to geography, including a brief summary of routes and populations. The last fragment, which indeed constitutes the corpus of the report, is completely devoid of sentimentalism and the expression of subjectivity, and is hence more officially public and more clearly a business document. What is of importance is clearly stated, namely, that there seems to be a great quantity of gold. Some of the gold has already been removed and worked upon, while more is still to be extracted. For the gold already mined, there is need of politics and policy; for the gold remaining, there is need of further appraisal and technology. This information is composed of in situ appraisal, partly of testimonial accounts, hearsay, and partly eyewitness accounts given by a hundred pairs of eyes. Raleigh writes:

> It hath also been concluded by divers, that if there had been anie such oare in Guiana, and the same discovered, that I woulde have brought home a greater quantitie thereof: first I was not bounde to satisfie anie man of the quantitie . . . . : but it is very true that had all their mountaynes beene of massie gold, it was impossible for us to have made anie longer staye to have wrought the same. , . . . There were on this discoverie, no lesse then 100 personnes, who can all witnesse. . . . and if we attempted the same the day following, it was impossible either to forde it, or to swim it, both by reason of the swiftnesse, and also for that the orders were so pestered with fast woods, as neither bote nor man could finde place, either to land, or to imbarque. ("To the Reader," 3)

In this document, as in all other documents of conquest, geography gives way to other more pressing interests. In the case of Raleigh, geography yields to mineralogy and geology, and both yield to politics. It becomes clear that the ports of entry are just a methodology to reach gold, but that reaching gold passes through the circle of fire of conquest.

Raleigh writes: "It is his [Atapalipa] Indian Golde that indaungereth and disturbeth all the nations of Europe," and "[t]hose princes which abound in treasure have great advantage over the rest" (4). Mineralogical knowledge and the extraction of gold are, then, the real purpose of the enterprise; ethnography, landscaping, taste, and the overcoming of difficulties are the means to obtain it. The hitch is to legally define the meaning of several terms and the pressing need for both technology and policy.[32] For instance, in landscaping minerals there is reference to mineral stones that Amerindians deemed to be gold—marcasite, *la madre del oro*, the scum of gold, which "must be found either in graines separate from the stone (as it is in the most of all the rivers in Guiana) or else in a kinde of hard stone, which we call the white Sparre, of which I saw divers hils" (3). Here wealth is a natural resource; hearing is the method to reach it.

Gold is a floating signifier: for the sentimental Spaniards, the site of the marvelous (Manoa, El Dorado); for the pragmatic English, it is simply wealth. But to reach the deposits, both groups need to know (explore) the terrain and map it, and to do that, they need to be scouted by Amerindians. Hence, they need to figure out a policy for treating the "Indians," and furthermore, they urgently need to come to terms with the "Indian" as a political signifier. Ethnography, then, is a necessary condition for the extraction of wealth. The human and the mineral map are thus intimately intertwined.

Given that all the Europeans traveling throughout Amazonia depended on Amerindian knowledge to make their *avanzadas*, pilots and languages are the two important go-betweens. As one moves inland, one is reminded that there are "Indians" guiding, "Indians" speaking tongues, "Indians" interpreting and translating, "Indians" thinking and forming an opinion of the Europeans and performing the hermeneutics of space.

In Raleigh, the original concept of "Indian" is politically and civically grounded. He acknowledges the Amerindians' territorial system, their jurisdiction over the land, tracing the lordships at the borders, and calling them "Lords of the border," or *caciqui*.[33] Whether the territorial boundaries being written by Raleigh are accurate or not is totally irrelevant. What is relevant is that he begins by recognizing jurisdictions, and that these jurisdictions named as borders imply, at the very least, a working hypothesis of where one hegemony ends and another begins. Raleigh also reports one of the fundamental guiding principles of this cartography, namely, the hypothesis of an inland city, which I surmise is a veiled reference to the Inca empire.

Given that the main European and English cities are ports, the thought of an inland settlement, which for all intents and purposes could be a real "empire," is a hypothetical abstract that makes the English cautious. Mesmerized by the idea of a sudden presence or possibility of an empire in the middle of the "dense beyond," the jungle is conceived as a forest, that is, as the edge of the clearing where the city/settlement ends and wilderness begins. As we saw in Carvajal, so too in Raleigh the selection of key spots to draw mental gardens in the middle of the jungle is part and parcel of his subjective understanding of the new land. Cities, El Dorado, the abundance of gold, and the well-wrought gold items the English have seen keep them cautiously hopeful of the reality of an empire that the Spaniards had not yet come up against and possessed. That explains why "Indian" parlance is carefully heeded, and why natives are regarded as authority, although in the texts they speak indirectly and within quotation marks: "I was informed by an Indian" (2), "by whom I understood" (50). Indians speak without words, or with and through someone else's words. Nonetheless, the "Indian," at this moment, still enjoys a human status, and some are directly positioned within the narrative as speaking voices whose life experience is worthy of narrating. Such is the case of Carapana, a king-resident in Trinidad, whose profile as "a man very wise, subtill, and of great experience" (29) is suggested as a model for policy making. He was taken to Trinidad by reason of a "civil war," and because he is very old, he has seen many "Christians both French and Spanish . . . by reason whereof he grew of more understanding, and noted the difference of the nations, . . . Carapana kept himselfe and his country in quiet and plenti: he also held peace with . . . his neighbors, and had free trade with all nations whosoever els had war" (ibid.). Therefore, Carapana deserves respect as a man of peace and commerce, abilities Englishmen hold in high regard because they are similes of their own culture, translatable points of contact. Maintaining peace in times of war is meant to indicate a man of good policy, politically astute, and able to negotiate. "[C]omparing the strength and armes of his country with those of the Christian" (ibid.), Carapana realized that might must be negotiated with words, and he is believed to have known what Crosby declares the real reasons of the strength of the conquering armies, namely, the fact that they could hit and run, that they had a rear guard and the possibilities of retreat. Carapana is thus an example of what Carvajal would call an "Indian of peace."

Some women also deserve special attention, and although the English policy is not to mix with them—to touch, rape, or take them as prisoners, for that is what distinguishes them from the Spaniards, who already enjoy ill fame for their abuses—Raleigh's English gaze, like that of Monk Lewis in the nineteenth-century Caribbean, rests on an Indian woman whose portrait is significant for her beauty, but principally for her manners: "She was of good stature, with blacke eies, fat of body, of an excellent countenance . . . *and it seemed she stood not in that aw of hir husband, as the rest, for she spake and discourst, and dranke among the gentlemen and captaines, and was very pleasant, knowing hir owne comelines, and taking great pride therein.* I have seene a Lady in England so like hir, as but for the difference of colour I would have sworne might have beene the same" (55; emphasis added). I argue here, as I did in the case of Monk Lewis, that this gaze is at best that of a man looking at a woman, that of a man admiring independence and grace in a woman; or, at worst, the gaze of the predatory eye before pouncing on its prey. It could also be, as in the case of John Lloyd Stephens's gaze looking at women cooking tortillas in Guatemala, the nostalgia of what development could do for ethnicities.

As far as population policy is concerned, the English offer political and cultural profiles of caciques but are also set to do some "damage control," and some "damage prevention." First, they distance themselves from the Spaniards. This distinction is based on their differential treatment of women and children, on the intuitive profitability of the respect for the family unit that Vieira will promote a century later, and on reversing the idea that all Europeans are alike. The climax is clarification by example: they are not, as the Spaniards have said they are, "cannibals." Spaniards "had persuaded all the nations, that we were men eaters, and Cannibals" (51). They take care of their interpreters and educate them; that is, they practice what Greenblatt calls "kidnapping languages." Raleigh writes:

> & by my Indian interpreter, which I carried out of England, I made them understand that I was the servant of a Queene, who was the great Casique of the north, and a virgin, and had more Casiqui under her than there were

trees in their island: that she was an enemy to the Castellani in respect of their tyrannie and oppression, and that she delivered all such nations about her, as were by them oppressed. (B4)

In their analysis, the English come to comprehend the greatest strengths and weaknesses of the Amerindian nations. Their strength is their knowledge of language and geography. Their weakness is their open system of thinking. What Inga Clendinnen observed about the Mayas, and their conception of war and enemies, is true for some of these nations. They do not uphold the principle of total war. Raleigh, like Clendinnen in Yucatán, reports how the Amerindians escorted their enemies, Martínez in this case, after he had been with them for seven months in Manoa, how the Inga asked Martínez "whether he desired to return into his own countrey, or would willingly abide with him; but Martynes not desirous to stay, obtained the favour of Inga to depart, with whom he sent divers Guianians to conducted him to the river Orenoque all loden with as much gold as they could carrie" (15).

In the twentieth century, the English concept of jungle reverted to the image of the frontier as Joseph Conrad's heart of darkness. Having been changed into a barbarian witch doctor with the power of the knowledge of plants that intoxicate white people, the English character portrayed by Alec Guinness in *A Handful of Dust* (1988) is a cross between the realistic picture of the fears of empire over Amerindian knowledge of plants and the Pfizer-like managing of medicaments by Sean Connery in John McTiernan's *Medicine Man* (1992).

ON ADMINISTRATION: TEACHING, LEARNING, GOVERNING

Around the middle of the seventeenth century, the English and Spanish exploratory discourse yields to the Portuguese discourse on colonization. In this section I read Father António Vieira's letters and sermons. Vieira, a Jesuit missionary, preacher, writer, and diplomat, born in Lisbon and living in Bahia since he was a child, was the superior of the Jesuit missions in the Amazon. His relations with the settlers were strained because the missionaries controlled the distribution of Indian labor to Europeans. Vieira's task was to curb slave expeditions and improve relations between the Company of Jesus and the settlers. In 1655, Vieira traveled to Portugal to bring a case against the settlers at court. In 1661, the settlers expelled Vieira and his fellow Jesuits from the Amazon. In 1663, he was arrested by the Inquisition for his writings against it. The king's death in 1656 had left Vieira—his preacher and confidant—open to attack. He could no longer protect him. Vieira was released in 1668 and he returned to Brazil in 1681. He dedicated the rest of his life to serving as a Jesuit administrator and editing his sermons for publication. The film *The Mission* (1986), by Roland Joffé, dramatizes some of the aspects of this confrontation.

In his *Sermons and Letters* of 1653, Father António Vieira addresses the needs of the Christian priests instructing Amerindians in the service of God, and, echoing Father Bartolomé de Las Casas, voices his concerns on the type of colonization that is depopulating the area.[34] He calls Amazonia *terras* and Amerindians *nações*. His sermons' purpose is to make transparent the relationship between those two terms. His worry regarding *nações* is twofold. He is concerned, first, with the instruction of the Christian doctrine, and, second, with the abuses perpetrated on the bodies of Amerindians. The first worry comes from the incredible flexibility of the receiving culture—that it believes and then disbelieves the doctrine—and the diversity of the spoken languages; the second is related to food production and hunger.

This section takes as a point of departure Vieira's letters LXII and LXIX of 1653 to King D. João IV, letter LXIII to Padre André Fernandes; letter LXIV to the head of the religious Jesuit province; and his sermon "Espirito Santo" to illustrate how his administrative model makes use of a two-pronged strategy, one seemingly directed toward the external world, the king, the civil society, and the administration of the colonies, and the other to the local world, a more mixed constituency, probably the local members of his religious order, and perhaps some of the indigenous communities of Amazonia.

In Vieira's writings, there is a clear line dividing the internal discourse (the sermon), directed to his order, and the external discourse (the letters), directed to a public at large. The division between internal and external is marked by a contrast in tone. The sermon is very passionate, belligerent, and didactic, made up of small phrases, anaphoric repetition of concepts, use of natural images—*terra, pedras, animais*. Vieira seems to be explaining to his religious order the difficulties of establishing Christian hegemony, that is, the art of exercising authority by persuasion. The letters are more subdued, imploring, and beseeching. They want to convince Vieira's interlocutors that his proposals are correct. The division between the two genres is also evident in the sign "Indian," which shifts from "barbarian" and "savage" in the sermon to "poor people" and "sheeps" in the letters. Thus, if his sermon is on learning, his letters are on government.

In his letters, Vieira addresses questions relative to administration—the rules governing labor, the politics of raids or *entradas*, population control, the common good, food production—and proposes to His Majesty and the provincial head of his order a daring plan. This plan consists in separating the areas of administration and production, and bringing the mediation of the church to bear on the relations between government and labor. Putting the church in charge of the material and the spiritual production will bring about good government, ensure the well-being of the colonies, and make them productive and just.

Vieira's first step is to draw up a classification of the population, divided between Portuguese and natural Amerindians; between Amerindians living with the Portuguese and those living in freedom in their own villages; between those who are part free, part captive. The purpose of classification is to address the relationship between the groups, and how it comes to manifest the abuses on Amerindians carried out by the Portuguese. Vieira's document bears witness to how the Portuguese torture, burn, and maim the bodies of Amerindians, as well as to how they sow destruction across the land. The moral of the story is that if the body is disrespected, if the space of the body is misused, the land will be depopulated; for disrespecting and abusing the body means not only inflicting torture and causing pain, but also taking Amerindian women away from their houses, and preventing Amerindians from cultivating their lands, from tilling the soil. In protecting the body, agriculture will be secured, and the land, territory (*terras*), and inhabitants (*nações*) preserved for the good of the empire. Without family and emotional or physical sustenance, no empire can exist. The abuse of indigenous populations renders a vision of duress and desolation—"the sad Indians are now almost defeated and consumed" (*Cartas*, 311).

The flip side of this analysis is that what Portuguese policies produce is war, and war fosters lawlessness—*desgobierno*. The Portuguese invade Amerindian lands and reduce Amerindians unjustly, take them captive by force or deceit, and then sell and/or exploit them. "This and similar terrors have made the name of the Portuguese hated in the fields, and has much disauthorized the faith, [a reason for which] many have retired to the interior of the forest, and others after living [with us] become disillusioned, others make war on us or inflict the damage they can upon us" (313).

His letter LXIX of April 6, 1654, to the king outlines a radical political, economic, and military system of administration that takes the military jurisdiction away from the captains and places it in Amerindian hands. The remedy Vieira offers is drastic: to close the *sertões*; to sever charity and justice from profit, and material ambitions from services and the well-being of the community; to render the *rescate* illegal, and to declare free all of those who had been taken by force. There is no question that the ideas concerning indigenous self-government and Vieira's own way of speaking about "human rights" are also a means for empowering the church and firming up colonial governance. The whole system is to be revised so that the church can exercise control by overseeing the *principales*. If there are *entradas*, their purpose must be to convert, not to reduce people to serfdom. The Amerindians themselves, with the assistance of the church, must carefully select the captain; what he obtains must be deposited within the central administration. A theologian and a *lengua* must always accompany an *entrada*. Thus Vieira writes a state of custody for the Amerindians, always in need of the mediation of a white protector if they are to obtain any type of justice.

In the control of the population, simplicity is advocated. A good population policy must populate, not depopulate. To populate is to feed, not to kill. This plan is to be implemented by putting an injunction on productivity. Neither governors nor captains should cultivate lands, nor give Amerindians in bondage, unless it is for defense and the construction of forts. Nor should churchmen be allowed to have personal investments, haciendas, tobacco, sugarcane, or any type of productive lands where Amerindians or slaves labor. The liminal zone between production and administration is traced through the ownership of land and the organization of labor, the two means by which the control of populations, both indigenous and Portuguese, will be undertaken.

Vieira's plan also contemplates a population census to keep track of settlements and resettlements and to know where people reside, thus facilitating administration and control. Amerindian villages must be adjoined.

Laboring to feed and to eat, rather than laboring to serve, must be deemed the most important activity. Amerindians must be left in peace to cultivate their lands, and if they work for the Portuguese, they must not be allowed to leave until they have tilled their soils. Furthermore, they must be paid in advance and their salaries deposited. Market activities must be fostered, allowing one every fortnight, thereby facilitating the entrance of Amerindians into monetary economies, and therefore, integration. Food production must be given preference over laboring in the tobacco and sugar plantations. *Reparticiones* (allocation of Indians to Portuguese) must be prorated depending on the number of Amerindians, beginning always with the poorest. The Amerindians must be placed where they are needed. To the degree that this project fosters local development, it is a better acculturation project. The caveat is that the key to acculturation is the teaching and learning of the Christian religion. Vieira's idea for implementing his plan is a full-fledged campaign of Christian conversion.

TEACHING AND LEARNING

In the discussion of conversion, three strands run parallel: one is the political struggle between church and state for the control of the Amerindian population; the second is the colonization projects of one and the other; and the third is the constitution of Amerindian new subjectivity as "barbarians." I will set aside the head-on collision between church and state that is to come fully undone in the writings of de Mendonça a century later, once the scores between those two institutions of governance are settled, and will focus on the interrelationship between the second and third strand: the construction of the new Amerindian subjectivity as "barbarian" in relation to the colonization project of the church.

"Barbarian" is the new identity with which Amerindian populations are going to circulate in the Western text during the whole period of the Enlightenment. In many ways, "barbarian" takes the place of the "good Indian" or the "Indian of peace," and is a sign that we have crossed an epistemological threshold. What is implicated in the construction of the "barbarian" is not solely the building up of a new subjectivity for Amerindians. It is also an indicator of how the church's colonization project itself comes up against a hermeneutic wall. Vieira explains these obstacles in terms of the nondialogic nature of languages. In his texts we come full circle to a discussion on the obduracy of languages with which this chapter began, but in a previous stage of development. Vieira's sermon "Espirito Santo" is the document that testifies to how languages obstruct the process of acculturation.

Let us begin with his discussion on languages. As in Acuña's and Figueroa's reports, in Vieira's "Espirito Santo" sermon, languages are relative to the numbers of Amerindian groups living in the jungle. The Amazon is so densely populated that the sheer numbers justify the comparison of Amazonia with Babel. The multiplicity of spoken languages in the region makes language learning an impossible task. However, for the Christian project of colonization to succeed, the priest must "estudar e saber la lingua" (study and know the language) (*Sermões*, 308). The problem is, Vieira writes, that in the Amazon languages are impossible to learn because they do not have a graspable structural system. He establishes the reasons for the difficulties: (1) one cannot distinguish the units of sound; (2) one cannot understand them conceptually; (3) "one cannot reduce [them] to grammar and precepts" (415); (4) one cannot distinguish names, verbs, adverbs, or prepositions, "the number, case, time, or mode with modes never seen, never imagined, like that of men as different in languages as in customs" (416); (5) one cannot pronounce (learn) them. Nheengaiba, Juruuna, Tapajo, Termembe, Mamaiana" are languages harder than Greek or Arabic (or, as de Léry said, High German) (416). Vieira cannot hear them because the pronunciation is "so obscured and closed . . . that it could truly be posited that they didn't have one" (415). He has been very attentive to "the mouth of the barbarian," and to that of the interpreter, but he has not been able to perceive syllables, vowels, or consonants, the same letter being confused with three similar ones. His strained ears do not perceive anything except the confusion, because the languages are "hard and rugged . . . interior and dark, suffocated in the throat . . . short and high . . . extended and multiplied so the ears perceive only confusion . . . only sound (ibid.). Amerindian languages sound like noises and grunts.

Once Vieira has determined that the problem is language, the question is, how does a language problem spill over and affect the colonization project of the church and its efforts at acculturation? In the "Espirito Santo" sermon, Vieira tries to answer this question by raising the problem of the learning of languages in conjunction with the teaching of the Christian faith. A common perception of the church—more than a perception, a conviction—is that the conversion of Amerindians to Christianity will result in acculturation. That means that Amerindians will shed their belief system and acquire new habits. Whether this acculturation will make Amerindians move from barbarism into citizenship is never spelled out. But the only way to reach Amerindians is to learn their language. Thus the church's project of colonization and the bases of its power demand doctrinal and linguistic expertise. Churchmen are already learned in the former; now they have to become proficient in the latter.

There are other sets of problems ensuing from the dialectics of learning and teaching. Both are vehicles for understanding the genealogy of the concept of "barbarian" as difference, and to grasp how colonial powers managed questions relative to human rights.[35] The fact is that one of Vieira's concerns is method: how is conversion to be achieved? What he recommends is "sabedoria e amor" (wisdom and love)—"é necessario maior amor que sabedoria" (more love than wisdom is necessary) (400). Like the priests of liberation theology today, Vieira declares love a method to approach Amerindians and to convert them to the Christian faith. Love is solidarity, a medium for good administration. Yet, in spite of all efforts, Vieira recognizes, with dismay, that "uns aprendem, outros não" (some learn, some do not) (398); that "Indians" easily believe and disbelieve: "faz que o seu crer em certo modo seja como não creer" (given that their believing is in a certain way like not believing) (406). Furthermore, he observes, with consternation, that the teaching and learning of the Christian doctrine, of ideology, faith, and religion, has become performance, pantomime. Amerindians are impervious and resilient. They just repeat the motions without internalizing the doctrine. The doctrine does not stick. A profound distress and bereavement result when the priest becomes aware that he is up against a hermeneutical wall and Amerindians before hermeneutic riddles. A steady indoctrination is a tall order. Vieira explains: "the Brasilians even after believing are still incredulous . . . for Brasilians, faith is or seems to be incredulity. . . . These men believed and disbelieved at the same time; because the faith with which they believed was so imperfect that on the one hand it seemed faith, and on the other it seemed incredulity; a faith that seemed incredulity, and an incredulity that seemed faith" (ibid.).

This tongue twister expresses his perplexity alongside his irritation and disappointment. The dialectics of belief/disbelief become an obsession, the mercurial adoption of something that for Vieira is the basis of power and authority related to obedience and disobedience. The indigenous *nações* "receive everything they are taught with great docility and ease, without arguing, without contesting it, without doubting it, without resisting it" (409). But obedience, as much as disobedience, is here related to what to me reads as the flexibility of the Amerindian epistemes, that which keeps Amerindians from sticking to the doctrine. The priests refuse to acknowledge this flexibility as the rules that govern the indigenous universe. The result is misunderstanding. There is no mediating structure, only a total hermeneutical incompatibility. There is no possible point of entry, only a degree zero of communication.

Where does the trouble lie? Vieira's hypothesis comes back to language. Languages are an obstructing element. Languages intercept and interrupt concepts. Languages act as non-conveyor belts. Languages are unknown and multiple, "nunca ouvidas, nem conhecidas, nem imaginadas as linguas" (never heard, nor known, nor imagined languages) (413). But languages, we all know, are clearly relational systems establishing meaning. So the problem is language, but it is also culture; hence, the concept of "barbarian." Barbarian is that opacity and impenetrability against European forms of knowledge, reasoning, understanding, and feeling.

De Mendonça will grab the topic of linguistic delusions and brandish it against the church's colonization project. He aptly uses Vieira's difficulties in learning Amerindian languages as fodder to feed his arguments against church governance and to corroborate the bridge of confidence established by the Christian missions on matters concerning faith. He has seen these churchmen disheartened because they could not communicate with the "Indians." He knows they have found themselves in the predicament of inventing a *giria* (lingua franca) to communicate with Amerindians, and he has observed religious men adopt this jargon as a way of thinking and being "to the extreme that there are today very few people in this city who speak Portuguese . . . [and according to their own testimony] they do not confess themselves except in the lingua franca, as they call it."[36] What is worse is that the Christian faith itself is drastically distorted. Going back and forth between Portuguese and the *giria* to negotiate the terms of the exchange between distinct belief systems produces a syncretism where "Indians" seem to enjoy the advantages. To achieve their purposes, he writes, churchmen make Amerindians learn the lingua franca and because of the lack of equivalences between words and ideas, they have come to admitting the plurality of gods. For instance, "the word Tupana in such jargon is God; the prefixes Acu e Mirim are the same as big and small, and such Indians are educated to explain God saying Tupana Acu = Big God; and the saints, their images and *verónicas* [religious images printed in cloth] Tupana Mirim = Small gods; and it is this that they say as a way of explaining, because they do not have in such a language the word Saint" (66).

Nothing is really new here. Father Francisco Ximénez made the same observation concerning the names of the Lord for the Quiché-Maya in the Guatemalan highlands. But Vieira himself had already pinpointed this problem and used translation to illustrate that which is lost and that which is gained.[37] The bigger problem he recognizes in translation is that of disadjustment between noun and object. Disadjustment triggers disbelief, and disbelief in turn accounts for Vieira's observation on the flexibility of Amerindian system—now they believe, now they don't. Disadjustment, "the old interplay between resemblance and signs," the process by which "words have swallowed up their own nature as signs," is what Michel Foucault calls a crisis of the analogue, the end of knowledge by similitude—a discontinuity that signals watersheds dividing epochs.[38] This process is evident in Vieira. Not knowing how to know and how to name what is known—whether by substitution or contiguity—is his nightmare.[39] The problem of knowledge and of governance has become a phonetic challenge; hence the intersection between politics and linguistics.[40]

It is important to notice that throughout his sermon Vieira is not complaining about the resistance of people so much as about the "nature of things." Amerindians are willing and ready to learn. Vieira's shortcoming is to explain resistance not as human agency but solely as that which is proper to a structure. This is not a social but a metaphysical quest that cannot be reduced to grammar or phonetics. Languages constitute epistemological and ideological clusters; they discriminate between meanings and promote some presences in preference to others; they prevent or facilitate access. From this point of view, Vieira's Amazonia is a very complex, conflictive, and afflicting landscape. Here the battle is for signs—how to say what, when, to whom. The creation of a mediating gadget, a *giria*, backfired because it radiated meaning in all kinds of contradictory directions.

From here we are to conclude that the most salient aspect of Vieira's narrative is frustration. The new Amerindian subjectivity is constructed in intimate relation to the churchmen's feelings of impotence. They simply could not come to grips with the Amerindian systems and internal structures. Faced with an epistemological obstruction, the result is the politics of blaming the other, now qualified as "barbarian and uncultivated nations and languages . . . among whom there were men as irrational as brutes, and as insensitive as tree trunks, and as hard and as stupid as rocks" (*Sermões*, 401). The subject emerging from Vieira's sermon is "stupid . . . ungrateful . . . inconstant . . . evil . . . the hardest to teach of any in the world" (404). Language learning and language teaching—*lenguas*; unknown topographies and guides—geographies; and ungovernability and lack of enlightened government are presented as three of the major stumbling blocks of empires and colonialism, Vieira's triad of the pillars of the mastery of Amazonia.

But if the "barbarian" is likened to inanimate, natural objects (rocks, tree trunks), priests are to cannibals. To be like a rock is to be dense, stubborn, thickheaded; to educate Amerindians is like sculpting on rocks. Missionaries are always working against the grain, against "the nature of the tree trunk and the humor of roots" (409), "teaching or taught, converting or converted, and making the made; made, so that it does not come unraveled; converted, so that it does not become perverted; taught, so that it is not forgotten; and finally helping incredulity, which is not incredulous, so that faith may not be faithless faith" (410–11). It is evident that the Amerindian hermeneutical condition invariably translates either into Christian frustration or into laymen's doubt. If we flip the question around, on the other side of the divide we can easily ascertain that it is priests who project onto Amerindians their own incapacity to translate, to convert or understand, or even to acknowledge the epistemes of diversity. *Sapientia* does not overcome *experiencia*. Education—that is, to convert dangerous animals into Christians, into men—is made analogous to eating: "and there is nothing more similar to teaching and indoctrinating than killing and eating. . . . God willing that Saint Peter taught the faith to those peoples, he told him to kill them and to eat them; because what is killed ceases being what it is, and what is eaten becomes the substance and the limbs of the one who eats. . . . First they should die, because they should stop being peoples; and then they should be eaten and transformed into limbs of Saint Peter. . . . In this manner, as nature makes beasts of men, killing and eating, so grace makes men out of beasts by indoctrinating and teaching" (426–27).

The culture of eucaristics as cannibalism and cannibalism as transubstantiation, as the main figure of acculturation, irony of ironies, is the most interesting analogue to explain *desgobierno* (ungovernability), cultural resistance, and resiliency. Is it here, perhaps, where Mário de Andrade's *Manifesto Antropofágico* is rooted?

It is left absolutely clear in Vieira's sermon that the constitution of the new subjectivities is inseparable from language learning and Christian teaching and that it is the obduracy of languages that results in the construction of the "barbarian." It is also clear that *barbarian* is the extreme of a predication and in this sense it constitutes itself into a radical and undesirable difference. If we now look at conversion as the colonization project of the church in Amazonia, the aporetic nature of its discourse gleams from afar; for conversion, aimed at normalization and homogenization, is premised on a notion of radical and seemingly insurmountable difference. If Vieira's task is not to sketch out a blueprint for explaining difference, the result is that peoples' diverse languages, behaviors, and cultures are the terrain on which the church's discourse will establish the radical differences between governing and governed.

TERRAS, NAÇÕES, ALDEIAS, FAZENDAS, MISSÕES, DOUTRINAS

A century later, Francisco Xavier de Mendonça Furtado will reiterate the same apprehensions using Vieira's arguments as counterarguments against the church. De Mendonça's contention is that the church's mission has failed, and that the state must have a try. In contrast to Vieira's proposal to divide the civic and religious spheres, de Mendonça's narrative of administrative utopias for the *capitanias do Maranhão* is based on the ideas of freedom fostered by the Enlightenment. If Vieira argued in favor of the church, de Mendonça argues in favor of the state.

In the eighteenth century, the struggle between church and state would be decided in favor of the state. The strength of the church, the strategy of its colonization project, was predicated on acculturation and based on language learning and teaching. It rested on the successful implementation of cultural linguistic strategies and methodologies and the creation of a lingua franca. De Mendonça's plans are radically different. Like G. E. Squier's in Central America, his project begins with the construction of accurate cartographies. His map of Amazonia can be read against the map of present-day Brazil, with a triangle inserted at the core signaling three positions: (1) the city of Barcelos, which was the old village of Mariua, (2) Vila Bela, then capital of Mato Grosso, and (3) Belém do Pará. The title of the map/project is "O Triangulo e os Pilares Mestres da Amazônia do Século XVIII" (The triangle and master pillars of Amazonia in the eighteenth century), and his aim is the integration of territories into what will become the Brazilian nation (see Figure 13).

On this map, the surrounding edges are all occupied by other European national groups: *Castelhanos* on all sides, except the northeast, which is occupied by the *Holandeses, Ingleses,* and *Franceses.* This geography spells out the dream of José de Pombal to found the Great Portuguese Empire in America whose baseline was the great Companhias Gerais de Comércio.

One of the interesting points in de Mendonça's map is his jurisdictional taxonomies—"aldeias, fazendas, missões e doutrinas" (villages, haciendas, missions, and doctrines)—that are very similar to those of Cortés y Larraz in the Guatemalan highlands in the same century. With the exception of *doutrinas,* the other nouns refer to productive, political, and administrative landscapes. In de Mendonça, geography is important because his project is commercial. Geography means routes and state governance. Legislating geographies is for him an end in itself. He speaks about law and order as the civil and military public administration of justice, counterposing military to religious regiments (Regimento das Missões). All this is related to entitlements, the civil rights of people, here narrated as "a decantada liberdade dos índios" (the delimited freedom of "Indians") (9).

As in the case of nineteenth-century West Indian travel narratives, de Mendonça's is drenched in the ideology, vocabulary, and spirit of the Enlightenment: but in the Amazon, to speak about the civil rights of "Indians" is to address questions pertaining to labor, then in the hands of the religious missions. The film *The Mission* dramatizes this protracted eighteenth-century struggle between church and state, making once more the bodies of Amerindians the terrain where freedom of commerce and the secularization of the state are battled. The duality of powers is coming to an end. Laws, "civil rights," "citizenship" will be enacted to settle disputes between the religious orders, the secular state, and the indigenous populations. Ironically, citizenship rights will undergird the program of Amerindians.

As the age of light meets the heart of darkness, de Mendonça's project is to engineer a "penetration design," to take possession, to administer. His goal is to dismantle church missions. De Mendonça puts forth a powerful lexeme, "enemy," that comes to replace "barbarian." Enemy is the concept that manages the politics of demonization. The structure of feelings no longer swings between fear and joy, the aesthetic sublime and the grotesque—as it did in Carvajal. Now the politics of sentimentalism is the

Figure 13. The Triangle of Pilares. Drawing by María Gabriela Patocchi; reproduced with permission from the artist.

technē for his aesthetic bedeviling of "enemies," and the canvas on which he is to draw their defeat. Enemies are all those who resist, those who do not obey, like Harris's Poseidon, or the Miskitus and Guatusos in Squier, those who do not work, those who escape to the innermost forest (the maroons), those who still live in subsistence economies.

The blinding glow of reason has reached the jungle, and de Mendonça's reason and reasoning spell out extermination under the guise of development. *Campinas* and *matas, sertões,* more than fifteen hundred leagues of land, are all tightly intertwined with vassals, which are always related to treasures, which are always related to souls and Christian piety. Targeting Vieira's most salient argument, de Mendonça asserts that Christian priests are nothing. They have not converted the people of the land; on the contrary, many Christians have already taken the costumes of the people (*indianos, aindiados*), "because having gone to look for them in the bush they have been brought to the villages; there they teach them a jargon they call lingua franca, . . . there they are lightly instructed in some mysteries of our holy faith, but so superficially that I believe the men of law are very few" (64).

The implacable redrawing of categories calls native hegemony over the land *desgobierno* (ungovernability), calls resistance, rebellion, and reluctance lack of reason. Sixteenth-century *naturales,* natives, caciques, *señores,* and even emperors become seventeenth- and eighteenth-century barbarians and enemies. Vieira's bestiary defines them as follows: "they were wolves, they were bears, they were tigers, they were lions, they were serpents, they were dragons, they were asps, they were basilisks. . . . They were barbarian and uncultivated nations; they were ferocious and indomitable, they were nations without humanity, without reason, and many of them without law" (403). The theoretical move in the conceptual description and its strategy results in the devolution of Amerindians. That is the legacy of the light of whiteness to the heart of darkness, a legacy that was to serve the eighteenth-century projects of development, the triangle and master pillars of Amazonia ("o triangulo e os pilares mestres da Amazônia").

chapter 7

THE AMAZON
A Modern Twentieth-Century Frontier

People died of horror and disgust at European civilization even more
than of smallpox and physical ill-treatment.

—CLAUDE LÉVI-STRAUSS, *Tristes Tropiques*

UNPATROLLABLE TERRITORIES

At the beginning of chapter 6, I gave a descriptive summary of the termi-
nological distinctions between forest, wood, wilderness, and jungle. My
purpose was to call attention to the porous nature of the words narrating
nature, and to make clear what set of words belonged to which set of
discourses. I argued that the representation of jungle rendered different
dividends when treated as a vast deposit of nonrenewable resources for
development (da Cunha's "real"), and when treated as a warehouse of
symbolic images (da Cunha's "imaginary"). Yet, both productions somehow overlap through the oxymoronic representation of an often insuffi-
ciently understood physical geography. I argued that the terminology
demarcated domains and differences, not only between different codifica-
tions of nature, but also between different epistemic systems. Whereas
wood, forest, parks, and timber lots are terms more pertinent to the positivistic narratives of progress where nature is already a predictable, controlled, codified, counted, and dominated matter, jungle, *manigua*, and *selva*
are more pertinent to Romanticism, where nature is still uncontrollable,
unmanageable, an open frontier, *una orilla*. I have interpreted the rhetorical conflation of all these terms as a stylistic anxiety, the belabored efforts

of writers struggling with the internal confusion and epistemological chaos of a not yet fully determined and historicized sign.

As in the case of highlands, also examined earlier, here too colonial narratives set the patterns for the representation of nature and of people and constitute the genealogy of modern and postmodern knowledges. In some cases, colonial narratives represent both people and nature as a commercial opportunity for the production of food or the extraction of wealth; in others, they dovetail with investment and aesthetics. I have argued that whereas ethnography manages Amerindians, aesthetics describe Europeans, and geography takes charge of wealth. The archaeology of the representation of this region from its inception to the present bears witness to this fact and is easily confirmed by the works I have examined in this piece. In Latin America, foundational narratives of nature are utopian and developmentalist, in that they envision well-developed geographies; they also set up the parameters for interethnic relations among Amerindians, mestizos, and criollos.

In the modern era, narratives of nature are, by definition, narratives of state, and most of them are still troubled by ethnicities. In fiction, the physical geographies, as *orillas,* underscore the problem of the ill-defined boundaries of the state, and therefore the Amazon is not a well-charted district or municipality, but river, forest, nature, the object of perpetual dispute between states as well as between tenants and landowners with conflicting deeds. The fact that three land surveyors (Euclides da Cunha, Wilson Harris, and José Eustasio Rivera) have produced three of the greatest fiction narratives of Amazonia is proof of the eminence of the frontier and the fact that it is even now an unresolved issue.[1] My task in this chapter is to turn to the works of Mario Vargas Llosa, Alejo Carpentier, and Wilson Harris to situate the imaginary modern jungle within the parameters of narrative intersections. My question is, do narratives of encounter/ confrontation reproduced in fiction find in jungle a propitious metaphor for development? Or, on the contrary, has jungle come to best represent that which has resisted possession, colonization, and expropriation?

HUBRIS: DISORIENTATION/DISORGANIZATION

In the twentieth century, the tropes of disorientation and disorganization dominate the modern literary representation of the Amazon as a jungle.

They betray the incapacity to grasp and to render, and underscore not only the antagonistic relationship between adversarial groups, ethnicities, genders, and sensibilities, but also a synergy between nature and Amerindians. In Vargas Llosa's *The Green House*, Adrián Nieves, a deserter from the army, thinks jungle as follows:

> he looks for channels and inlets to follow, and it is not difficult, the whole region is full of waterways. . . . [H]ow will he find his way, these uplands are not his country, the water has risen a lot? . . . [W]here he is going now, the channel seems to spin around him and he is navigating in the dark, the woods are thick, the sun and the air can barely penetrate, it smells of rotting wood, mud, and so many bats besides. . . . Neither backward nor forward, neither going back up the Marañón, nor reaching the Santiago.[2]

In Harris's *The Secret Ladder*, the jungle stands for political epistemic chaos exposing and defeating what the eye can see. To try to map the jungle is to try to measure the incommensurable—in Guyana the "bush" or "the interior":

> the jungle kept crawling and returning, stretching its ancient wiry knuckles and long grassy sleeves high up as well as across the black face of the river . . . the encroaching image of the forest leaning into the riverside . . . a haphazard billowing of land, changing and declining into swamp . . . of the inchoate Amazon basin. . . . It was this sensation of exposure and defeat, amounting to confusion. . . . the jungle turned blind as a shuttered place and the eye learnt to relinquish the neighboring sun for a tenebrous, almost electrical gloom.[3]

The juxtaposition of horror and peaceful images, plainly displayed in Werner Herzog's film *Fitzcarraldo* (1982), is the transparent model of these narratives of national development. So, what matters is that disorientation and disorganization are tropes that take the reader into the wilderness, a free zone inhabited by the figurative "Indian." In Caribbean literatures this is a slot occupied by the "black maroon," as in the fiction of Harris. In the novels I will examine in this chapter, the figure "Indian" is a sign radiating in opposite hermeneutical directions. One direction is the "premodern" "Indian," the barbarian; the other is the menacing "Indian" construed as the *interruptus* of development.[4]

Disorientation and disorganization are thus narrative strategies that situate the narrator outside the well-constituted parameter of the nation-
state—outside his city and his country, and inside the "Indian" wilderness.
This strategy allows the formation of a national self as separate and different from "Indians." "Indians" are the narrator's opposite, a menacing
adversarial counterimage. This composition is obtained by launching a
descriptive offensive against the "Indians" whose solid ground rests on an
ethnographical discourse of uses and customs. What is the end result of
the constitution of these modern regimes of subjectivity? The end result is
for the national-subject-narrator to rewrite the jungle as the "enchanted"
forest of economic development. Economic development is the end of his
journey to the untrodden frontier.

NATURE/HISTORY/GEOGRAPHY: THE AMORPHOUS NATURE OF NATION-STATES

The first novel I will examine is Mario Vargas Llosa's *The Green House*
(1966). In it, this well-known Peruvian writer turns his attention from the
city to the jungle, a labyrinthine world vast and unbridled. In this text, a
very experimental narrative technique weaves together five threads, which
tell the stories of two Peruvian regions—coast and jungle. The provincial
city of Piura in the coast and Santa María de Nieva in the jungle are two
areas of the nation totally isolated from each other. Piura is represented as
a parochial and narrow-minded provincial town, a city of layabouts, a
place lacking in vitality and whose conservative way of life unfolds in the
burning of "The Green House," the house of ill repute that corrupts the
town. The jungle is the embodiment of barbarism itself, inhabited by
indigenous groups who roam about the forest, cultivating rubber and selling it for nothing to the merchants who mercilessly exploit them.

The five stories that are interwoven in the novel are that of "The Green
House"—the brothel opened by Don Anselmo; the story of the Uncon-
querable—a group of friends from La Mangachería who live their life perpetually partying, boozing, and whoring; the story of Lituma—a civil
guard who becomes a decent human being but later reverts back to his old
mores of the Mangachería; the story of Fushía and his journey through the
vast web of Peruvian Amazonian rivers; and finally, the story of the captured Amerindians—mainly little girls who are taken by the nuns to the

mission to be saved from "ignorance" and "paganism." The voices of these five stories are constantly intersected and interrupted, thus presenting each of them as a part of a broken whole. The connecting thread between the two regions and the five stories is Bonifacia, *la selvática*, who, as a girl, is abducted from her indigenous group and taken into custody by the nuns in the mission. When she grows up, she becomes a prostitute in the Piura brothel "The Green House."

My interest in this novel lies in its portrayal of the relationship between mestizos, criollos, and "Indians" in Peru. My claim is that for Vargas Llosa, the Peruvian nation is constituted through the identification of populations with territorialities—"Indian" and wilderness—and that, through the trope of the journey, he sets the stage for a drama in the jungle whose main protagonists are the church, the state, commerce, and "Indians." Trailing down the path established by the early colonial writers—such as Friars Gaspar de Carvajal and António Vieira—Vargas Llosa reproduces verbatim the tropes of people and jungle inherited from a racist colonialist past and firms up the idea that "Indians" are ballast. His obsession is development and modernity and he holds "Indians" responsible for the "backwardness" of Peru.

In *The Green House*, nature accounts for the amorphous makeup of nation-states, or, perhaps, in a more strictly Hegelian fashion, for the absence of the state. The title of the novel itself serves as a metaphor for that part of the nation that is still a geography—jungle.[5] The structure of the text and the organization of the story line reproduce the tropes of foundational narratives apt to mirror the conflation of history and geography, which in turn highlight the baffling voices of ethnography. The style is achieved through the mixing of the written and the oral that constantly coil and recoil. The diegetic process is thus permanently set adrift, and the same story is told and retold. Rhetorically, this narrative structure, reinforced by the juxtaposition of oral and written discourses, reproduces the feelings of vertigo elicited by former representations of the jungle. Metaphorically, the disorderly voices stand for wilderness, and wilderness in turn for the fragmentation of the story line that portrays a broken nation. Thus, the style of the novel introduces the reader to a radical critique of nation formation that underscores the necessity of disengaging the tropes of nature (geography) from human events (history). In Vargas Llosa, as in Carvajal, history, human incidents, and events—for example, the escape of the "Indian" girls from the mission, the smuggling activities of Fushía, the story of the Mangaches and the Mangachería, the role of the army in the jungle—do not measure up to the backdrop provided by the jungle, which is the subject matter overwhelming the narrative. All human incidents are of little consequence when compared with the jungle. In the midst of this ill-charted geography, institutions, ranks, hierarchies, mores, ethics—all the props of the state—dissolve into nothingness.

With the exception of leading characters in the position of state representatives, the protagonists of *The Green House* are consolidated as the abhorrent subalterns, the outlaws who populate all the porous spaces of the state beyond citizenship—the *mangaches*, the *gallinacera*, prostitutes, blind people, orphans, drunkards, invalids, abused women, fugitives, delinquents, merchants, and "Indians."[6] These protagonists travel through entire geographies of Peru: Santa María de Nieva, Iquitos, the Ucayali, the Marañón, Lima, Piura, the charted points of reference that frame their "history," their incidents and events. But beyond these well-known geographic names, there are other proper names that blend with the generic, and we pass through them as readers of the mestizo or criollo narratives of progress in their attempt to establish a national identity. In point of fact, proper names establish distinctions between real citizens and the rest. For instance, in the names Chunchos, Aguarunas, Urakusas, Shapras, Lupunas, Huambisas, "Indians" name what is not citizenship, what is not Peruvian. "Indians" are one extreme, the opposite pole of the Peruvian state. As the habitat of the "Indian," jungle comes to represent the lack of secured borders and true citizenship. It is, rather, a free-for-all narrative space where criollos now, as European colonizers before them, deliberate the feared and highly besieged counterhegemony of Amerindian cultures.

Thought of as jungle, that part of the national territory itself is conceived as unexplored basic "natural" resources, raw materials that, if properly exploited, can eventually bring Peru's positivist national utopia of development to fruition. For the sake of development, Amerindians must be ideologically, rhetorically, and physically removed. However, the irony is that in this catachresis, the "Indians" become the metaphor for the unvanquishable. This is certainly a reversal very much at odds with that narrated by geographers, anthropologists, and witnesses for peace, whose work speaks about the extermination of the indigenous populations and the conquest of the jungle.[7]

LOS SELVÁTICOS: JUNGLE PEOPLE

In Vargas Llosa, as in Carvajal and Vieira, the civilizing mission of the church is represented as a perennial mediation between governance and ethnicities. Twentieth-century fiction writers no longer plot the discrepancies between church and state that mortified Vieira's and Pombal's writings. A pax social has been established and the nuns now, as the friars before, manage a religious mission in the middle of the jungle for the benefit of the state. Their role is to foster progress, to civilize, and to modernize. To do so, they carry out resettlement and acculturation programs. They take the young Aguarunas away from their places of residence, give them Christian names, and change their habits in eating, cleansing, and clothing. The effect of the church's work is first to transform Amerindians into orphans, then into wards of the church, and finally to relocate them within the productive area of services within the national economies. And although church and state are somewhat disjointed, they never work at cross-purposes.

As in colonial times, the church's role is to discipline ethnicities, the by-product of which provides more laborers to the menial workforce. When the Amerindian children grow up, the church becomes an employment agency, providing domestic workers to a society predicated on using poor Amerindian women as servants, sexual workers, or both. To be transplanted from the jungle to the mission, and from the mission to a private house in the city to do housework or sexual work, is here, as it was in the works of geographers and naturalists, the essence of the religious modernizing program for ethnicities. As far as disciplinary action is concerned, as a halfway house, the church moves Amerindians from the fields of ethnography in the jungle to the fields of sociology in the city. Never does Vargas Llosa critically narrate this relationship between church and state regarding Amerindians. He limits himself to show the difficulties, if not the impossibility, of combining piety and charity with programs of development. His text reproduces in fiction the ideas and narrative structures of a colonial heritage combined with the lexemes of positivism. As such, it constitutes itself into an all-out offensive against the aboriginal people living in the Amazon.

In *The Green House*'s mission, as in the colonial missions, programs of acculturation are put into effect. A literacy program includes the teaching of rudimentary Spanish, learning to wear Western-style clothes, sleeping in beds, maintaining Western standards of hygiene and health. Through this program Amerindian girls are taught shame and rejection of their own cultures. Later on, through meager salaries, they are introduced to an informal monetary economy. In this manner, fiction refurbishes and modernizes the identity "Indian." Once they pass through the crucible of church education, "Indians" no longer fit into the concept of the "barbarian." They become what is called a "premodern" subject. A "premodern" condition is embodied in what is most conspicuous—clothing, diet, hygiene. Thus the body and its habits will become the focus of debate in fiction.

Amerindians' nakedness constitutes the first flank of attack. "Indians" in Vargas Llosa go around naked. Their bodies, firm legs and thighs, strong arms, and round buttocks are always contrasted with the fully clothed parts of nuns. The narrative lingers over these bodies, focusing on their parts. Not even their genitalia are spared the onlooker's penetrating gaze. Vargas Llosa calls them *calatos*, the U.S. films "bare-asses"; both words stand for the "natural state" that is equated with savagery and is a sign of their animal condition and primordialism. There is nothing new in this representation of Amerindians. Vargas Llosa just paints another reinforcing coat over the layerings provided by tradition.

Diet is another targeted topic. Amerindians' eating habits are described as disgusting. Two of the most selected details are the preparation of an intoxicating yucca beverage and the eating of grubs. The careful detail with which this food preparation is observed, and the fact that it is a leitmotif stretching from at least Central America to Brazil, is an indication of how much this habit has impressed the minds of the narrators and how fiercely they oppose it. The yucca beverage is produced with the mouth. First, women chew the yucca so that the saliva ferments it. Then they spit it into containers. When it is ready, the beverage is served in vessels made from horns or skulls. Amerindians drink it with relish. Europeans and criollos feel like throwing up.[8] The effect of this narrative is to foreground barbarism and illustrate antihygienic habits. The eating of grubs is also a chastised practice and used as evidence against the "premodern" Amerindians.

Hygiene is also the object of vigilance. Women are portrayed picking lice from their children's heads, or children preening other children, and placing the lice between their teeth. In *The Green House*, Bonifacia picks lice from the head of the young kidnapped Aguarunas. In Vargas Llosa's narrative, as in filmic portrayals of Amerindians, the message illustrates filth, ignorance, the undesirable animal in humans. I read it as a sign of tenderness and companionship. Echoing Franciscan, Dominican, and Jesuit patterns of colonization, and Amazonian films produced in the United States, in *The Green House*, the mission's mission is to reverse those habits and to create new ones.[9]

Once the body is totally besieged, the offensive moves on to language and religion as syllabary. That is why *silabariolima, limagobierno* (Lima-syllabary, Limagovernment) are two words collapsed into one by Jum, the main Amerindian protagonist of *The Green House*. The conflation of words expresses his understanding of the relationship between government, letters, and civis, as well as Vargas Llosa's indictment of his illiteracy. However, the different moments of Christian teaching and learning are all related to following, interpreting, and obeying the rules of the state taught by the church. Nuns and priests are bridges carrying "Indians," *calatos*, "bare-asses" from nudity to governability. The sergeant in the novel says:

> You're sorry for the kids because you don't know how they're treated in the villages. . . . They open up holes in the noses and mouths of newborn babies. And when the Indians get liquored up they screw right in front of everybody. . . . They don't care how old the woman is, and the first one they can grab, their daughters, their sisters. And the old women open up the girls with their hands. . . . And then they eat the cherries so that it brings them good luck. (112–13)

In this interaction between the sergeant and his troops, a culture's rights are repealed. The sergeant, a Mangache, described *selváticos* as rapists. The Mangaches are poor people from Piura, subalterns who live in the poor neighborhoods. They make up the army, the prostitutes, the bartenders, the *garimpeiros* (merchants), the rubber collectors, the outlaws. The intelligentsia assigns them the role of characterizing other subalterns as rapists.

As becomes evident in my reading of Vargas Llosa's novel, high culture feeds on colonial and positivistic works, and reproduces their cultural parameters. Thus, it contributes to legitimizing and/or fossilizing the definition of the aboriginal populations. Narratives of progress are then spun out of quotations, interventionary proceedings, injunctions, and perennial recontextualizations, reconfigurations, and transculturations, forms of mimicry, and positional politics. In *The Green House*, Vargas Llosa creates a rift between the population of mestizos and the Amerindians, and makes mestizos the frontier dividing Amerindians from citizens. It is an object lesson against mestizos themselves as well, a timely warning not to turn back into what they once were. If they slip, they will fall into the other category. Mestizos are allowed to deny that possibility by chastising the "Indian" within them. Viewed this way, high culture is a demonstration of regional and ethnic solidarity, a lesson in obedience and discipline, an excercise warning the subaltern Mangaches against all forms of "Indian" behavior.

Let me turn now to the question of hegemony and domination. Positivistic narratives of development dominate Amerindian cultures through negation. In the deployment of paralinguistic codes, the body uncovers the basic signs of consensus it has stored in its memory. Reading body language, elites come to understand the signs of self-negation as a proof of allegiance. Verbal debasement, to refrain from raising the voice, to smile submissively, is a demonstration of the stigmatizing of oneself. Conversely, to be loud, not to make room for criollos or mestizos, not to keep quiet when they speak, to overgesticulate and overdramatize, are all signs of rebellion. For Jum to be self-reliant is a telling sign of disobedience, evidence that he refuses to accept his construction as an "Indian," and a defiant demonstration of his culture as a mnemonic form that underscores the continuities of his affects and resiliencies.

Reminiscent of nineteenth-century English abolitionist narratives in the Caribbean, the method Vargas Llosa uses to teach self-negation is irony. Laughing at and ridiculing the indigenous is a steady element in structuring his plot. There is a dual movement in this derision: first, it is used to distance himself from the "Indian," and second, to distance "non-Indian" from "Indian" protagonists. Distancing himself from the "Indians," as Julio Ramos notes that Sarmiento does from the gauchos, gains him recognition as a national writer, constitutes his subjectivity as that of a civilized elite, and brings him closer to the European or U.S. writer. Disciplining and punishing the bodies of "Indians" distances "non-Indians" from "Indians," constituted as different.

Vargas Llosa pegs Amerindians through the conflation of body postures and decoration, habits, and incorrect use of Spanish. However, describing "the Other" is just a form of describing oneself. From this viewpoint, negating the "Indian" is an exercise in self-reflection and an attribute of the politics of constitution of selves as subjects. In denigrating "Indians," Vargas Llosa's fiction constitutes itself as good literature, an elite narrative for elite consumption, a self-directed narrative that reinforces consensus through the rhetorical repetition of colonial tropes. Yet, reading ethnographies, historiographies, and fiction in reverse, all the signs of negation become signs of self-preservation and self-affirmation, when not of mobilization. Thus, when Jum protests the price he receives in exchanging his product for money, when he continues to shave his head himself as a sign that he has been shaved to be shamed, his small but meaningful actions, unequivocally read as signs of opposition and resistance, as counterhegemonies and obedience to different cultural paradigms.

Furthermore, domination demands the constant drilling of the idioms of self-negation. In Vargas Llosa, the offensive never relents. The Aguarunas are described in animalistic terms. They grunt softly, and, like breathing animals, without moving from the spot, sit up little by little, stretching out their necks like snakes, "sunning themselves on a river bank when a steamboat comes along, and something frightens them, dilates their pupils, and the chest of one puffs up, the tattoo grows clear, is erased, grows clear, and they gradually approach Sister Angelica, very attentive, serious, silent" (11). This way of portraying the Aguarunas' behavior through the description of their bodies in fear will be highlighted throughout the text, as will be the rejection they bring upon themselves. They are like *animalitos* (little animals). They want to be savages. In these portrayals we see displayed all the lexemes of domination: "the system of concepts by means of which the members of a given group provide themselves with a representation of their social relations . . . tacitly laying down the dividing line between the thinkable and the unthinkable, thereby contributing towards the maintenance of the symbolic order from which it draws its authority."[10]

Encoding the Aguaruna's body across as many semiotic systems as possible is a rich vein that provides lucrative capital for Latin American fiction. In addition to body movements, the written tradition of modernization records the language of the Aguarunas as noises and grunts. The echoes of Vieira strongly resonate in this fiction. Words do not serve to communicate: they become hated and distrusted signs always signifying within an alien semiotic apparatus. Syllabaries are among the most distinguished gadgets of a very well-oiled semiotic system of repression. Exactly as in the seventeenth century, "Indians" don't speak. They roar. Speech resonates as sound bridges between natural beings and religious/cultured subjects and the names of people are reduced to simple onomatopoeic sounds—Jum, Kua-Ko, Cla-Cla. Thus, vocabulary, phonology, and morphology in translation are repulsive to both interlocutors because they demarcate the line of obedience and disobedience, governance or chaos.

JUNGLE: THE ULTIMATE LIMIT OF ONESELF

"For two days we had been crawling along the skeleton of the planet, forgetting History and even the obscure migrations of the unrecorded ages."[11]

In Alejo Carpentier's *The Lost Steps* (1956), more than in any other writer—with perhaps the exception of Euclides da Cunha—nature and jungle, Amazonia, are cultural and historical boulevards, sites of the "real marvelous," the terrain where the wealth of narratives describing the continental mainland are replotted and redeployed so that the rich cultural past unravels and the national subject can constitute itself as the regional continental *latinoamericano*. In Carpentier, jungle stands for a momentous cultural icon and a criollo repositioning of self.

The Lost Steps tells the story of a Latin American man who works for a museum in New York and obtains some funds to travel to the center of the jungle in search of the instruments that will prove the origin of music. The novel plots the journey of this intellectual, who travels from the most modern to the most "premodern" of all possible worlds. The importance of this journey is twofold: to enable the protagonist to recover his own sense of self, and to illustrate the natural marvels of the Latin American continent. As the protagonist moves from modern to "premodern," a world of insects, illnesses, political upheavals, and overall discomforts surrounds him. These discomforts persuade his companion, a French woman by the name of Mouche, to leave him. Mouche's leaving is the necessary precondition for the protagonist to meet Rosario, the earth-woman. Thus the duality modernity/"premodernity" is gendered in the duality Mouche/Rosario. Rosario guides this man's journey to the center of "prehistory," where he discovers the sublime in nature alongside the abject in humans. After a long and fruitful journey, the aesthetic enjoyment of the protagonist comes to an end when he realizes that he cannot record his findings regarding the origin of music because he has no paper to write on. Missing the tools of civilization, he decides to return, trusting that he will be able to weave his way back through the river web of the forest and reach again the center of the jungle. But the passageways to this occult magic kingdom are hidden and the codes only open to those who inhabit it permanently. So, at the end, his modern arrogance and overconfidence lock him out of this marvelous world. Here I am interested in establishing the intersection of time and space in the modern narratives of self-formation.

As in all narratives of self-formation, this one has well-known points of departure. Geographically, the point of departure resembles that of Francisco de Orellana in Peru. Historically, the point of departure is modernity. A travel through space replays a travel through time. However, the trip is not narrated so much as a geographical exploration but as a metaphor of a journey to the center of an inner meaning or identity. There are several steps taking us to this center, each bringing the subject closer to his own self and meaning, until meaning dissolves into the incomprehensible, formulated as the first day of creation. In this place of time without time (the "premodern," the Paleolithic), the self simultaneously perceives his identity and his difference. In "primitive man," man before writing, a specimen that ties the theories of natural evolution to the first narratives of religious creation, he encounters the abject:

> At dusk we stumbled upon the habitat of people of a culture much earlier than that of the men with whom we had been living the day before. We had emerged from the Paleolithic . . . to enter a state that pushed the limits of human life back to the darkest murk of the light of ages. These beings . . . were nevertheless men. . . . I looked at the faces of the people . . . realizing the futility of words, knowing beforehand that we could not even meet in the coincidence of a gesture. (181–82)

This quest to the center of self is written in the form of an autobiography, a genre that subsequently slips into a parody or allegory of exploration narratives and that the narrator calls novels of conquest. As in any historical allegory, all the characters stand for other characters, so their original functions are preserved: there is the crew, and in the crew, a priest (Fray Pedro), a captain (El Adelantado as Felipe de Utre), an astrologer (the Greek man), and the "Indians." But in this allegory there is only one character and one function that skips the slippage and that is the "Indian." "Indians" remain "Indians."

In allegory's logic of equality in difference ($x = y$), I take this identity to mean a reiteration of the conqueror's logic. "Indians" are not human yet, and that is why the author can write sentences like "we were 12 men and three Indians" (165). This phrase, repeated by the Adelantado, is uttered, the narrator warrants, "without malice," an assertion that attempts to foreclose all commentary on racism or cultural domination, and excuses men from talking about other men as "Indians." Having offered this disclaimer, the allegory proceeds to represent the native populations as the cultural artifacts of the past, not as ($x = y$), but as a tautology ($x = x$), namely, "Indians" are "Indians."

Another sign that Carpentier's jungle is an allegory of the colonial texts is that, as in colonial literature, the jungle lacks all coordinates, horizontal or vertical. Everything is generic: "Two yards from where we were, stood a tree trunk, exactly like the others" (159). This is a geography of loss, later metaphorized as the convergence of all historical time into a vortex of "nonhistorical time." The reflection of the vegetation in the water causes a mirage and is absorbed by the vegetation itself; there is "the loss of the sense of verticality, a kind of disorientation, and a dizziness of the eyes" (161). This geography is putrid, dampness clinging to body and clothing, "all the nameless insects . . . , dried wasps, bits of wing, antennae, half-sucked shells . . . a dead alligator, its flesh rotting, under whose hide swarms of green flies came and went" (ibid.). Nature is unpleasant noises: "croaking of enormous frogs . . . metal combs, saws whining through wood, harmonica reeds, the quavering stridulation of the crickets . . . the peacock's cry, belly growls" (162). Because the jungle is the ultimate limit of oneself, it becomes murky, ambiguous, and threatening: "the primeval slime . . . a sour reek like a mud of vinegar and carrion" (160); the uncanny and arcane: "depths bristling with hairy talons where everything seemed a slimy tangle of snakes" (ibid.).

No coordinates are given in this journey for there is no previous geographic knowledge to rely on. There is just the usual semiosis combining weather, ambition, and the extraction of wealth. Knowledge is a privilege reserved for the natives or *naturales*, those who live there. Foreigners have no clue. To reach the interior, travelers must always be guided, and the visitor today, like the visitors during the colonial period, is forever at the mercy of expert Amerindian navigators—what Julio Schvartzman calls "barbarian teachers." To modern visitors, the lack of roads and maps reads as chaos. However, this same lack of knowledge gives the journey an aura of mystery, makes it maddening and exotic, and transforms jungle in a tropicalist stage set. To underscore this aura of mystery, the entrance to Carpentier's jungle is secret, demarcated by a sign on a tree visible only to those who know, to those who often navigate its waters. The sign is noticeable only when the waters are low; when they rise, it vanishes. The biological refugium theory is surreptitiously introduced in the midst of the narrative to support the idea of a natural man and a self-preserving wilderness.

As the protagonist-visitor moves deeply into the forest, his sense of disorientation parallels the perceived disorganization of nature. He experiences a sense of discomfort, uneasiness, and ultimately a terror bordering on hysteria. To convey bodily discomfort, Carpentier has his character first come into the jungle as a simile for entering a prison—"a kind of low colorless jungle growth . . . which threw up a solid fence" (159). Vegetation imprisons because its borders are not drawn, because jungle is a perennial lawlessness. Here we can read Carpentier's staging of the jungle through Greenblatt's experience of wonder. Wonder is the internal response to something amazing, a physical feeling, "a sudden surprise of the soul" (*Marvelous Possessions*, 20), derived from the element of revelation, a result of a suspension or failure of categories, the absence of normal associative mechanisms, something that Greenblatt dramatically compares to a heart attack. Writing experience as wonder relocates, rewires feelings. The experience of jungle feels like danger charged at once with desire, ignorance, and fear, the response to a propitious first confrontation. This is none other than Kant's idea of the sublime, that which produces terror and registers the compelling powers of the real. When an explorer/conqueror speaks of jungle, he is not just noting the unusual but creating a hyperbolic intensity.

Each time Carpentier wants to take us deeper into the jungle, there is a further narrowing of the gorge. Once we have left the obscure jungle for good, we come into "the roaring jungle" of rapids, flinging currents, whirlpools, torrents and watersheds, chill winds, huge waves, whirlwinds, cyclones. The dangerous rivers in jungles are nothing out of the ordinary.

Nonetheless, they are depicted following the guidelines of a Sturm und Drang type of sensibility that is noticeable in a devotion to lightning and to torment. As a few years later in Herzog's *Fitzcarraldo*, torrents, rapids, and tropical rain are the elements the narrator uses to constitute the illuminated horror of natural danger. Menacing obscurity complements menacing clarity. Clarity illuminates the uncanny, creating images of tenebrosity and mean silhouettes. But after this second moment of terror, each terror constituting a passing of a test, we come into a definitive landscape, one made out of rock, "[a] Titans' city . . . with Cyclopean stairways . . . vast terraces guarded by strange fortresses . . . whose role seemed to be to guard the entrance of some forbidden kingdom. . . . There, against a background of light clouds towered the Capital of Forms, an incredible mile-high Gothic cathedral . . . situated on a conical rock (172).

This city of Titans is a transition that dovetails the uncanny experience of jungle with the aesthetic sublime. Utopia subtends this transition in that it is always the unknown, and in this narrative in particular, it invokes the romantic idea of the "primitive" as an ideal state of nature. Once the narrator has overcome his sense of terror contemplating nature as prison and begins contemplating nature as landscape, the language of utopia comes into play. Utopia is presented as something romantic, past:

> When the light came once more . . . I was sharing with the thousands of men who lived in the unexplored headwaters of the Great Rivers the primordial sense of beauty, of beauty physically perceived, equally shared by body and spirit, reborn with each rising of the sun. . . . [D]awn in the jungle always renews the intimate, the atavistic rejoicing, carried in the bloodstream, of ancestors who, for thousands of years, saw in each dawn the end of their nocturnal fears. (163)

In another passage Carpentier writes: "[A]ncient dead forest," "towering obelisks of a drowned city," "the largest trees I had ever seen . . . their branches forming unreal aerial boscages that seemed suspended in space, from which hung transparent mosses, like torn lace" (164). And thus, fear of the unknown transcended, and bodily discomforts taken heed of, the metaphorical forest and "the real jungle" come to be one and the same.

When nature is historicized, we are already in another stage of the voyage, and confront other typologies. For instance, the transit from the

Paleolithic Age to the Glacial Age or creation is introduced in two ways, through the "Indians" and through the Cathedral of Forms—that comes to sublimate the idea of the city of Go(l)d. The "Indians" make their entrance through the narratives of conquest. Portrayed first by El Adelantado as possessions or hands, the hands that pole the rafts are now briefly introduced as barbarians by Fray Pedro, who, like Fray Gaspar de Carvajal, invokes decapitation, torture, and skirmishes as being metonymic of "Indians." All time thus predates itself. Once the jungle provides the space in which civilized men are reoriented through their disorientation, jungle becomes their inner eyes that come to see what their physical eyes would not. Nevertheless, in all instances, ambitions for lucre (gold, slaves) define the existence of the protagonists, the perpetual cycles of time in which they are trapped like Sisyphus. Amerindians are never represented as confused. But their clear perceptions are systematically transferred to the area of the sublime, their consciousness and knowledge displaced to make way for the transformed consciousness of the city man, or citizen. Thus nature makes way for reason in unreason.

And here we can see fully deployed the project of Carpentier's narrative to convert nature into culture. For him, jungle is simultaneously and contradictorily history and "prehistory." It is history in that foliage, verdure, flora, fauna, and "Indians" could not be narrated without having recourse to high culture. His nature is built up with all the tropes of colonial narratives of conquest and exploration. But the manner in which he narrates jungle presents different cultural moments, angles, and projects. Going into the jungle is a narrative of exploration; inside the jungle are high-European plastic arts and cultural anthropology. He sees geology through wilderness and "Indians" through Frobenious (or Lévi-Strauss), and rivers, trees, and rapids through German Romanticism.

In a revealing point of contrast, Wilson Harris narrates the same journey in *The Palace of the Peacock*, the first novel of his *Guyana Quartet*, but his main focus is the conflation of postcolonial and colonial narratives of identity onto the jungle and the indigenous peoples. His crew is composed of all the mixed bloods and conquered peoples meeting in the New World: the (East) Indian, the Native American, the Asian American, the African American, and the European American. In *Palace* there is a contract; Amerindians are metonymized as woman/slave/concubine, a constantly morphing figure marking the liminal points between material and immaterial jungle in the eyes of the workers and the search party's scribe.[12] Whereas the men are perpetually transformed into their racial ancestors, the Amerindian woman Mariella is the vessel, the guide; the jungle, the secret the jungle keeps to itself. She is not, then, a woman—raped, enslaved, beaten—but a metaphor, a vehicle without a history, fashioned for articulating the object of the perpetual cycles of development. Where Harris is pessimistic and Carpentier hopeful, each conflates jungle with "Indian" on the other side of culture and history, that is, on the other side of *civitas* and citizenship. Thus the narratives of the state and its predicate, the nation, are indirectly narrated.

Both Carpentier and Harris use nature as a double articulation, to deploy the psychic inner world and the physical interior of the nation as backlands. Continually repeated is an idea of nation reduced to geography, and of national identity reduced to intimate landscape. Jungle is that in between us (Latin American criollos and Creoles) and them ("Indians"). Carpentier's subject unfolds into an omniscient male narrator who sees and comments, a protagonist within the text who takes the position of the writer/intellectual-*escribano*, the one who, like Carvajal, translates landscapes into culture and law. There is a sense of—or wish for—the natural preservations that are projected. The defense of the refugium theory on the basis of symbolic and figurative impenetrability sublimates the fact that the jungle is entirely—and persistently—penetrable.[13] The authenticity of the narrated (subject) is established by the setting: the jungle. Jungle is the generic nature and empty slot, the likes of caves and hideout places known only by maroons in Jamaica's anonymous 1827 novel *Hamel, the Obeah Man*.[14]

Neither Carpentier's nor Harris's narrative is directly a narrative of positivism proposing development. In their cultural relativism, they could even be considered antipositivistic in that they review concepts of race, ethnicity, and barbarism, explaining them as other states of culture. There is no direct monetary or economic interest in the transcription of this vision. The writers are not driven by a narrow nationalistic project. Rather, they validate the different components of landscape as historical and cultural geographies. What is striking is the perdurability and startling transnationality of a vision centered on nature as frontier. And as long as nature is mirrored in the speculum of culture, becoming a museum, a monument, a reservoir, nature/jungle and the narratives encoding it become, through literature, national-state projects, patrimony.

The counterpoint to this type of fiction is Darcy Ribeiro's project of cultural anthropology, which undertakes a revision of concepts such as race, ethnicity, savagery, and the literary making of the Amerindians into primitive ancestry, linking them to any primitive men. Ribeiro, one of Brazil's leading twentieth-century intellectuals and a member of the Brazilian Academy of Letters, has written innumerable studies on anthropology, but he has also contributed to Brazilian letters. In his novel *Maira* he narrates the story of the Mairum society, a product of Ribeiro's work with the Caduvoeo and Urubu groups. In this novel, he describes the devastating effects of the contact between Amerindians and white Brazilians from the standpoint of the indigenous people. Ribeiro places the aborigines in the "theater of their existence," outside of the literary first day of Genesis, of the timeless landscape—people absent from history—and portrays them just as any other human beings. The anthropological message is that, seen in their localities and situated inside their own paradigmatical frames, "Indians" stop being discursive entities and become flesh-and-blood transnational subalterns. This is one way of disentangling the minuscule, the *petit récit* of ethnicities, from the aristocratic cultural monuments elaborated by Carpentier and Harris. In Ribeiro's novel, a reconstruction of Amerindian societies from within is attempted. If at the high end of Carpentier's scale there is nature, rock formations, vegetation, at the human scale of Ribeiro there is the Society for the Protection of "Indians," the National Indian Foundation, but, above all, human beings, Amerindian "Indians."

HIDDEN ANCESTRY

"He liked to think of all the rivers of Guyana as the curious rungs in a ladder on which one sets one's musing foot again and again, to climb into both the past and the future of the continent of mystery" (Harris, *The Guyana Quartet*, 367).

In the 1960s, the Guyanese writer Wilson Harris, who began his training as a land surveyor in 1939, and was hired in 1942 to trace the path of the innumerable waterways in the Guyana jungle, published his *Guyana*

Quartet (1960–64), a group of three novels that document the confrontation between the dense jungle and development. In *The Secret Ladder*, one
of the novels of *The Guyana Quartet*, Fenwick, the protagonist, a land surveyor, is put in charge of measuring and counting, ordering and classifying rivers, savannas, and fields, a remiss and secretive landscape opaque to
the modern gaze. In the process of carrying out his work, he finds himself
at odds first with his labor crew, then with the inhabitants of the jungle,
and finally with himself. The first discrepancy occurs over management—
one of the workers advises him against all kinds of sentimentalist and pop-
ulist stances; the second occurs over the interpretation and meaning of the
gauging and measuring instruments—an old surviving maroon sees in them
not his salvation but his destruction; and the third occurs in the quandary
these two opinions present with respect to his own faith in modernization.

The absolute blackness of the jungle is not broken by the measuring
instrument, neither is the vast brown, mighty river accountable to the
national project. The ciphers never tally; meanings never reach consensus. The history of Guyana fictionalized in this novel renders the lay of
the land incommensurable with the needs of its people. The overpower-
ing weight of the jungle underpins the artificiality of modernity, whose
mighty weight is threatened by the weak gaze of a destitute, surviving
maroon and his rudimentary clarity. The disenfranchised subaltern casts a
gaze that is devastating to the surveyor. It demarcates the limits of the project and confronts the history of nation and development head-on. The
imperial heights of technology perish in the jungle and all social relations
and identities unravel at its seams. Administration collapses when it comes
into contact with the jungle and wants to measure everything in the bush.
I examine here the tensions created by the narratives of development and
modernity in the regimes of subjectivity constituting the national selves.

Almost at the end of *The Secret Ladder*, the novel that closes Harris's
Guyana Quartet, Russell Fenwick, the mestizo/creole protagonist, writes a
letter to his mestiza/creole, almost-white English mother in which he relates his encounter with Poseidon—a symbolic black maroon father: "I
wish I could truly grasp the importance of this meeting. If I do not—if
my generation does not—leviathan will swallow us all" (384). What is the
importance this "I" has to grasp and why is he posing himself and his generation as a last hermeneutical frontier? To attempt to answer this question,
which Fenwick himself does not answer, we must first traverse his jungle.

In Harris's jungle, there is emptiness and desolation. The indomitable jungle and the ungovernable crew of *The Secret Ladder* parallel each other in this landscape of despair, where human hubris is relentlessly gauged by the figure of the state in the character of a land surveyor. In one of his multiple attempts to apprehend the jungle, the protagonist has named it "Palace of the Peacock after the city of God, the city of gold set somewhere in the heart of Brazil and Guyana" (367). If, in Carpentier's novel, all members of the imaginary crew parodied the Spaniards, reproducing their functions, in *The Secret Ladder*, as in *The Palace of the Peacock*, the crew is the image of multinational and multiethnic migrancy, a result of the mostly forced migration of those then without nation-states—Asians (Weng, Chiung), Africans (Jordan, Bryant, Dominic), Hindu East Indians (Van Brock, Perez, Stoll)—all the substrata of the empire whose meeting place is Amazonia.

Gauging and measuring, the tools of positivistic science, seem futile in the context of the jungle. The figure of the land surveyor represents this uselessness as well as the weakness and indifference of an absent government. Drastically differing from E. G. Squier, the geographer of Central America whose mission is supported by a flourishing metropolitan commerce, Fenwick, the land surveyor, is a lonely man out in the wilderness, looking like the Canje River whose banks are "brittle in places, scored and ravaged by itinerant streams" (363). Jordan, his aide-de-camp, knows this, and, as Vargas Llosa's Mangaches, whose function is to scoff at Amerindians' own subaltern condition, he advises against insecure liberal policies. Fenwick cannot be a romantic in his conduct toward the people; he cannot make himself vulnerable. A popular sensibility, a sort of populism will not do in the jungle. Solidarity with the poor must not be allowed in governance. Speaking of the relationship between men and women, in analogy to the state and productive government, he warns:

> One would never be worried to ask who entertained whom . . . so that it never materially affected the order of government. . . . a social expedition should [not] ever be so cornered that it had to discover who kept company with whom. This was always the beginning of the end of oneself and everything. An open invitation . . . to the ghosts of chaos. . . . Not only distress of conscience. But the immortal foul sisters—hope and progress. (447–48)

The "brilliant land surveyor" denies any analogy between himself and the government: he is not the Colonial Secretariat, the law of the jungle in the jungle. Nevertheless, the game of governance persists in *The Secret Ladder*. As with Susan Hecht and Alexander Cockburn, Richard Price and Sally Price depict intellectuals, consultants, and developers as being tied to projects, and projects to progress.[15] Cultural technicians are always embroiled in displacing people, in telling the story of displacing and deterritorializing peoples. But, paradoxically, there is always a perplexity, an ambiguity, and an engaged disengagement in the representation of the intellectual's journey into the jungle looking for the nation, or the borders of the nation, and finding people instead. In a critical flaw—endemic to strangers in Amazonia—in Harris's novel, the character comes to convince himself that jungle people are his ancestors, an essential component of his mestizo or creole self. His encounter with Poseidon, the old black maroon, is important to understand or to decipher, as important for him as an "I," as an "Us," the collective of his generation, the last one with a chance.

In this narrative of confrontation, Poseidon, as a black maroon, takes the place of the Amerindians in the Latin American and European or U.S. frontier narratives. By this time, the maroons have become mythical figures in the official pantheon of the nation, and Poseidon stands alone, a product of a "labyrinthine genealogy" that took him back to a runaway African slave "turned into a wild cannibal man in the swamps" (369). What ultimately matters about this prefiguration is the encounter, his presence as the counterfeited vision invoked by and through the national imaginary, "an unkempt sheep's back. The black wooden snake of skin peeping through its animal blanket was wrinkled and stitched together incredibly" (371). How can we come to trust the vision of this unseeing subject lurking in the woods, a stranger in a habitat who suddenly "appears in the opening of the bush" (370) like Rima, the woman in Hudson's *Green Mansions*?

When the mestizo/Creole meets his hidden ancestry, past ("premodern," "precivilized") confronts present and projects the undesirable image of a future of despair, "the immortal foul sisters—hope and progress" (448), where any temporality is alike, where history folds in on geography, the arena where there are no human deeds, but only jungle. That is the primary reason for the importance of grasping the meaning and weight of the encounter or misencounter with incomplete, peripheral, unequal, "premodern" man. There they stood, facing each other, and Fenwick, like the male narrator in Carpentier, cannot "help fastening his eyes greedily upon him as if he saw down a bottomless gauge and the river reflection" (370). There is a parallel moment in Carpentier, when, looking at the edge of a muddy hole, he sees "the most horrible things [his] eyes had ever beheld. They were like two fetuses with white beards from whose hanging lips came sounds resembling the wail of a newborn child. . . . 'They are prisoners,' said the Adelantado sarcastically, 'prisoners of the others, who consider themselves the superior race, the sole rightful owners of the jungle'" (183). But there is a difference to be traced between these two narratives already and that difference is made by Poseidon's attire. His dress is an unmistakable sign of his *mestizaje* and his decrepitude: "a flannel vest, flapping ragged fins of trousers on his legs" (370).

The encounter of self with his hidden ancestry is provoked, desired, invoked, reiterated, and necessary. Fenwick narrates the encounter following the precepts of a tradition. He is the modern intellectual who writes over what the colonial intellectual (his white ancestor) wrote for him. The narrative is thus a river flowing to the confluence of the mestizo with his African-American and Amerindian ancestry. In the language of his white European ancestor, "one dead seeing eye and one living closed eye" (19); in the language of his black African ancestor, a series of incomprehensible grunts—Poseidon's "mouth moved and made frames which did not correspond to the words he actually uttered" (371). Fenwick has to explain this apparition to his mother, and in a letter he attributes the hallucinatory vision, as does Albert Camus's protagonist in *L'Étranger*, to the heat, the influence of the sun. Horrified at the vision of self as destitute maroon, he insists that he is not a politician: he is an intellectual and his interests consequently are not political. The issue for him is fundamentally psychological—or aesthetic.

However, despite the psychological confusion these aesthetics frame, there is another explanation for the perplexity produced by this sudden unexpected encounter. Fenwick's job is to record and analyze a network of tidal readings. In the process, "his reconnaissance surveys—conducted with chain and compass—had disclosed glaring inconsistencies between his plot and the maps compiled from air photographs" (387). These discrepancies in cartography correspond to discrepancies in judgment that, at another level, mirror the incongruities between Fenwick and those who employed him, as well as between Fenwick and Poseidon. In the first case, the disagreement reveals the divergence between landlord and government; in the second, between the meaning and value assigned to technology. The interest represented by all these sectors embroils the narratives of progress in innumerable clashes; the one that concerns us here refers to the oral narratives of subsistence economies. What Poseidon—and Jum in Vargas Llosa, the Amerindians in Carpentier, and Kua-Ko in Hudson—stand in for are the subsistence economies cheated first by trade (how many balls of *jebe* (rubber) are tradable for a knife in Vargas Llosa) and then by land surveyors representing the interest of the sugar estates, or the rice lands in the case of Harris, the cattle estates, or the incommensurable financial world in the case of Augusta Dwyer, Hecht and Cockburn, Pedro Casaldáliga, and others.

Fish, rubber, and land are not fairly exchanged. Discrepancies in prices correspond to discrepancies in value. The difference lies in the value assigned to things in relation to the value assigned to people. What mediates between people, what degrades people, is unequal exchange, the hampering of their freedom of trade, the restricted crystal ceiling imposed on their capacity to set a fair price for their goods, and ultimately the relationship between subsistence economies and capitalism, between ethnicities and progress. Freedom for Poseidon is not hitched, as the narratives of progress mistakenly assume, to running rampant in the middle of the jungle, but to his capacity to earn a living, the possibilities of staying alive, his ability to reproduce his environment, the difference between the hours it takes him to produce the object of exchange and the unfair return he gets for it.

This is what Poseidon and Jum defend when they are allowed to speak—were they allowed to speak against the voices of progress. But neither is allowed. Jum interjects, at most, a composite word—*Limagobierno, silabariolima.* Poseidon is, once more, the narrated, the enunciated, when Fenwick points to the ladder of numbers and claims that the measurement of the river is for their own good, for him and "everybody else who lives in the river," and asks him to

Tell the people so. . . . Poseidon moved his head blindly as if he were deaf and dumb. He had nothing to say . . . staring solemnly and thoughtfully at the gauge; then at the Dumpy level and tripod. . . . He distrusted these, seeing in them the heartless instruments of science which were aimed like sentient forces at him (and whose monstrous profession would turn the tables on him, and rob him of the last freedom he possessed). (394–95)

As in the case of Jum, who can see the stealing of his labor in the unfair exchange for the sale of his rubber to *Limagobierno* and *silabariolima*, Poseidon can see in the gauging instruments his destruction, and the destruction of the river peoples. This encounter is an instance of a war of positions, of the relation between hegemony and dominance. For Fenwick and his kind, the technological and scientific possession of the river is an instance of the exercising of freedom to achieve progress. For Poseidon and his kind, this very same act signifies death. The secret ladder symbolically portrays the struggle between subsistence and monetary economies at work within "the national." This struggle is mediated by the mestizo cultures. In alliance with the ideologies of capitalism and progress, Fenwick's conflict resides in his absolute conviction that these cultures cannot survive. Thus, although he is appalled at this inhuman condition, he must leave it behind. Talking to one of his crew, who manifests his solidarity with Poseidon, Fenwick states:

Plain wholesome understanding of history and facts and possibilities is important, Bryant. Take the unadorned facts of science, the plain economic structure of society shorn of worshipful emotion, shorn of this fiction of freedom you say Poseidon alone possesses. I am glad we can see him as he is so that we can know what this life is, the hard business of this life, here and now. . . . and indeed we can see . . . the necessity for human freedom. (396)

In the conflation of freedom with progress, progress with science, and science with the well-being of people, all poetry fades out. The voice of research and development speaks for the interest that is financing it. For Harris's protagonists, the question is clear. Meeting his other half as "black," or "Indian," the brilliant mestizo intellectual could never, anymore, rid himself of the demon of freedom and imagination and responsibility. "Poseidon [like Jum, Kua-Ko, *La Selvática*, primitive men] had been hooked and nailed to a secret ladder of conscience however crumbling and extreme the image was" (371). After being in touch with him, a

nightmare overcomes Fenwick. He dreams of a tall horseman. Like the
conqueror, he is armed with the sword and the spear. Armed knight and
ragged maroon come with relentless passion to hunt the mestizo narratives
of progress. These hordes of mounted, obscure horsemen decapitate a
mare, leaving the headless trunk quivering. The image teaches us

> the terrifying depth of our human allegiance, our guilt in the face of
> humanity, our subservience to the human condition. But he [Poseidon,
> Jum, Kua-Ko] cannot force us, surely, to make an idol of this present de-
> grading form—crawl on our bellies in order to make ourselves less than he
> is, tie ourselves into knots in order to enslave ourselves deeper than he is.
> (397)

In this novel, modernity or postmodernity signify the technical services
rendered by intellectuals to the financial world of the beyond. Beyond is
what pays for the voice-over narrating Fenwick from London, Amerindians from Paris, or them all by us from the United States. This narrator,
this voice-over, is not Fenwick's, or our own. It is the voice of the invisible land surveyor historicizing geographies and gauging the power of resistance, the short life of resistance represented by alternative economic
forms and forums, by different freedoms and authorities, and designing
the time, mode, and model of extermination—high finance, low-intensity
warfare, or both. It is, then, the voice of the consultant over the voice of
the native intelligentsia, or the voice of money over the voice of the consultant. In his letter to his mother, Fenwick proves prophetic: "I wish I
could truly grasp the importance of this meeting. If I do not—if my generation does not—leviathan will swallow us all" (384).

CONCLUSIONS

In modern Latin American fiction, the representation of jungle swings
back and forth between ethnological descriptions and history of art. In
Harris and Carpentier, jungle becomes architectonic landscape. This
brings back the memory of paradise, the founding image of nature that
opened this study, except that the disorganized prose of the founding
relatos is now superseded by the troubled discourses of the state. Measuring, gauging, mapping, the tools provided by positivist sciences to subdue

the jungle, are, however, to no avail. Plotting settlements, investments, and commerce is thus once more extrapolated to beauty in the frozen descriptions of nature presented as the new archaeology of knowledge. In *Palace*, jungle is the palace of the peacock—everything and nothing, every man's dream and accomplishment, every man's destruction and obliteration. The apotheosis of landscape as jungle is simultaneously vortex and senselessness.

Harris's *Guyana Quartet* provides a sharp metaphor to capture the dilemma of jungle, namely, "one dead seeing eye and one living closed eye" (19). The novel opens with a shot that rings out and kills a horseman. In a moment, the horseman is alive and revealed as the brutal landowner whose Amerindian slaves have all fled into the interior. A journey to capture the runaways is immediately begun. The narrator is none other than the landowner's brother. A divided self, one side entrepreneur-landowner, the other intellectual-writer—"one dead seeing eye and one living closed eye"—vividly captures the split. The metaphor also introduces the double nature of Amazonian narratives: blind to what they see, revealing in what they do not see. Despite the apparent disparity between the two brothers, one the tyrannical leader and the other the liberal writer, they are both members of the same family, united by blood. Thus, one brother's brutal chase is the other brother's pretext to narrate the journey of development that ends in an all-out war between workers and maroons. The ideal, according to the moral of the story, would have been never to undertake the journey. The curse is that each and every character—with the exception of the Amerindian female guide—is caught up in an inexorable cycle, doomed to repeat the journey over and over again.

Living with "one dead seeing eye and one living closed eye" accounts for the differences in perception. The unseeing closed eye changes over the vision of landscape from physical to intellectual. In the change, all of the putrid, noisy, threatening, and arcane elements paradoxically become rhetorical figures representing the exquisite—*locus amoenus*, garden, paradise: the palace of the peacock—the orderly, the regulated, the accountable. These are the layers of the journey of meaning. The signifying chain obtains the aesthetic: a beautiful nature, nature fashioned into garden, into woods, a palace as glorious as a peacock, "a far journey," "a whole armor," "a secret ladder"—Harris's metaphors—that ironically introduce the "prehistory" or "premodern" humankind. Amazonia, the jungle—whether plotted in Carpentier's metonymic chain as the Genesis, "year 0," "the Paleolithic Age" (Carpentier, *The Lost Steps*, 179), "a timeless setting" (169), "the dawn of History" (179), "the darkest murk of the night of ages" (82), or "the skeleton of the planet" (185)—becomes the zero degree of writing: a "significant absence," a zero-sum game.

Therefore, the structure of these narratives—Vargas Llosa's, Carpentier's, Harris's—presumes a journey from a metropolitan, civilized, modern city to the interior of an unknown "barbarian" and "underdeveloped" nature. If the character succeeds, he will be fully rewarded with aesthetics and jungle will become a sweet dream, a *locus amoenus*, a (super)natural cultural highway. If he fails, the character will be punished with the ethnological inferno and jungle will become his nightmare. At the end of Harris's *Guyana Quartet*, the eye soars over the wreckage of history to close the circle of time, to usher in a new dawn. In Carpentier, the rewards are multiple—the discovery of courage, the contemplation of beauty, the prizes of cultural anthropology offered by the "prehistory" of culture in pottery, musical instruments, old ways of being. It is at the heart of jungle that Carpentier's "Indians" meet Vargas Llosa's "Indians," the objects of his reflection, the "Indians" as borders and obstacles of (un)constituted nation-states, the "Indians" as primitive beings. Carpentier's Fray Pedro repeating Fray António Vieira had already given us a preview of this narrative by calling them barbarians. But then, when Fray Pedro celebrates Mass, just as in Harris, nature and "Indians" are conflated with tree trunks and hanging leaves that hide dangers: "And around us were the Gentiles, the idol-worshipers, gazing upon the mystery from a narthex of lianas" (Carpentier, *The Lost Steps*, 176).

The echoes of early colonial narratives ring out loud in the modern narratives examined here. Colonial paradigms are recycled and early exploration narratives are mirrored in the speculum of the modern. Modern and colonial narratives plot nature, in this case the Amazon jungle, either as utopia—a cultural terrain to ponder and enjoy; the place of wilderness in frontier narratives of adventurers, pilgrims, ambitious military men— or as a setting to exploit, later to become a topos for development. And just as space permits Father Gaspar de Carvajal to project himself in time, in his case a future time, so it serves the contemporary writers, whose projections in time are, in reverse, toward the past.

Today, the idea of converting jungle into parks springs from the film *Jurassic Park* (1993) by Steven Spielberg. This idea works in tandem with tourist investment projects targeting pleasant geographies like the Caribbean. That *Jurassic Park* was filmed in Costa Rica's rain forest speaks eloquently of the impossibility of using Amazonia, which, in its grandiosity, would have been a more apt stage. In the film, there is a desire to mount a monumental scenery to match the dimension of dinosaurs, and to use the power of the televisual image to render an imaginative contemporary reconstruction of the appalling imagination of the first European explorers. Only U.S. pragmatism and the availability of special effects allowed Spielberg to avoid the pitfalls of Werner Herzog, still able to enact the meeting of past, present, and future, yet avoiding nostalgia and keeping in tune with utopia. There are no natives in *Jurassic Park*.

NOTES

INTRODUCTION

1. The adjectives this I/eye uses to describe the "new" are *barbarian, unknown, ungovernable, paradisiacal.* What becomes evident in this subject's descriptions, however, is how the social imaginary expresses perplexity before the "new." Awe and wonder are the master terms informing Stephen Greenblatt's interpretation of the documents. His hypothesis is that there is a specific political reason for the performance and production of wonder. The marvelous confirms the power and validity of the Spaniards' claims against those skeptics who ask for more tangible signs. Wonder is gold, a calculated rhetorical strategy, the conjuring of an aesthetic response in the service of a legitimating process. See Mary Louise Pratt, *Imperial Eyes: Travel Writing and Transculturation* (London and New York: Routledge, 1992); Stephen Greenblatt, *Marvelous Possessions: The Wonder of the New World* (Chicago: University of Chicago Press, 1992).

2. Michel Foucault, *The Order of Things: An Archaeology of the Human Sciences* (New York: Vintage Books, 1973), xv. Speaking about *tierra* as nature, Foucault maintains that it is "trapped in the thin layer that holds semiology and hermeneutics one above the other" (29). He defines hermeneutics as "the totality of the learning and skills that enable one to make the signs speak and to discover their meaning," and semiology as "the totality of the learning and skills that enable one to distinguish the location of the sign" (ibid.). In unraveling the sign *tierra*, however, "this superimposition necessarily includes a slight degree of noncoincidence between the resemblances" (29–30). In this sense, *tierra* is the site of noncoincidence, a meaningless, unlocalizable, silent sign that is the reverse of nature in that nature "is neither mysterious nor veiled" (29).

3. Ibid., 131.

4. Greenblatt (*Marvelous Possessions*) makes his case in three steps: the first is related to the observation and collection of data as signs. The second moves on to the

interpretation of signs. The third is taking possession. He believes Europeans first make the unfamiliar coincide with the familiar, explaining any unfamiliar feature as wonder either in the positive (Columbus as a science-fiction writer) or in the negative (Jean de Léry as the producer of sublime horror). Here is where the Kantian and Foucauldian traditions overlap and are constituted into master narratives. For Kant, the idea is that of the sublime aesthetic, which basically consists of the ascription of beauty or ugliness to something that is analogous to or different from us. For Foucault, this is related to the four forms of analogy stated at the beginning of this note.

5. For Greenblatt, "words in the New World seem always to be trailing after events that pursue a terrible logic quite other than the fragile meanings that they construct. . . . The possession of weapons and the will to use them on defenseless people are cultural matters that are intimately bound up with discourse: with the stories that a culture tells itself, its conceptions of personal boundary and liability, its whole collective system of rules" (ibid., 63–64). His thesis is that the European system seems to be paradoxical, mobile, and dependent on improvization. Paradox is the figure that justifies his hypothesis that in the colonial discourse words are empty signs (tabulae rasae, mimetic beings), always trailing and looking like quotes, "a glass through which Columbus looks to find what he expects to find" (88), and "to confirm what he already knows" (89), what Richard Mulcaster calls enfranchisement or "making the 'stranger denisons' of other tongues 'bond to the rules of our writing'" (88). When the signs are in disagreement, "when the pressure of articulating the known on the site of geographical or cultural difference becomes overwhelming [is when] the representational system itself significantly changes" (89), which is the case of the seventeenth-century Don Quixote in Foucault, and the narratives of the initial confrontation for Greenblatt. He recommends hermeneutical caution, for exchanges are frequently fraught with obstacles. Language is not transparent, as a brief glance at Mayan glyphs immediately demonstrates. The stories of the initial exchange of signs must be passed through the Cartesian sieve and researchers must question the power of performances, charades, and pantomimes, for communication is contingent upon a shared gesture system: "the Europeans and the interpreters translated such fragments [of communication] as they understood or thought they understood into a coherent story" (95–96). But was that which is narrated what really happened?

6. For further discussion on this matter, see Antonio Benítez Rojo, *The Repeating Island: The Caribbean and the Postmodern Perspective*, trans. James E. Maraniss (Durham, NC: Duke University Press, 1992); Arjun Appadurai, *Modernity at Large: Cultural Dimensions of Globalization* (Minneapolis: University of Minnesota Press, 1996).

7. Susan Kirkpatrik, "The Ideology of Costumbrismo," *Ideologies and Literature* 2.7 (1978): 28–44.

8. For a thorough comparative discussion on lands, land patterns, and land-tenure systems, see Patricia Seed, *Ceremonies of Possession in Europe's Conquest of the New World: 1492–1640* (Cambridge: Cambridge University Press, 1995).

1. PARADISE

1. My primary sources for chapter 1 include Edmundo O'Gorman, *The Invention of America: An Inquiry into the Historical Nature of the New World and the Meaning of Its History* (Bloomington: Indiana University Press, 1961); idem, *Cuatro historiadores de Indias: Martir, Oviedo, Las Casas, Acosta* (Mexico City: Secretaría de Educación Pública, 1972); Tzvetan Todorov, *The Conquest of America: The Question of the Other*, trans. Richard Howard (New York: HarperPerennial, 1984); Margarita Zamora, *Reading Columbus* (Berkeley: University California Press, 1993); Beatriz Pastor, *The Armature of Conquest: Spanish Accounts of the Discovery of America, 1492–1589*, trans. Lydia Longstreth Hunt (Stanford, CA: Stanford University Press, 1992); José Rabasa, *Inventing America: Spanish Historiography and the Formation of Eurocentrism* (Norman: University of Oklahoma Press, 1993); Antonello Gerbi, *The Dispute of the New World: The History of a Polemic, 1750–1900*, trans. Jeremy Moyle (Pittsburgh: University of Pittsburgh Press, 1973); idem, *Nature in the New World: From Christopher Columbus to Gonzalo Fernández de Oviedo*, trans. Jeremy Moyle (Pittsburgh: University of Pittsburgh Press, 1985); Pratt, *Imperial Eyes*; Walter D. Mignolo, *The Darker Side of the Renaissance: Literacy, Territoriality, and Colonization* (Ann Arbor: University of Michigan Press, 1995); Peter Jackson, *Maps of Meaning: An Introduction to Cultural Geography* (London and New York: Routledge, 1994); Greenblatt, *Marvelous Possessions*; Peter Hulme, *Colonial Encounters: Europe and the Native Caribbean, 1492–1797* (London and New York: Routledge, 1986).

2. *The Voyage of Christopher Columbus: Columbus' Own Journal of Discovery Newly Restored and Translated*, ed. John Cummins (New York: St. Martin's Press, 1992), 186.

3. Ibid., 104.

4. For a discussion on the hegemony of the scientific method, see Richard Rorty, "Method, Social Science, and Social Hope," in *The Postmodern Turn: New Perspectives on Social Theory*, ed. Steven Seidman (Cambridge: Cambridge University Press, 1994), 46–64.

5. The following texts discuss this idea in more detail: Asad Talal, *Anthropology and the Colonial Encounter* (London: Ithaca Press, 1973); Francis Barker et al., eds., *Europe and Its Others: Proceedings of the Essex Conference on the Sociology of Literature* (Colchester: University of Essex, 1985); Henri Baudet, *Paradise on Earth: Some Thoughts on European Images of Non-European Man*, trans. Elizabeth Wentholt (Westport CT: Greenwood Press, 1976); Robert F. Berkhofer Jr., *The White Man's Indian: Images of the American Indian from Columbus to the Present* (New York: Alfred A. Knopf, 1978); Urs Bitterli, *Los "salvajes" y los "civilizados": el encuentro de Europa y Ultramar*, trans. Pablo Sorozabal (Mexico City: Fondo de Cultura Económica, 1982); Bernadette Boucher, *Icon and Conquest: A Structural Analysis of the Illustration of de Bry's Great Voyages*, trans. Basia Miller Gulati (Chicago: University of Chicago Press, 1981); Edward Topsell, *The History of Four-Footed Beasts and Serpents and Insects* (New York: Da Capo Press, 1967).

6. Foucault, *The Order of Things*; Graham Burchell, Colin Gordon, and Peter

Miller, eds., *The Foucault Effect: Studies in Governmentality with Two Lectures by and an Interview with Michel Foucault* (Chicago: University of Chicago Press, 1991).

7. Gerbi, *The Dispute of the New World*, 54.

8. Ibid.

9. Ibid., 55.

10. Roberto González Echeverría, *Myth and Archive: A Theory of Latin American Narrative* (Cambridge and New York: Cambridge University Press, 1990).

11. *The Voyage of Christopher Columbus*, 106.

12. Gerbi, *The Dispute of the New World*, 224.

13. Ibid., 80.

14. Walter Mignolo's postcolonial answer to the dispute on knowledge is to make a case for the recognition of multicultural hermeneutical presences and against the denial of coevality. He proves that all kinds of knowledge have been generated by different people at different times, not only by Europeans, although the discourses of colonialist texts would have us believe otherwise. Knowledge of the world is contingent on the tension created by the power of cultural ethnicities. Mignolo's strategy is to place alternative views side by side and to entwine ethnicity and power within "coexisting territorial representations" (*The Darker Side of the Renaissance*, 23). Illustrations of the coevalness of knowledge are later supplemented by Mignolo, with representations taken from the Islamic world as well as from European descriptions of non-European cities, such as Cuzco and Tenochtitlán. He takes this notion of European power on to the "new *tierras*," to the redrawing of territorialities, and hermeneutics to reinterpret the silence of the indigenous populations. If Ricci, Durán, and Sahagún are the moments of conflicting representations of cosmography and territoriality, at the end of the sixteenth century the point is ethnic hegemony. The discussion between ethnicity as power and cosmography as representation of that power is useful in many other ways. For instance, in Mignolo's outlining of indigenous maps, he tells us that "the quadripartite division" used by Aztecs "is valid not only for the organization of space and time, but also for the entire organization of urbanity and social life" (248). Coexistence, like coevolution, is the other supporting pillar of Mignolo's structure, one very useful today because the remapping of extension and duration once more has to contend with the existence of indigenous people.

15. *The Four Voyages of Christopher Columbus*, trans. and ed. J. M. Cohen (London: Penguin, 1969), 217–18.

16. Todorov, *The Conquest of America*, 25 . Subsequent references are given in the text.

17. O'Gorman, *The Invention of America*, 18–19.

18. Cummins, *The Voyage of Christopher Columbus*, 96.

19. Michel de Certeau, *Heterologies: The Writing of History*, trans. Tom Conley (New York: Columbia University Press, 1988).

20. David Spurr, *The Rhetoric of Empire: Colonial Discourse in Journalism, Travel Writing, and Imperial Administration* (Durham, NC: Duke University Press, 1993), 28. Subsequent references are given in the text.

21. Rabasa, *Inventing America*, 71.

22. Ibid.

23. For further discussion on this topic, see Stuart B. Schwartz, *Implicit Understandings: Observing, Reporting, and Reflecting on the Encounters between Europeans and Other Peoples in the Early Modern Era* (Cambridge: Cambridge University Press, 1994).

24. W. J. T. Mitchell, ed., *Landscape and Power* (Chicago: University of Chicago Press, 1994).

25. More discussion on this topic can be found in Karen Ordahl Kupperman, ed., *America in European Consciousness: 1493–1750* (Chapel Hill: University of North Carolina Press, 1995); John Huxtable Elliott, *Spain and Its World, 1500–1700* (New Haven: Yale University Press, 1989); idem, *The Old World and the New, 1492–1650* (Cambridge: Cambridge University Press, 1970).

26. Zamora, *Reading Columbus*, 131, 130. Subsequent references are given in the text.

27. For more information on this logic, see the insightful articles of Sylvia Wynter, "Beyond the Categories of the Master Conception: The Counterdoctrine of the Jamesian Poiesis," in *C. L. R. James: A Reader*, ed. Henry Paget and Paul Buhle (Durham, NC: Duke University Press, 1992), 63–91; idem. "1942: A New World View," in *Race, Discourse, and the Origin of the Americas: A New World View*, ed. Vera Lawrence Hyatt and Rex Nettleford (Washington, DC: Smithsonian Institution Press, 1995), 5–57.

28. Rabasa, *Inventing America*, 58.

29. Greenblatt, *Marvelous Possessions*.

30. Ibid., 91.

31. In his geographical study of maps and their meanings, for instance, Peter Jackson (*Maps of Meaning: An Introduction to Cultural Geography* [London and New York: Routledge, 1994]) unravels the terms that engage the polemic of culture versus landscape. For him, the notion of landscape is rooted in human mediation. He opposes Carl Sauer's idea of "landscape as a peculiar unit of geography, a peculiar geographic association of facts" (25), because this concept, Jackson argues, excludes or ignores human agency, the imprint that humans work upon an area. In total agreement with Jackson, W. J. T. Mitchell proposes that the concept of nature as landscape naturalizes cultures, and puts forth the notion of "circulating sites" associated with the dissonance between class and national interests in the same style as does Raymond Williams. Other critics in other disciplines, among them the historian Inga Clendinnen, also move away from the natural representations of landscapes and explain the Mayan countryside as a complex and organized construction, as webs of symbols. She argues that the organization of space and the interrelationship between conceptions of time-space enabled the indigenous cultures of Yucatán to be resilient and resist the cultural offensive of colonial Spanish friars. The physical world, the world of nature, is, then, always historically and culturally constituted. See Inga Clendinnen, "Landscape and World View: The Survival of Yucatec Maya Culture under Spanish Conquest," *Comparative Studies in Society and History* 22.3 (1980): 374–93.

2. INFERNO

1. My primary sources for chapter 2 are Matthew Gregory Lewis, *Journal of a West Indian Proprietor* (London: John Murray, 1834; New York: Negro University Press, 1969), and R. R. Madden, *A Twelve Month's Residence in the West Indies, during the Transition from Slavery to Apprenticeship; with Incidental Notices of the State of Society, Prospects, and Natural Resources of Jamaica and Other Islands* (Westport, CT: Negro University Press, 1970). Subsequent references to Lewis and to Madden are given in the text.

2. William Beckford, *A Descriptive Account of the Island of Jamaica, with Remarks upon the Cultivation of the Sugar-cane, throughout the Different Seasons of the Year, and Chiefly Considered in a Picturesque Point of View; Also, Observations and Reflections upon What Would Probably Be the Consequences of an Abolition of the Slave-Trade, and of the Emancipation of the Slaves* (London: Printed for T. and J. Egerton, 1790 [microfiche]); Edward Long, *History of Jamaica* (New York: Arno Press, 1972); Bryan Edwards, *The History, Civil and Commercial, of the British Colonies in the West Indies* (London: Printed for J. Stockdale, 1794).

3. But, at this point, representation wavers between what the Cuban philosopher Luz y Caballero called the beauties of the physical world, paradise, and the horrors of the moral world, the inferno Cintio Vitier (*Ese sol del mundo moral: para una historia de la eticidad cubana,* 1st ed. (Mexico City: Siglo XXI Editores, 1975).

4. Alejo Carpentier, *El siglo de las luces* (Havana: Editorial de Arte y Literatura, 1974); idem, *The Lost Steps,* trans. Harriet de Onis (New York: Alfred A. Knopf, 1956).

5. Claude McKay, *My Green Hills of Jamaica* (Kingston: Heinemann, 1979).

6. Appadurai's reading of Edward Said's *Orientalism* supports my observations linking the representation of East and West (Indian) colonies in the politics of numbers. His argument on exoticization (tropicalism, in our case) and enumeration completely coincides with mine. Discussing Orientalism as a discourse that generates exoticism, strangeness, and difference, he says: "that rhetorically speaking orientalism is absolutely anatomical and enumerative, to use its vocabulary is to engage in the particularizing and dividing of things Oriental into manageable parts" (Appadurai, *Modernity at Large,* 115). My general argument is that exoticization and enumeration were complicated strands of a single colonial project and that in their interaction lies a crucial part of the explanation of group violence and communal terror.

7. B. W. Higman, *Jamaica Surveyed: Plantation Maps and Plans of the Eighteenth and Nineteenth Centuries* (Kingston: Institute of Jamaica, 1988), 7. Subsequent references are given in the text.

8. Francisco Arango y Parreño, "Discurso sobre la agricultura de la Habana y medios de fomentarla" and "Proyecto," in *De la factoría a la colonia* (Havana: Talleres de Cultura, 1936), 1–113, 94–112.

9. Ileana Rodríguez, "Romanticismo literario y liberalismo reformista: el grupo de Domingo del Monte," *Caribbean Studies* 20.1 (March 1980): 35–56.

10. James Clifford, *The Predicament of Culture: Twentieth-Century Ethnography, Literature, and Art* (Cambridge: Harvard University Press, 1988).

11. Simone Schwartz-Bart, *Bridge of Beyond*, trans. Barbara Bray (London: Heinemann Educational Books, 1982); Jean Rhys, *Wide Sargasso Sea*, intro. Francis Wyndham (London: Deutsch, 1966). See also Ileana Rodríguez, *House, Garden, Nation: Space, Gender, and Ethnicity in Postcolonial Latin American Literatures by Women* (Durham, NC: Duke University Press, 1994).

12. This depiction of black cultures works in tandem with Mikhail Bakhtin's notions of the grotesque in which the images of the body acquire "a considerable and substantial development in the popular, festive. . . . the grotesque concept of the body forms the basis of abuses, oaths, and curses" (Mikhail Bakhtin, *Rabelais and His World*, trans. Helene Iswolsky [Bloomington: Indiana University Press, 1984], 27). See also Javier Sanjinés, *Literatura contemporánea y grotesco social en Bolivia* (La Paz: Instituto Latinoamericano de Investigaciones Sociales, 1992).

13. Frantz Fanon, *Black Skin, White Masks*, trans. Charles Lam Markmann (New York: Grove, 1967); Albert Memmi, *The Colonizer and the Colonized*, trans. Howard Greenfeld, intro. Jean-Paul Sartre (Boston: Beacon Press, 1970).

14. Benita Parry, "Problems in Current Theories of Colonial Discourse," in *The Post-Colonial Studies Reader*, ed. Bill Ashcroft, Gareth Griffiths, and Helen Tiffin (London and New York: Routledge, 1995).

15. Richard Price and Sally Price, *Ecuatoria* (New York and London: Routledge, 1992).

16. In the nineteenth century, pictures representing cultural landscapes are drawn in ink and pen; in the twentieth, bright colors are used. Their tropes are small villages, fruit trees, clusters of birds, hillsides, lovely plains, luxuriant fields, guinea grass, laurel-looking coffee patches, sugar mills, rarefied air, wagons, oxen, puffs of smoke, seaside views, noble harbor vessels, merchantmen, people going about their daily chores. E. G. Squier's texts on the geographies of Central America are all fully illustrated using these techniques, which represent what the culture of politics has labeled "Banana Republics."

17. In reference to Yarico, Peter Hulme claims that her story with Inkle is the product of a society that chose to tell and retell itself as a romantic episode at a time when "the purity of true love would often be the product of a 'natural' society destroyed by some form of European corruption, calculation or double-dealing," what Renato Rosaldo calls "imperial melancholia" (Peter Hulme, *Colonial Encounters: Europe and the Native Caribbean, 1492–1797* [London and New York: Routledge, 1986], 229).

18. Cirilo Villaverde, *Cecilia Valdés* (Havana: Cultural, 1941).

19. Jamaica Kincaid, *A Small Place* (Toronto: Penguin, 1988); McKay, *My Green Hills of Jamaica*; Rhys, *Wide Sargasso Sea*.

20. McKay, *My Green Hills of Jamaica*, 3.

21. A contrasting attitude can be found in the works of the historians William Beckford, Edward Long, and Bryan Edwards, who are intellectuals living in the islands and members of the planter class.

22. Gayatri Chakravorty Spivak, "Can the Subaltern Speak?" in *Marxism and the*

Interpretation of Culture, ed. Cary Nelson and Lawrence Grossberg (Urbana: University of Illinois Press, 1988), 275.

23. Philip D. Curtin, *The Two Jamaicas: The Role of Ideas in a Tropical Colony, 1830–1865* (New York: Greenwood Press, 1968); Richard Pares, *Yankees and Creoles: The Trade between North America and the West Indies before the American Revolution* (Hamden, CT: Archon Books, 1968); Gordon K. Lewis, *Main Currents in Caribbean Thought: The Historical Evolution of Caribbean Society in Its Ideological Aspects, 1492–1900* (Baltimore: Johns Hopkins University Press, 1983).

24. Manuel Moreno Fraginals, *The Sugarmill: The Socioeconomic Complex of Sugar in Cuba, 1760–1860*, trans. Cedric Belfrage (New York: Monthly Review Press, 1976).

3. BEACHES

1. Carrol B. Fleming, *Adventures in the Caribbean: The Sierra Club Travel Guide to Forty Islands of the Caribbean Sea* (San Francisco: Sierra Club Books, 1989), 9–10.

2. Simone Schwarz-Bart, *Ti Jean L'Horizon* (Paris: Points, 1981).

3. Henry Miller, *Tropic of Cancer* (New York: Grove Press, 1961).

4. Fredric Jameson, *The Geopolitical Aesthetic: Cinema and Space in the World System* (Bloomington: Indiana University Press, 1992).

5. Michelle Cliff, *No Telephone to Heaven* (New York: Dutton, 1987).

6. Ernest Hemingway, *The Old Man and the Sea* (New York: Charles Scribner's Sons, 1952).

7. Suzanne Slesin, Stafford Cliff, Jack Berthelot, Martine Gaume, and Daniel Rozensztroch, eds., *Caribbean Style* (New York: Clarkson N. Potter, 1985), 1; emphasis added.

4. CULTURAL GEOGRAPHIES

1. Pedro de Alvarado, "Cartas de relación a Hernando Cortés," in Jorge Luján Muñoz, *Inicios del dominio español en Indias* (Guatemala City: Editorial Universitaria, 1987), 79–98. Subsequent reference are given in the text.

2. J. Eric S. Thompson, *Maya History and Religion* (Norman: University of Oklahoma Press, 1990).

3. The towns mentioned in the first *relación* are Zapotulán, Quecaltenango, and Utatlán (Luján, *Inicios del dominio español*, 79–98); in the second *relación*, Alvarado lists the towns in the following sequential order: Uclatán (Utatlán), ciudad de Guatemala, another city (which could be Sololá or Panajachel, since it is located by a lake), Yzcuyntepeque, Atiepar, Tacuylula, Taxisco, Nacendelán, Pacaco, Mopicalco, Acatepeque, Acaxual, Tacuzcalco, Miaguaclán, Atebuán, Cuzcaclán, Tapalán (ibid.).

4. *The Ixquín-Nehaib Title*'s route is Palahunoh, Chuabah, Chuaraal, Pachah (ibid., 70–72).

5. I take threshold to mean a stop or a detour sign that makes the reader veer off in a different direction or unwittingly move across another surface. As such, threshold

can be used as a heuristic device that permits the localization of voices and of fields and enables us to understand the cross-cultural as much as the cross-disciplinary. By using the notion of threshold, we can argue the idea of resistance or insufficiency as that point where the text becomes obscure and all kinds of negotiations and discrepancies become available. Understood in this manner, discursivity permits the construction of "meaningful relationships" by allowing the coexistence of counter-positions and, in our case, opening a space for the introduction of Amerindian subjects and discourses within the colonial corpus. For a development of this concept, see Burchell, Gordon, and Miller, *The Foucault Effect*.

6. Bernal Díaz del Castillo traces the route from Mexico City to Teguantepeque, Soconusco, Zapotitán, Quetzaltenando, Utlatán (Luján, *Inicios del dominio español*, 100). Then, as an afterthought, he mentions Izcuintepeque, a town that appears to lie on another road.

7. Fuentes y Guzmán has Alvarado's army come through the Peñones of Guélamo, Teguantepeque, Soconusco, to the province of Sapotitlán (today Suchitepeques or San Antonio), Zamala, Quetzaltenango, Utatlán, ending at Olintepeque.

8. What follows is Villacorta's reconstruction of the indigenous populations and their territorialities at the time of the Conquest. I include this extensive quote to give an idea of the density of population of the Quiché-Maya area and to indicate the difficulties in understanding the topographies of the Guatemalan highlands at the time of the Conquest. Unless otherwise noted, all translations from here on are Derek Petrey's. "The Amerindian population was located in the region comprised between the mountainous foundations of the Cuchumatane range in the west, the Santa Cruz sierra to the north, and the Mines range at due south, whose southern slopes form the basin of the Motagua River. . . . In that extensive region, between the rivers Suchiate and Cuilco to the west and the Coatepec to the east, the Mames inhabited, being people of cold climates, Sachena to the west of Ixbul hill, Menton on the banks of the river of the same name, Hista over the *vertientes* of Hista and Chiantla by the river Selegua. The region was watered by the Cuilco River; along its margins lived the Tapilzaya and Cuilco inhabitants, to the north of the rough summit of Ixtatán, finding Zakuleo and Chinajabul to the east. . . . Descending toward the coast were the towns of Ixtahuacán, Tejutla, and Tajumulco, and already by the sea, Malacatán and Ayutla. . . . In the neighborhood of the Mames toward the east was the Quiché nation . . . whose dominions extended . . . from the Xupiltepec coast in the south to the region watered by the rivers Chixoy and Lacantun to the north; the Tzutujiles, Cakchiquels, and Pokonchis tribes remained to the east.

"To the north were the towns of Nebaj, Cotzal, Chajul, and Ilóm, enjoying a temperate climate, the same as Jocopilas, Zacapulas, Cunen, and Uspatán. . . . To the east, the Quiché extended themselves through Zmaneb and Rabinal, and traded with those of Cubulco and Joyabaj in the left bank of the river Motagua, in which confluents, which gave it origin, appeared to be seated within a picturesque valley, protected by high hills, the city of Utatlán or Gumarkaaj, capital or residence of the Quiché lords, and those of Chichi, Chiguita, Tzibanul, and Chiquila, which were close to the

Cachiquel towns. . . . The rivers of the southern slope of the cordillera descend to the southern coast through uneven lands . . . and in which banks the Quichés established some towns that played an important role in the struggles of these towns for their freedom in the seventeenth century. . . . The largest of those rivers is the Samala, which originates near Chugui-Mikena (Totonicapán), leaving to the north the towns of Tzolonche (Momostenango) and Cugui Tzak, and turning sharply to the south, watered the countrysides of Banabaj, Olintepec, Tzalcaja, Xelaju, Tzunil, and Retalhuleu, this last one fully on the coast. . . . To the west of Samala run the waters of the Tilapa River, and to the west those of the Nima, whose source originates from the Tzamaac. . . . Nahualate, probable border with the Tzutujiles, descends from the mountains, where the towns of Nahaula, Tzamayac, and Ixtahuacan stand. . . . A volcanic line crosses the territory, beginning in Gagnaxul or of Quezaltenango, the Xezuk (Santa María), the Xetocoy or Tzunil, and the Tzunun-Choy (San Pedro), also called Pacajil, which overwhelmed the nearby town with frightening eruptions. . . . In the southern banks of the charming lake Atitlán or Panajachel were found the brave Tzutujiles, whose main city, Atitlán or Tzupitayaj, lies on its banks, at the foot of the majestic Atital-Huyo, or Atitlán volcano, the territory extending itself through the fertile and hot lands of the coast, where Zapotitlán and Xupiltepec are located. . . . To the north of river Motagua, between Chixoy to the west and the Atlantic to the east, the extended region of Tezulután stretches out. Its inhabitants were of Manche, Quikchi, and Pokomchi origin. Its principal towns occupied the central part between the rivers Cankuen, Motagua, and Chixoy. The rivers Polochic and Cajabon irrigated the area. United, these rivers merge into lake Izabal, as well as Icholay, Yalmalchac, and Chinayan, which separate the high tops of the Chama sierra.

"Over the Cajabón, which at its source irrigates the town of Tactic, the populations of Caboan, main city of that Lanquin lordship, stand.

"The river Polochi shelters in its banks the towns of Tamaju, Tucurú, Teocinte, and Sinacán, of the Pokomchi race, whose territories bordered those of other tribes, those of Alahuilac, whose main city was Acasahuatlán.

"Zamaneb was by the river Salama and there resided great lords, and over a branch of the Polochic was Chacujal, visited by Cortés in 1525.

"To the east of the Quiché nation, in the high peaks of Tecpán, where the first waters of the river Motagua spring, in the region of Mucubaltzip, or 'Place where the clouds hide,' a river that there is called Xalbaquiej or Sepela, the Cakchiquel nation was found, which to the east extended itself all the way to the Poco plains or Chimaltenango, bordering in the same direction with Cacatepequez, which had very recently overcome the Cakchiquel yoke, establishing an independent lordship whose principal city was Ayampuc, and its most important town Ucubil (San Pedro and San Juan Sacatepequez).

"The most important Cakchiquel city was Iximché, a rival of Gumarkaaj, and just as powerful, and when the Spanish arrived there Belejep-Cat governed as Ajau Ajpop, and Caji Imox as Ajpop Camja. The mountains of Pantzik, Paraxone, Chinajilay, Pacibakul, and Pacaguet-Quijil defended the towns from the northern winds. In the proximity of the river Pixcatoyatl was the town of Mixco.

"Bordering with the Quiché monarchy, the Cackchiquels possessed Panajachel or simply Ajachel, Sololá, and Cabaja, in the valley of Panchoy Almulunga, near the majestic volcanos of Belej-chi Junajup (of Water) and Belej-Chicaj (of Fire), and Acatenango, which the Quichés called Pecul.

"The towns of Comalapán and Tzumpancu, of hardworking and brave people, also belonged to the Cackchiquel town of Actenango. . . . To the east of the Cakchiquels, the Pokomanes established some towns of a certain relevance such as Pinula, Petapa, and Amatitlán. . . . To the south of the lake rises the Pacayatl volcanic system and at the end of the Orient, the towns of Jumay and Xilotepec. The Sincas occupy the coastal regions and its principal towns were Xutiapan, Comapán, Jalpatagua, and Quaxinicuilapán, which provided valiant soldiers to the caciques of Taxisco, Guazacapám, Chiquiulja, and Naxintlán in the war against the Castilians. To the east of Sacatepequez and to the south of Lake Izabal, all the way to the mountains of Merendón, were located the *cacicazgos* of Chorti origin, whose towns, Chiquimula, Jocotán, Zacapa, Tuculutral, and Copánts, bear witness to how populated they were. On the banks of the magnificent Lake Izabal, numerous towns, such as Xocolot and Tzuitzumpán to the south of the Xux-Chupan sierras, whose outskirts reached the Sactun, the English Sarstun, had their abode. The most important Chorti town was Copán, bravely defended by its Galel against the Castilians. . . . On the Pacific Coast, from Michatoyal to Lempatl, remained the populations of Pipil origin, such as the Panatacaltal lordship, whose most important city was Izcuintlán" (José Antonio Villacorta C., *Prehistoria e historia antigua de Guatemala,* trans. Derek Petrey [Guatemala City: Tipografía Nacional, 1938], 305–9). Subsequent references are given in the text.

9. Adrián Recinos's reconstruction of Quiché topographies, alongside studies by scholars such as Robert Carmack, John W. Fox, and George W. Lovell regarding Mayan social formations, are additional instances where texts have demonstrated a need to cast some light on the tangled web of Quiché-Maya topographies, which, together with Villacorta's, dovetail with the efforts of indigenous documents such as the *Popol Vuh* (which I see as a counterpart to Alvarado's document) to both preserve and reconstruct the Quiché-Maya past. The *Popol Vuh* retraces the steps of the Quiché people's migrations from the northeast until they settle in Gumarcaaj, the city we know as Utatlán, which the Spaniards subdued.

10. Alfred W. Crosby, *Ecological Imperialism: The Biological Expansion of Europe, 900–1900* (Cambridge: Cambridge University Press, 1986).

11. For a bibliography on the *Titles,* see Robert M. Carmack, *Quichéan Civilization: The Ethnohistoric, Ethnographic, and Archaeological Sources* (Berkeley: University of California Press, 1973); Dennis Tedlock, *Popol Vuh: The Definitive Edition of the Maya Book of the Dawn of Life and the Glories of Gods and Kings* (New York: Simon and Schuster, 1996).

12. Anonymous, *Isagoge histórica apologética de las Indias Occidentales y especial de la Provincia de San Vicente de Chiapa y Guatemala,* Preface by J. Fernando Juárez Muñoz (Guatemala City: Sociedad de Geografía e Historia, 1935), 186. Subsequent references are given in the text.

13. See, for instance, the meticulous works of Robert Carmack, *The Quiché Mayas*

of Utatlán: The Evolution of a Highlands Guatemala Kingdom (Norman: University of Oklahoma Press, 1981), *Rebels of Highlands Guatemala: The Quiché-Mayas of Momostenango* (Norman: University of Oklahoma Press, 1995), and Dwight Wallace and Robert Carmack, eds., *Archaeology and Ethnohistory of the Central Quiché*, Institute for Mesoamerican Studies, Pub. 1 (Albany: State University of New York Press, 1977).

14. One example of this is the *Libro viejo*, but also the works of all the Spanish friars, particularly Vásquez and Remesal. See Anonymous, *Libro viejo de la fundación de Guatemala y papeles relativos a D. Pedro de Alvarado*, Preface by Jorge García Granados (Guatemala City: Sociedad de Geografía e Historia, 1934).

15. For a discussion of this topic, see Ileana Rodríguez, "Entre lo aurático clásico y lo grotesco moderno: la mayística moderno como campo de inversión y empresa postcolonial," in Ricardo Salvatore, ed., *Re-pensando el imperialismo* (Buenos Aires: Temas, forthcoming).

16. Las Casas is full of these references. See Bartolomé de Las Casas, *Apologética história sumaria,* ed. Edmundo O'Gorman (Mexico City: Universidad Nacional Autónoma de México, 1967).

17. Carmack lists the following documents: post-Hispanic native documents: *Popol Vuh, Título Totonicapán, Título Tamub, Títulos Nijaib, Título Sacapulas, Título C'oyoi, Título Huitzitzil Tzunun, Título Zapotitlán, Título Santa Clara, Rabinal Achí*; major documents of groups related to the Quiché: *Annals of the Cakchiquels* (*Memorial de Sololá*), *Títulos Xpantzay, Título Chajoma, Relación Tzutujil, Título Cajcoj*; minor Quichéan documents: *Título Paxtoca, Título Retalhulew, Título Chuachituj, Título Chacatz-Tojin, Título Lamaquib, Título Uchabaja, Buenabaj Pictorials, Testament Catalina Nijay, Relación Pacal, Títulos Felipe Vásquez, Testament Ajpopolajay, Título San Bartolomé, Título Mam, Título Chama, Título Chamelco, Testament Madgalena Hernández*; native documents cited by later writers: by Fuentes y Guzmán: *Título Ixtahuacán Tzumpám, Título Ixtahuacán Torres Macario, Título Xecul Ajpop Quejam, Título Pipil, Título Xawila Tzumpám, Título Gómez Ajtz'ib, Título Tzutujil* (by Brasseur de Beaubourg), *Fragment of the Crónica Franciscana* (by an anonymous Franciscan) (Carmack, *Quichéan Civilization,* 20–79).

18. For a discussion of the confrontation between Spaniards and Amerindians and its lasting effects, see Antonio Cornejo Polar, *Escribir en el aire: ensayo sobre la heterogeneidad socio-cultural en las literaturas andinas* (Lima: Editorial Horizonte, 1994).

19. Antonio de Remesal, *Historia General de las Indias Occidentales, y en particular de la governación de Chiapa y Guatemala, escribese juntamente los principios de la religión de nuestro glorioso padre Santo Domingo* . . . (Guatemala City: Tipografía Nacional, 1932; Madrid: Ediciones Atlas, 1964–66), 302.

20. Mercedes de la Garza, ed., *Literatura Maya* (Caracas: Ayacucho, 1992), xi–xii.

21. Quetzil Castañeda, *In the Museum of Maya Culture: Touring Chichén Itzá* (Minneapolis: University of Minnesota Press, 1996), ix–x.

22. David Freidel, Linda Schele, and Joy Parker, *Maya Cosmos: Three Thousand Years on the Shaman's Path* (New York: William Morrow, 1993), 16.

23. Ibid.

24. Dennis Tedlock, "Hearing a Voice in an Ancient Text: Quiché Maya Poetics in Performance," in Joel Sherzer and Anthony C. Woodbury, eds., *Native American Discourse: Poetics and Rhetoric* (Cambridge: Cambridge University Press, 1987), 142. Subsequent references are given in the text.

25. Speaking about the spelling of words and their meaning, J. Eric S. Thompson makes a distinction between Nahuat and Nahuatl (and Nahua?), the former being a dialect of the latter. Speaking about Francisco Zipaque, who had succeeded Hernán Azbaque as a Putun ruler after the conquest, Thompson claims that Zipace is "a corruption of Acipac, which with locate affixes, Putun *ta* and Nahuatl *co*, reappear as the geographical entity Tabasco. Cipaque . . . is surely the Nahuatl day name Cipactli, first of the twenty days" (*Maya History and Religion*, 9).

26. Francisco Ximénez, *Las historias del origen de los indios de esta provincia de Guatemala, traducidas de la lengua Quiché al castellano para más comodidad de los ministros del S. evangelio* (Vienna: Gerold e Hijo, 1857), 194. Subsequent references are given in the text.

27. Adrián Recinos, trans. and ed, "Los *Popol Vuh* o *Popolhuun* míticos, históricos y proféticos," in de la Garza, *Literatura Maya*. In reference to the name of Guatemala itself, Recinos explains that it comes from the Nahuatl *Quauhtlemallan*, probably the Tlaxcaltecan translation of *Quiché—Quiché, queche, quechelah*—a noun meaning "forest." Quiché in turn comes from *qui(y)*, an adverb of quantity signifying many, and a noun *che*, signifying tree. Therefore, Guatemala means "forest," the tropical rain forest situated to the south of Mexico where the Maya lowlands were located—or is it what we call in Spanish *altiplano*, the highlands? Guatemala, then, connotes the whole region, and not only one city; not only Iximché, the capital city of the Cakchiquel nation, which the Tlaxcaltecan who arrived with Pedro de Alvarado called Tecpán-Quauhtlemallan; not only Utatlán, the seat of Quiché-Maya power. In fact, Quauhtlemallan and Tecolotlán (today's Verapaz), Recinos adds, named the territory located to the south of Yucatán and Petén-Itzá. Already in the nineteenth century, Domingo Juarros had stated that the word *Guatemala* comes from *Quanhtemali* (which in the Mexica language means a decayed log of wood), because "the Mexican who accompanied Alvarado found near the court of the kings of Kachiquel an old worm-eaten tree, and gave this name to the capital. . . . Some writers have derived it from U-hate-z-mal-ha, words that, in the Tzendal language signify a mountain that throws out water" (6). And in a footnote he states that "[f]rom the name Jiutemal the word *Guatemala* may derive its origin; for it is very natural that the country should at first be called the kingdom of Jiutemal [the name of the eldest son of Acxopil, a Quiché prince], and afterward by corruption it might become Guatemala" (89). But what is more meaningful about Recinos's reconstruction is that in interpreting the topographies of the *Popol Vuh*, he superimposes mythical or metaphorical locations. For instance, he derives a geographic location for Xibalba, a subterranean region inhabited by the enemies of the human race—for David Freidel, "the place of awe" (*Maya Cosmos*, 35). In the passage where four messengers from Xibalba bring a message to Hun-Hunahpu and Vucub-Hunahpu, who are playing a ball game called Nim-Xob

Carcháb, Recinos explains that the great Carcháh was an important population center in Verapaz, the mythical place where the Quiché-Mayas located their mythological occurrences of *Popol Vuh*. From Carcháh, the Quiché-Maya and Cakchiquel "went to populate Subinal, in the middle of Chacachil, in the middle of Nimxor, in the middle of Moinal, in the middle of Carcháh (nicah Carcháh). Some of these places keep their ancient names and can be easily identified in the region of Verapaz" (de la Garza, *Literatura Maya*, 31–32). From this mythical and circular location of culture, Recinos moves on to suggest that the names of ravines and caves are clearly marked topographical data indicating that the Quiché-Mayas had a very precise idea of the location of the kingdom of Xibalba, a place in the coastal areas, which merciless and despotic chieftains inhabited, and to whom they were made subjects in mythological times. In chapter 2 of the *Popol Vuh*, the point of departure of the Xibalba route is Carchá, a town today located near Cobán, the capital city of the district of Alta Verapaz. On the way out of Carchá, the road goes down through ravines and caves, among which runs a fast river. This is the way from the mountains to the lowlands of Petén, dominated by the Itzaes, or Itza, a group that was the last to fall to the Spanish Conquest. Hence Xibalba, which begins as a naming of an ethical condition, a symbolic place, or a mythically encoded character, is then interpreted by Recinos as meaning perhaps Ah-Tza, Ah-Tucur, the owls or evil ones. "Or the words could be read as 'those from Itza' (Petén), and 'those of Tucur,' that is, Tocolotlán [Mexicans today call owls *tecolotes*], the land of the owls (Verapaz). Those are the two regions to the north of Guatemala, well known to the ancient world, up where the Quichés could not extend their conquests. . . . These inhabitants of the north were the Mayas of the Old Empire, one of which branches, the Itzas, was the last to surrender to the Spaniards at the end of the seventeenth century" (32). This reading links Recinos's interpretation to Thompson's studies on Maya migration, particularly those of the Itza peoples. According to other documents, the lords of Xibalba came from out of a deep abyss, perhaps the lowlands of the coasts, "the place beside the sea" (Tedlock, *Popul Vuh*, 179), from which they had to climb to reach the highlands. The people dominating that area, as Recinos interprets the document, were not gods but tyrants, hypocrites, envious men with false hearts.

28. Ruth Bunzel, *Chichicastenango: A Guatemalan Village* (Seattle: University of Washington Press, 1959), 6. Subsequent references are given in the text.

29. Inga Clendinnen, *Ambivalent Conquests: Maya and Spaniard in Yucatán, 1517–1570* (New York: Cambridge University Press, 1988), 23.

30. Clendinnen, "Landscape and World View," 375.

31. Pedro Cortés y Larraz, *Descripción geográfico-moral de la diócesis de Goathemala, hecha por su arzobispo, el Illmo. Sor. Don Pedro Cortés y Larraz del Consejo de S. M. en el tiempo que la visitó, y fue desde el día 3 de noviembre de 1768 hasta el día 1.0 de julio de 1769, desde el día 22 de noviembre de 1769 hasta el día 9 de febrero de 1770, y desde el día 6 de junio de 1770 hasta el día 29 de agosto del dho. 1770*, vol. 22, Preface by Adrián Recinos (Guatemala City: Sociedad de Geografía e Historia, 1958). Subsequent references are given in the text.

32. Francisco Antonio de Fuentes y Guzmán, *Historia de Guatemala o Recordación Florida. Escrita en el siglo XVII por el capitán D. Francisco Antonio Fuentes y Guzmán, vecino y regidor de la ciudad de Guatemala*, ed. Justo Zaragoza (Madrid: Luis Navarro, 1883). Subsequent references are given in the text.

33. Luis Antonio Díaz Vasconcelos, *Apuntes para la historia de la literatura guatemalteca: épocas indígena y colonial* (Guatemala City, 1950), 153–57; Antony Higgins, *Constructing the Criollo Archive: Subjects of Knowledge in the Bibliotheca Mexicana and the Rusticatio Mexicana* (West Lafayette, IN: Purdue University Press, 2000). Subsequent references are given in the text.

34. Severo Martínez Pelaez, *La patria del criollo: ensayo de interpretación de la realidad colonial guatemalteca* (San José, Costa Rica: EDUCA, 1981; Mexico City: Fondo de Cultura Económica, 1998).

35. For a discussion on testimonials, see Georg M. Gugelberger, *The Real Thing: Testimonial Discourse and Latin America* (Durham, NC: Duke University Press, 1996).

36. Although the Quichés had developed a civic-religious hierarchy that gave them some negotiating power, by the middle of the eighteenth century they had become thoroughly transformed into peasants. The population was dispersed widely over the land, "rarely forming towns; rather, [the people lived] in hamlets [*parajes*], where the land was good, generally in low places and canyons; there the family or clan [*chinamital*] lived, not together, but each one in his milpa" (Ximénez, *Las historias del origen de los indios*, 12). The most important economic activities, cattle and sheep raising, were in the hands of Spaniards, mestizos, or *latinos*. Cattle often broke into the natives' fields, and haciendas had the reputation of being havens for mestizo thieves, who carried off the few sheep owned by native peasants, as Cortés y Larraz's narrative reports. The indigenous population lived in rural settlements. Their agricultural economic activity supplied food to the haciendas, and as late as 1830 towns like Antigua still received food from the Quiché. Haciendas gave little in return. Miraculously, a few native craftsmen or merchants survived within colonial society. An early seventeenth-century official stated that the inhabitants of Chichicastenango were "all rich Indians, half-merchants and great workers . . . for they have more than three thousand mules for their work" (Martín Alfonso Tovilla, *Relaciones histórico-descriptivas de la Verapaz, el Manché y Lacandón en Guatemala* [Guatemala City: Editorial Universitaria, 1960], 223). They traded cloth for coastal cacao and cotton. Most visitors to the town mentioned only its agricultural production, which suggested that trading was curtailed as the colonial economy was more fully implanted. Spanish, or rather *criollo*, hegemony assimilated or acculturated the authority and respect of native chiefs.

37. Don Domingo Juarros, *A statistical and commercial history of the kingdom of Guatemala, in Spanish America: containing important particulars relative to its productions, manufactures, customs, &c. &c. &c. With an account of its conquest by the Spaniards, and a narrative of the principal events down to the present time: from original records in the archives; actual observation; and other authentic sources*, trans. John Baily (London: J. Hearne, 1823). Subsequent references are given in the text.

38. See also Díaz Vasconcelos, *Apuntes*, 170–71.

39. Of Juarros we can say what González Echeverría states about Sarmiento: "Sarmiento's relationship to Facundo Quiroga is homologous to the one his book establishes with the discourse of scientific travelers and thinkers whose names he mentions and whose texts he quotes or uses as epigraphs throughout. The role of this web of texts . . . is to lend authority to Sarmiento's discourse, to serve as a model, and to give Sarmiento legitimacy as author" (*Myth and Archive*, 99–100). Except that in the case of Juarros, his work is totally disqualified and dismissed by those very same scientific travelers, such as E. G. Squier, on the basis that it is a copy of the earlier inaccurate documents written by friars. Most important in relation to the history of intellectual life in America is the observation that "[i]t is with fascination and repulsion that Sarmiento approaches Facundo Quiroga, like someone delving into the darker recesses of his or her own subconscious. The grandeur of the book is predicated on this antithetical origin, a cauldron or warring contraries in which author and protagonist embrace like Dioscuric twins, joined and separated by their correlative differences" (99).

40. For a more contemporary explanation of the relocatings of the Spanish capital city, see Julio Galicia Díaz, *Destrucción y traslado de la ciudad de Santiago de Guatemala* (Guatemala City: Editorial Universitaria, 1976).

41. Munro S. Edmonson, *The Ancient Future of the Itza: The Book of Chilám Balám of Tizimin* (Austin: University of Texas Press, 1982), xx. See also idem, *Meaning in Maya Languages: Ethnolinguistic Studies* (The Hague: Mouton, 1973), and *The Book of the Year: Middle American Calendrical Systems* (Salt Lake City: University of Utah Press, 1988).

42. What follows is Alvarado's battles as reconstructed by José Antonio Villacorta, whose aim is to correct the accounts of "Herrera, Torquemada, Remesal, Fuentes y Guzmán, Vásquez, the *Isagoge Histórica* and of Juarros and other historians who have followed the steps of the first [and which] do seem erroneous." "The battle of Zapotitlán lasted at least four days. . . . The author of the '*Memorial* of Tecpán-Atitlán' recorded the battle of Zapotitlán, which he calls Xetulul [*Prehistoria e historia*, 330; trans. Derek Petrey]. . . . Tecúm-Umám had established his general headquarters . . . in Chugui-Mekena, a town that later on the Tlascaltecas called Totonicapán; and he chose this place to be closer to the theater where the episodes of those campaigns developed rapidly during the first three months of 1524. . . . From there he sent out troops to cover the rough roads that led from the Xuchiltepeque coast in the direction of the principal towns in the mountains, such as Xelaju, Tzalcaja, Chugyi-Mekena [331]. . . . The road the Spanish army followed to ascend to the hilltops [mountain chain] was the ancient route that went from Cuyotenango to Xelaju-Quiej, passing through Pazulin, Zunil, and Almolonga in the valley closed off by the Samala River, which descends from near Suja and passes through the extensive ravine formed by Quemado Hill or Quetzaltenango volcano, the Seven Ears, and the Excamul or Santa María in the west, and the Zunil and Santo Tomás in the east, a rough road cut through by various tributaries of said river, which is turbulent near Patio de Bolas, where the waters form rapids between the cliffs that serve them as beds. . . . The day 1 Ganel, a date that, according to the '*Memorial* of Tecpán Atitlán,' the battle of Zapotitlán was

undertaken, corresponds to February 22 of that year [1524]; thus Alvarado took over its march again the twenty-third of that month, and on the twenty-fourth he began climbing a port or narrow and steep road, seven leagues in length, in the midst of which he rested that night, and the opening was so marshy, he could barely take the horses; and the next day in the morning, February 15, he continued and on top of an outcropping he found a woman who was sacrificing a dog, and according to what he was told from a translator, that was a sign of defiance. . . . The Spanish army was thus on the outskirts of the Excanul volcano (today Santa María) [332]. . . . The next day, the twenty-fourth, the Spanish army settled a league from there, always to the north, near some water fountains . . . and having dismounted the horses and drinking, they saw a lot of warriors coming upon them. . . . This combat took place on February 25, near Zunil probably. Advancing a bit further, perhaps near Almolonga and the foot-hills that form the base of Quemado Hill or the Quezaltenango volcano, another skir-mish took place with the Utatlán troops commanded by Ahau-Ahzumanche [333]. . . . that battle . . . was drawn in the Tlascalan *lienzo* . . . figuring in lamina 77 [334]. . . . After the Quezaltenango battle, the Spanish army took over that city . . . a military action which we have corroborated that took place February 27, 1524. . . . Thursday, March 3 . . . the Quiché army presented itself with the intention of recovering the city; it was led by that one chosen by the Casa Caguek himself, Tecúm-Umán. . . . the Quiché nobility and its invincible lord Tecúm-Umán perished there, in a site called Pakaja, near Pachab" (335).

43. For the constitution of research fields, see Mark T. Berger, *Under Northern Eyes: Latin American Studies and US Hegemony in the Americas 1898–1990* (Bloomington and Indianapolis: Indiana University Press, 1995). For the relationship between the Maya field and the different investment institutions, see Castañeda, *In the Museum of Maya Culture.*

5. BANANA REPUBLICS

1. E. G. Squier, *The States of Central America; Their Geography, Topography, Climate, Population, Resources, Productions, Commerce, Political Organization, Aborigines, Etc., Etc., Comprising Chapters on Honduras, San Salvador, Nicaragua, Costa Rica, Guate-mala, Belize, the Bay Islands, the Mosquito Shore, and the Honduras Inter-Oceanic Railway* (New York: Harper and Brothers, 1858). Subsequent references are given in the text.

2. De Certeau, *Heterologies*, 36, 94.

3. Here is what de Certeau says. Strategy is "the calculation (or manipulation) of power relationships that becomes possible as soon as a subject, with will and power (a business, an army, a city, a scientific institution) can be isolated. It postulates a place [alien and foreign] that can be delimited as its own and serve as the base from which relations with an exteriority composed of targets or threats (customers or competitors, enemies, the country surrounding the city, objectives and objects of research, etc.) can be managed" (ibid., 36).

4. See, for instance, Jaime Incer, *Nueva geografía de Nicaragua* (Managua: Editorial Recalde, 1970); José Coronel Urtecho, "Rápido tránsito," in *Prosa de José*

Coronel Urtecho (San José, Costa Rica: EDUCA, 1972); Ileana Rodríguez, "Lugares minúsculos/grandes narrativas," in Salvador García, ed., *Literatura de viajes: el viejo mundo y el nuevo* (Madrid: Castalia, Ohio State University, 1999), 287–98.

5. See Ileana Rodríguez, "Modernización y formaciones discursivas estatales: Las identidades regionales como productos de la transculturación," in Mario Valdés, Linda Hutcheon, eds., *Latin American Literary History* (London: Oxford University Press, forthcoming).

6. See Ileana Rodríguez, "Entre lo aurático clásico y lo grotesco moderno," in Salvatore, *Re-pensando el imperialismo.*

7. John Lloyd Stephens, *Incidentes de viaje en Centroamérica, Chiapas y Yucatán,* trans. Benjamín Mazariego Santizo (San José, Costa Rica: EDUCA, 1982); *Incidents of Travel in Central America, Chiapas, and Yucatán,* ed. Karl Ackerman (Washington, DC: Smithsonian Institution, 1993). The pagination used in this text corresponds to Ackerman's version. Subsequent references are given in the text.

8. Homi K. Bhabha, *The Location of Culture* (London and New York: Routledge, 1994).

9. For further discussion on the animal representation of people, see Roger Bartra, *El salvaje artificial* (Mexico City: Era, 1992); idem, *La jaula de la melancolía y metamórfosis del mexicano* (Mexico City: Grijalbo, 1987).

10. Severo Martínez Pelaez, *La patria del criollo: ensayo de interpretación de la realidad colonial guatemalteca* (San José, Costa Rica: EDUCA, 1981; Mexico City: Fondo de Cultura Económica, 1998); idem, *Motines de indios* (Guatemala City: Ediciones en Marcha, 1991).

11. Fernando Ortiz, *Cuban Counterpoint: Tobacco and Sugar,* trans. Harriet de Onis, Intro. Bronislaw Malinowski, Preface by Herminio Portell Vila, new Intro. Fernando Coronil (Durham, NC: Duke University Press, 1995).

12. For further discussion of the difference between acculturation and transculturation, see Cornejo Polar, *Escribir en el aire*; Friedhelm Schmit, "¿Literaturas heterogeneas o literatura de la transculturación?" in José Antonio Mazzotti and U. Juan Zevallos Aguilar, eds., *Asedios a la heterogeneidad cultural: libro en homenaje a Antonio Cornejo Polar* (Philadelphia: Asociación Internacional de Peruanistas, 1996).

13. González Echeverría, *Myth and Archive,* 113, 131. Subsequent references are given in the text.

14. Arthur Morelet, *Travels in Central America, Including Accounts of Some Regions Unexplored since the Conquest,* Intro. and Notes by E. G. Squier (New York: Leypoldt, Holt & Williams, 1871). Subsequent references are given in the text.

15. Theodor W. Adorno, *Prisms,* trans. Samuel Weber and Shierry Weber (Cambridge: MIT Press, 1983).

6. THE VOID

1. "Ao defrontarmos o Amazonas real, vemo-lo inferior a imagem subjetiva ha longo tempo prefigurada" (99). (Euclides da Cunha, *Um paraiso perdido* [Petropolis:

Instituto Nacional do Livro, 1976], 99). Unless otherwise indicated, all translations are Derek Petrey's.

2. As Antonello Gerbi has documented it, in the sixteenth century Gonzalo Fernández de Oviedo and Peter Martyr had debated exactly the same question (Gerbi, *The Dispute of the New World;* idem, *Nature in the New World.* Reading the nineteenth-century Argentine writer Domingo Faustino Sarmiento, Julio Ramos refers to this distance between empirical reality and the subjective understanding of it as "the filling up [of] the void," "to populate the American desert with the structures of modernity," a void and a desert observed from a distance that is just as geographical as it is cultural (Julio Ramos, *Desencuentros de la modernidad en América Latina: literatura y política en el siglo XIX* [Mexico City: Fondo de Cultura, 1989], 19, 20). Annette Kolodny addresses the same concerns in U.S. literature of the same epoch. Her interest in tracing "the imagery through which the landscape is rendered and assimilated into meaning" is yet another instance of this representational breach, a distance that in both U.S. and Latin American studies is alluded to as frontier literature (Annette Kolodny, *The Land before Her: Fantasy and Experience of the American Frontiers, 1630–1860* [Chapel Hill: University of North Carolina Press, 1984], xii; idem, *The Lay of the Land: Metaphor as Experience and History in American Life and Letters* [Chapel Hill: University of North Carolina Press, 1975]. Referring to this same emptiness, Michel de Certeau writes it poetically as that gesture which in its attempt "to embrace everything . . . clasp[s] only wind" (de Certeau, *Heterologies,* 72), echoing Antonio Cornejo Polar's "writing in the air" (*Escribir en el aire*). Subsequent references to Cornejo Polar are given in the text.

3. In this study I am sidestepping all the daunting issues concerning environmentalism. However, I want to acknowledge the outstanding studies of Susan Hecht and Alexander Cockburn, Augusta Dwyer, and David Cleary. What I found most astonishing about Cleary's work is his affirmation that contrary to the perceptions that the Amazon is stubbornly unrepresentable, "the Amazon is actually an easier subject for environmental historians than some other parts of the world," ironically owing to "the detail awareness of biological complexity and regional variation" (David Cleary, "Towards an Environmental History of the Amazon: From Prehistory to the Nineteenth Century," *Latin America Research Review* 36.2 [2001]: 69; see also idem, *Anatomy of the Amazon Gold Rush* [London: Macmillan, 1990]). See also Susan Hecht and Alexander Cockburn, *The Fate of the Forest: Developers, Destroyers and Defenders of the Amazon* (London: Verso, 1989; New York: Harper, 1990); Augusta Dwyer, *Into the Amazon: The Struggle for the Rain Forest* (San Francisco: Sierra Club Books, 1991).

4. Far from filling up this void, writing does quite the opposite. In de Certeau, writing is the principal device of heterologies, "the fabrication and accreditation of the *text [and of the enunciating subject] as witness of the other*" (*Heterologies,* 68). Roman Jakobson called this particular rhetorical style "metonymic aphasia," by which he meant that anxiety expressed by the incapacity to quite say what the subject really means (Roman Jakobson, *Lingüística y poética,* Estudio preliminar de Francisco Abad [Madrid: Ediciones Cátedra, 1981]).

5. See, for instance, the following passage: "Primeval (or primitive), as applied to a forest, a nation, or a period of time, is a word of rather indefinite signification, and generally but of relative import. If every wild forest, densely covered with trees, on which man has never laid his destroying hand, is to be regarded as a primitive forest, then the phenomenon is common to many parts both of the temperate and the frigid zones; if, however, this character consists in impenetrability, through which it is impossible to clear with the axe, between trees measuring from 8 to 12 feet in diameter, a path of any length, primitive forests belong exclusively to tropical regions" (Alexander von Humboldt, *Views of Nature: or, Contemplations on the Sublime Phenomena of Creation with Scientific Illustrations*, trans. E. C. Otte and Henry C. Bohn [London: Henry G. Bohn, 1850], 193). Subsequent references are given in the text.

6. Claude Lévi-Strauss, *Tristes Tropiques*, trans. John Weightman and Doreen Weightman (London: Penguin, 1992).

7. *The Burden of Dreams*, directed by Les Blank and Maureen Gosling, Flower Films, 1982; quoted in Jean Franco, "High-Tech Primitivism: The Representation of Tribal Societies in Feature Films (1993)," in Mary Louise Pratt and Kathleen Newman, eds., *Critical Passions: Selected Essays* (Durham, NC: Duke University Press, 1999), 181–95.

8. In reference to *orillas*, the older English connotation of heath, that which lay outside the cities and villages, refers to ethnicities. Those uncouth, uneducated people living in the middle of it are called "heathens."

9. Fray Gaspar de Carvajal, *The Discovery of the Amazon according to the Account of Friar Gaspar de Carvajal and Other Documents as Published with an Introduction by Toribio Medina*, ed. José Toribio Medina and H. C. Heaton, trans. Bertram T. Lee (New York: Dover Publications, 1988). Subsequent references are given in the text.

10. Kenneth Clark, *Landscape into Art* (New York: HarperCollins, 1991).

11. This is particularly true in Robert Saint John de Crèvecœur. See *Saint John de Crèvecœur, sa vie et ses ouvrages (1735–1813) avec les portraits de Crèvecœur et de la comtesse d'Houdetot, gravés d'après des miniatures du temps* (Paris: Librairie des Bibliophiles, 1883).

12. For further discussion on this subject, see Philip P. Boucher, *Cannibal Encounters: Europeans and Island Caribs, 1492–1763* (Baltimore: Johns Hopkins University Press, 1992).

13. As de Certeau proposes, following Jean de Léry's founding work on ethnography, the discipline organizes itself "around two strategic questions, cannibalism and polygamy" (*Heterologies*, 69). The fruitful consequences of this distinction are long-lasting and will become evident in the works of Vieira and de Mendonça. Some of the modern effects of the distinction will endure in the tropes of Ariel (the noble savage) and Caliban (the cannibal) used by criollos, grafting racism into their nation-building struggles and discourse.

14. Cristina Iglesia calls the route of conquerors the "route of hunger," and points out how, for Ulrico Schmidl, in his descriptions of Amerindian groups, the first thing to notice and write about is what they eat: "They also have great provision of Turkish

wheat, *mandiotín, mandioca-pepira, mandeporí*, potatoes, peanuts, *bocaja*, and other roots, which today cannot be described. They also have meats like deer, Indian domestic and wild sheep, ostrich, ducks, geese, chicken, and other poultry, but this time I don't know how to write them all" (Cristina Iglesia and Julio Schvartzman, *Cautivas y misioneros: mitos blancos de la conquista* [Buenos Aires: Catálogos Editora, 1987], 22).

15. For further discussion of this topic, see Sanjinés, *Literatura contemporánea y grotesco social en Bolivia*; Bakhtin, *Rabelais and His World.*

16. War and hunger are without question two tropes key to understanding the construction of all the subjectivities involved. In 1986, in his book on the Canary Islands, Alfred W. Crosby confronts head-on two of the most important arguments on war studied by postcolonial students of colonial confrontations. These are (1) the numerical argument (there were more Amerindians than Spaniards) and (2) the weapons argument (Europeans possessed better weapons). Crosby subverts these two arguments from the inside by turning the question around and reading victory and defeat as a result of agricultural production. His claim is that colonial wars are always fought in the colonies and therefore the local populations, engaged in their own self-defense, neglect the production of food. In fact, Crosby's originality lies in downplaying the importance of gold and silver, and in highlighting the usefulness of iron, an irresistible metal for making fishhooks. Thus he dovetails his arguments on war with those on sustenance. To the ordinary tropes that explain the victory of the colonizers—the visitors who would come from heaven on a white horse; the cultural disorientation or reorientation caused by the encounter itself; the power of the alphabet—Crosby explicitly adds agriculture, the fellow life-forms the Europeans brought with them, which "set off ecological oscillations" (Alfred W. Crosby, *Ecological Imperialism: The Biological Expansion of Europe, 900–1900* [Cambridge: Cambridge University Press, 1986], 91; subsequent references are given in the text). In the eighteenth century, Vieira is to make the same argument; in the twentieth century, Crosby's lexemes of iron and fishhooks, food and development, are to be found in the contemporary narratives of Brazil today, as in Antonio Callado's *Quarup* (Rio de Janeiro: Civilização Brasileira, 1967).

17. To see the land as rich and fruitful is a rhetorical tradition inaugurated by Christopher Columbus in the Antilles that we constantly read in the works of Central American friars as well as in Gonzalo Fernández de Oviedo or in Fray Fernando de Espino's narrative of Honduran forests. For Central America, see Gonzalo Fernández de Oviedo y Valdés, *Historia general y natural de las Indias, islas y tierra firme del Mar Océano*, ed. Amador de los Ríos (Madrid: Spanish Royal Academy of History, 1851–55); Fray Fernando de Espino, *La relación verdadera de la reducción de los indios infieles de la Provincia de Taguisgalpa llamados Xicaques* (Managua: Banco Central, 1983).

18. Appleton writes that in exploratory narratives the European eye "scans the landscape as a strategic field, a network of prospects, refuges, and hazards" (Jay Appleton, *The Experience of Landscape* [New York: John Wiley, 1996], 16). Paul Shepard adds thay they spot "food that holds still and enemies that move" (Paul Shepard, *Man in the Landscape: A Historic View of the Esthetics of Nature* [College Station: Texas A&M

University Press, 1991], 8). This is a predatory disposition that is fixated and focused on danger. The point of this analogy is that in narrating the territory as perilous, a semantic bond between this seeing imperial self and his animal behavior is established.

19. See Cornejo Polar, *Escribir en el aire*; Todorov, *The Conquest of America.*

20. See Hulme, *Colonial Encounters*; Roberto Fernández Retamar, *Caliban and Other Essays*, trans. Edward Baker, Foreword by Fredric Jameson (Minneapolis: University of Minnesota Press, 1989).

21. Or at least so he is considered by Jay Appleton (*The Experience of Landscape*). He advances the thesis of the predatory nature of the colonial subject, which helps us read in Carvajal the procedures of a seeing eye that organizes nature as a series of obstacles to overcome.

22. For the theoretical consequences of omissions and ellipsis, see Ranajit Guha, "The Small Voices of History," in Shahid Amin and Dipesh Chakrabarty, eds., *Subaltern Studies IX: Writings on South Asian History and Society* (Delhi: Oxford University Press, 1996), 1–11.

23. The embattled nature of the confrontation has been discussed in different terms by other scholars. See Pratt, *Imperial Eyes*; Bhabha, *The Location of Culture*; de Certeau, *Heterologies.*

24. For a discussion on this subject, see Greenblatt, *Marvelous Possessions.*

25. Jean de Léry, *History of a Voyage to the Land of Brazil, Otherwise Called America*, trans. Janet Whatley (Berkeley: University of California Press, 1990), 162. Subsequent references are given in the text.

26. Francisco de Figueroa, Cristóbal de Acuña, et al., *Informes de Jesuitas en el Amazonas, 1660–1684* (Iquitos, Peru: IIAP-CETA, 1986), 77.

27. Quoted in Alain Gheerbrant, *The Amazon: Past, Present, and Future*, trans. Mark Paris (Paris: Gallimard, 1988), 99.

28. To get an idea of the types of Amerindian societies and how they were annihilated by the Conquest, see Sherburne F. Cook and Woodrow Borah, *The Indian Populations of Central Mexico, 1531–1610: Essays in Population History: Mexico and the Caribbean* (Berkeley: University of California Press, 1972), 79; Gonzalo Aguirre Beltrán, *Estructura de casta y clase* (Lima: Instituto de Estudios Peruanos, 1966); Darcy Ribeiro, *Maira* (New York: Vintage Books, 1984).

29. An interesting take on this issue is Giovanni Arrighi, who is of the opinion that the conquest of America was based on the superiority of force. This superiority is the condition for the European primitive accumulation of capital. However, he adds that the condition of liberation from oppression is the pairing of the superiority of force with the superiority of courage (Giovanni Arrighi, *The Long Twentieth Century* [London: Verso, 1994]).

30. Enrique Dussel, *1492. El encubrimiento del Otro. Hacia el origen 'mito de la Modernidad'* (La Paz: Facultad de Humanidades y Ciencias de la Educación, 1994), 35. Subsequent references are given in the text.

31. Sir Walter Raleigh, *The Discoverie of the Large, Rich and Bewtiful Empyre of Guiana, with a relation of the great and Golden Citie of Manoa (which the Spanyards call*

El Dorado) And of the Provinces of Emseria, Arromaia, Amapaia, and other Countries, with their rivers, adioyning. Performed in the yeare 1595 by Sir W. Raleigh Knight, Captaine of her Maiesties Guard, Lo. Warden of the Stanneries, and her Highnesse Lieutenant Generall of the Countie of Cornewall (Amsterdam: Da Capo Press, 1968). A facsimile of Robert Robinson's imprint in London, 1596: *The discoverie of the large, rich and bewtiful Empyre of Guiana/by Sir Walter Raleigh,* ed. Neil L. Whitehead (Norman: University of Oklahoma Press, 1997). Subsequent references are given in the text.

32. For further discussion on this topic, see Seed, *Ceremonies of Possession.*

33. Carvajal had already recognized the existence of jurisdictions, rendering an onomatopoeic listing of the names of the Amerindian overlords—Aparia the Great and the Lesser, Machiparo, Celis, Ica, Oniguayal, Omagua, Paguana, Tinamoston, Arripuna, and Nurandalguguaburabara—eleven in all. These names wash away all illusions concerning empty lands and consequently all construction of agrarian utopias must pass through the crucible of war, for the spaces have to be taken from the natural owners, the so-called *naturales,* by persuasion or by force.

34. António Vieira, *Sermões,* ed. Gonçalo Alves (Porto: Lello & Irmão Editores, 1959); *Cartas no Padre António Vieira,* vol. 1, ed. J. Júcio D'Azevedo (Coimbra: Imprensa de Universidade, 1925). Subsequent references to these works are given in the text.

35. For a critique of this position, see Scott Michaelsen and David Johnson, eds., *Border Theory: The Limits of Cultural Politics* (Minneapolis: University of Minnesota Press, 1997).

36. Marcos Carneiro de Mendonça, ed., *A Amazônia na Era Pombalina: Correspondencia Inedita do Governador e Capitao-General do Estado de Grão Pará e Maranhão: Francisco Xavier de Mendonça Furtado, 1751–1759* (Rio de Janeiro: Instituto Historico e Geografico Brasileiro, 1963), 67. Subsequent references are given in the text.

37. One of Vieira's examples is the word *river.* It is simply insufficient and inadequate for talking about the Amazon. *Pará* or *Maranhao,* sea or great sea, is more appropriate, for the Amazon is "truly a sweet-water sea, bigger than the Mediterranean at the entrance of the mouth. The Mediterranean in the largest part of the mouth is seven leagues, and the Amazon River eighty; the Mediterranean from the straight of Gibraltar to the Syrian beaches . . . is one thousand leagues, and the Amazon, from the city of Belém up, has already been counted three thousand, and still the beginning is not known" (*Sermões,* 414).

38. Foucault, *The Order of Things,* 46, 48.

39. In Foucault's words, the age of deceiving senses defined by metaphor, simile, and allegory has been disjointed and "from then on, the noble, rigorous, and restrictive figures of similitude were to be forgotten. And the signs that designated them were to be thought of as the fantasies and charms of a knowledge that had not yet attained the age of reason" (ibid., 51).

40. An interesting note on this question is struck by Julio Schvartzman, who says that for the cases of Peru and Paraguay, "to listen [is] a necessity. But what for? To speak. . . . He who hears receives the language of the Indians. He who speaks,

disseminates the Gospel *in* that language" (in Iglesia and Schvartzman, *Cautivas y misioneros*, 129). Thus, in an ironic twist, a Jesuit becomes "a disciple of the barbarians." To listen correctly, to learn to listen, is profitable, and "the function of the indigenous interlocutor . . . is that of correcting: to verify in the mimetic discourse of the missionary if this one understood well. Paucke asks his Indians for this type of collaboration: 'I would be grateful, because I want to understand your language perfectly in order to be able to teach you'" (129–30). The oxymoronic relation between barbarian teachers and enlightened Amerindians, simultaneously rhetorical master and serf, ought to foster humility, modesty, or, at the very least, a recognition of the expertise and agency of the interlocutor.

7. THE AMAZON

1. José Eustacio Rivera, *La Vorágine* (Buenos Aires: Losada, 1976); da Cunha, *Um paraíso perdido*; Wilson Harris, *The Guyana Quartet* (London: Faber and Faber, 1985). Subsequent references to Harris are given in the text.

2. Mario Vargas Llosa, *The Green House*, trans. Gregory Rabassa (New York: Harper and Row, 1968); 91. Subsequent references are given in the text.

3. Wilson Harris, *The Secret Ladder*, in *The Guyana Quartet*, 358–59.

4. De Certeau has clearly marked the directional aspects of these types of figures in Western writings: "The cannibal is a figure on the fringe who leaves the premises, and in doing so jolts the entire topographical order of language" (*Heterologies*, 12). "The 'savage' drifts toward 'natural' . . . and takes as its opposite an 'artificiality' that alters nature. . . . this sliding gives the word 'savage' a positive connotation. The signifier moves, it escapes and switches sides. The ferret is on the run" (72).

5. For further discussion on this topic, see Ileana Rodríguez, *House, Garden, Nation: Space, Gender, and Ethnicity in Post-Colonial Latin American Literatures by Women*, trans. Robert Carr with the author (Durham, NC: Duke University Press, 1994).

6. Another novel with a similar title, *Green Mansions: A Romance of the Tropical Forest* (New York: Random House, 1944), by the naturalist fiction writer W. H. Hudson, plots the endeavors of an insurgent Venezuelan patriot lost on the borders of the nation-state. Hudson's character decides "eventually to go back upstream, and penetrate to the interior in the western part of Guyana, and the Amazonian territory bordering on Colombia and Brazil" (12). He ascends the Orinoco, the Meta and Guaviare rivers, and then becomes lost in the uncharted spaces of unmapped and unpossessed territorialities—Manapuri, the Queneveta Mountains, Curicay, Parahuari, and beyond, sites of tribes such as the Maquiritari.

7. Susan Hecht and Alexander Cockburn (*The Fate of the Forest*) and Augusta Dwyer (*Into the Amazon*)—and in Guatemala and Mexico Ricardo Fallas and Carlos Montemayor—speak about the extermination of the indigenous populations and the conquest of the jungle. Fallas is able to ascertain the destruction of at least four hundred villages, and the extermination of seventy-five thousand "Indians." He lists many of them by name and draws sketches of their villages in his anthropological

testimonial, as does Carlos Montemayor in his novel *Guerra en el Paraíso* (Mexico City: Diana, 1991).

8. Observing like traditions in the Miskito Coast of Central America, an English text from the eighteenth century also reproves Amerindian habits as nauseating: M. W., "The Mosqueto Indian and his Golden River; being a familiar Description of the Mosqueto Kingdom in America, with a Relation of the Strange Customs, Ways of Living, Divinations, Religion, Drinking Bouts, Wars, etc., of those Heathenish People; together with an account of the Product of the Country," in Awnsham Churchill, *A Collection of Voyages and Travels*, vol. 6. (London, 1744); "Los Indios Miskitos y su Río Dorado. Sencilla descripción del Reino Miskito en América: con una verdadera relación de sus extrañas costumbres, manera de vivir, credulidades, religión, borracheras, guerras, matrimonios, entierros, etc. de ese pueblo pagano; y también informes de los productos de la región," written in 1659 by M. W., printed by Henry Lintot and John Osborn, in Golden Ball Pater Noster; in *Nicarauac: Revista Cultural* 3.8 (Managua, Nicaragua) (October 1982): 47–65.

9. For a discussion on the topic of higiene and body behavior in relation to state formation, see Beatriz González Stephan, "The Teaching Machine for the Wild Citizen," in Ileana Rodríguez, ed., *The Latin American Subaltern Studies Reader* (Durham, NC: Duke University Press, 2001), 313–40.

10. Rajanit Guha, "Discipline and Mobilize," in *Subaltern Studies 6* (Delhi: Oxford University Press, 1989), 40.

11. Carpentier, *The Lost Steps*, 185. Subsequent references are given in the text.

12. Robert Carr, *Black Nationalism in the New World: Reading the African-American and West Indian Experience* (Durham, NC: Duke University Press, 2002).

13. See Hecht and Cockburn, *The Fate of the Forest*.

14. Anonymous, *Hamel, the Obeah Man* (London: Hunt and Clarke, 1827).

15. Richard Price and Sally Price, *Equatoria* (London and New York: Routledge, 1992).

INDEX

Ileana Rodríguez is Humanities Distinguished Professor of Spanish and teaches Latin American literatures and cultures at Ohio State University. Among the books she has authored and edited are *Women, Guerrillas, and Love: Understanding War in Central America* (Minnesota, 1999), *House, Garden, Nation,* and *The Latin American Subaltern Reader.*